Expressions

Meaningful English Communication

David Nunan

Teacher's Annotated Edition

HEINLE & HEINLE
™
THOMSON LEARNING

Australia · Canada · Mexico · Singapore · Spain · United Kingdom · United States

HEINLE & HEINLE

THOMSON LEARNING

Editorial Director: Nancy Leonhardt
Production Director: Elise Kaiser
Editorial Manager: Christopher Wenger
Senior Development Editor: Sean Bermingham
Development Editors: Colin Toms, Maria O'Conor
Production Editor: Tan Jin Hock

Senior Marketing Manager: Amy Mabley
Interior/Cover Design: Christopher Hanzie, TYA Inc.
Illustrations: Raketshop Design Studio, Philippines
Cover Images: Photodisc
Composition: TYA Inc.
Printer: Seng Lee Press

Additional editorial support provided by David Bohlke.

For more information, contact Heinle & Heinle Publishers, 20 Park Plaza, Boston, MA 02116 USA. Or you can visit our Internet site at http://www.heinle.com

UK/EUROPE/MIDDLE EAST:
Thomson Learning
Berkshire House
168-173 High Holborn
London WC1V 7AA
United Kingdom

CANADA:
Nelson/Thomson Learning
1120 Birchmount Road
Toronto, Ontario
Canada M1K 5G4

ASIA (including India):
Thomson Learning
60 Albert Street
#15-01 Albert Complex
Singapore 189969

AUSTRALIA/NEW ZEALAND:
Nelson/Thomson Learning
102 Dodds Street
South Melbourne
Victoria 3205, Australia

LATIN AMERICA:
Thomson Learning
Seneca 53
Colonia Polanco
11560 México, D.F. México

SPAIN:
Paraninfo/Thomson Learning
Calle Magallanes 25
28105 Madrid
España

For permission to use the material from this text or product, contact us in the US by
Tel   1 (800) 730-2214
Fax 1 (800) 730-2215
www.thomsonrights.com

Every effort has been made to trace all sources of illustrations/photos/information in this book, but if any have been inadvertently overlooked, the publisher will be pleased to make the necessary arrangements at the first opportunity.

ISBN 0-8384-2242-X

Printed in Singapore
1 2 3 4 5 6   04 03 02 01

Contents

AUTHOR'S ACKNOWLEDGMENTS

As always, in a project of this magnitude, there are many people to thank. First and foremost, I would like to acknowledge and thank Christopher Wenger, ELT Editorial Manager for Asia at Heinle & Heinle/Thomson Learning. It was Chris who first saw the potential of *Expressions* and did more than anyone to bring it to fruition. To Grace Low for her contributions to the Read On sections. To John Chapman for his workbooks. To Colin Toms for his detailed and insightful editing. To Nancy Leonhardt for her faith in this project and in me. To Christopher Hanzie, Stella Tan and the staff at T.Y.A. for their round-the-clock efforts under nearly impossible deadlines.

I am indebted to numerous other folks within Heinle & Heinle: Amy Mabley, John Lowe, Ian Martin, Francisco Lozano, Carmelita Benozatti, Sean Bermingham and Tan Jin Hock who, as always, are a joy to work with. I can't thank you enough for your support.

In addition to the above, I would like to extend my thanks to the following professionals who have offered invaluable comments and suggestions during the development of the series:

• Esperanza Bañuelos	CECATI, Mexico City, Mexico
• Graham Bathgate	ELEC, Tokyo, Japan
• James Boyd	ECC Foreign Language Institute, Osaka, Japan
• Gunther Breaux	Dongduk Women's University, Seoul, Korea
• Robert Burgess	NAVA Language Schools, Bangkok, Thailand
• Connie Chang	ELSI, Taipei, Taiwan
• Clara Inés García Frade	Universidad Militar 'Nueva Granada,' Santafé de Bogotá, Colombia
• Rob Gorton	Kumamoto YMCA, Kumamoto, Japan
• Randall Grev	ELSI, Taipei, Taiwan
• Ross Hackshaw	IAI Girls' Junior & Senior High School, Hakodate, Japan
• Ann-Marie Hadzima	National Taiwan University, Taipei, Taiwan
• Gladys Hong	The Overseas Chinese Institute of Technology, Taichung, Taiwan
• Ching-huei Huang	Oriental Institute of Technology, Taipei, Taiwan
• Ivon Katz	Asian University of Science & Technology, Chonburi, Thailand
• Tim Kirk	Asian University of Science & Technology, Chonburi, Thailand
• Clarice Lamb	ATLAS English Learning Centre, Porto Alegre, Brazil
• Lee Bal-geum	Seul-gi Young-o, Seoul, Korea
• Mike Lee	ELSI, Taipei, Taiwan
• Susan Lee	Seul-gi Young-o, Seoul, Korea
• Jisun Leigh	Hankook English Institute, Seoul, Korea
• Hsin-ying Li	National Taiwan University, Taipei, Taiwan
• Ian Nakamura	Hiroshima Kokusai Gakuin University, Hiroshima, Japan
• Luis Pantoja	Colegio Particular Andino, Huancayo, Peru
• Juan Ramiro Peña	Preparatoria - Benemérita Universidad, Autónoma de Puebla, Puebla, Mexico
• Susanna Philiproussis	Miyazaki International College, Kano, Japan
• Leila Maria Rezende	Solivros, Brasilia, Brazil
• P. Robin Rigby	Hakodate Shirayuri Gakuen Chugakko, Hakodate, Japan
• Lesley D. Riley	Kanazawa Institute of Technology, Ishikawa, Japan
• Mercedes Rossetti	Inglés en Línea S.A., Buenos Aires, Argentina
• Fortino Salazar	Instituto Benjamin Franklin, Mexico City, Mexico
• Beatriz Solina	ARICANA, Rosario, Argentina
• Carolyn Teh	ELSI, Kuala Lumpur, Malaysia
• Daisy William	ELSI, Kuala Lumpur, Malaysia

Welcome!

It is my pleasure to introduce you to *Expressions: Meaningful English Communication*. The purpose of this course is to help learners develop their communicative ability in English. The course is comprised of three levels, and includes student books, workbooks, teacher's annotated editions, audio tapes, audio CDs, a website, and an assessment package.

Expressions provides learners with **opportunities to practice all four skills**— listening, speaking, reading, writing—as well as vocabulary, grammar, and pronunciation. The topics have been carefully chosen to provide learners with meaningful situations through which to practice everyday English. This series embodies many of the principles that have shaped my own beliefs as a language teacher and learner, which I've outlined below. I wish you and your learners great success with *Expressions*.

Schema Building

Schema theory is based on the idea that **our past experiences allow us to create 'mental frameworks,' which help us make sense of new experiences**. We have schemata for the many different aspects of our life, such as 'restaurant' schemata, 'school' schemata and so on.

Because schemata are built from our past experiences, they are both personally and culturally determined. Our learners, of course, have very rich schemata, and many of these will match related schemata in the target language and culture. Our task is to show them how to express in the target language things they already know in their first language. In other instances, however, the target language schemata will be different from their first language. In this case, we have to help learners build new schemata. In each unit of *Expressions*, learners are given opportunities to see, hear and use the target language in rich, communicative, schema-building contexts.

Transparency

Transparency has to do with the relationship between the goals of a language program and the learning opportunities provided to learners. I have been involved in many studies recently where the pedagogical agenda was not spelled out to the learners, often resulting in confusion. There is plenty of support in the literature for the notion that **we should make instructional goals explicit to learners**. Studies of successful classrooms show that this is an important characteristic of exceptional

teachers. *Expressions* achieves transparency by setting out the key communicative goals at the beginning of each unit. The detailed *Scope and Sequence* chart at the beginning of each student book also provides teachers and learners with a detailed outline of what is covered in each level.

Consistency

Task sequencing should follow a consistent pattern so that learners can anticipate what is to come in an instructional sequence. This notion of consistency has been found to characterize successful classrooms. While such a concept can seem almost commonsensical, or even unimaginative or routinized in terms of teaching behavior, **consistency in presentation serves an important purpose for language learners**. When tasks are presented in a consistent manner, learners can focus more clearly on the tasks themselves, without having to work out what is happening each new lesson. In *Expressions*, consistency is achieved through a regular and predictable cycle of tasks in each unit.

Receptive vs. Productive Tasks

Another useful principle for sequencing tasks is to work from receptive to productive tasks. A receptive task involves learners in processing language through reading and listening tasks, which keep speaking and writing to a minimum. In the early stages of the learning process, receptive tasks are important because learners simply do not have the language to engage in production to any significant extent. **Receptive tasks take the pressure off**

learners and help to lower the anxiety that many feel in the early stages of the learning process. In *Expressions*, learners get to see and hear the target language before they are required to produce it.

From Formulaic to Creative Language Use

Another sequencing principle involves moving learners from formulaic through reproductive to creative language use. **Formulaic language** is 'chunks' of language that learners can use to achieve communicative ends without being able to break them down into their grammatical constituents. These are very useful, particularly for beginning learners. **Providing learners with these formulae, in the form of short model sentences and dialogs, enables them to 'outperform their competence,'** that is, to communicate more interesting and sophisticated meanings than would otherwise be possible. **It also allows them to build confidence** in using the target language, another important factor in successful language learning.

The next step in the learning process is for learners to begin to break down these unanalyzed chunks of language through **reproductive language tasks**. They are called 'reproductive' because they require learners to reproduce language models provided by the teacher, the textbook, or some other source. Most drills and exercises require reproductive language use, although communicative tasks can also involve reproductive language use. For example, a classroom survey in which a student has to identify classmates' food preferences is both reproductive (the speaker will be using a predictable language form 'Do you like hamburgers?') and also communicative (he or she doesn't know how the interlocutor will respond). **Creative language use** involves recombining familiar elements (words, structures, sounds) in new ways. It is when learners are engaged in creative language tasks that opportunities for language acquisition are maximized. A key principle in sequencing the tasks in *Expressions* was to move from formulaic/reproductive tasks at the beginning of the unit to creative language tasks in the second half of the unit. This is made explicit in the next principle.

Task Dependency

A source of confusion in many communicative classrooms is related to the selection and sequencing of tasks within a lesson or unit of work. In some instances, tasks are too challenging or confusing for the learners. In other instances, where the tasks are at an appropriate level of difficulty, there is no logic to the sequencing, and succeeding tasks are not connected to prior tasks by anything other than the most tenuous link. It is therefore **important to sequence tasks so that prior tasks provide a 'platform' for ones to come**, so that succeeding tasks 'depend' on those that have come before—thus the notion of 'task dependency.' This principle was key in deciding how the tasks in *Expressions* should be ordered.

Focus on Strategies

Strategies are "the mental and communicative procedures learners use in order to learn and use language" (Nunan, 1999: 171). One or more strategies will underlie any given pedagogical task. Common classroom strategies include selective listening, skimming, scanning, classifying, brainstorming, practicing, memorizing, and reflecting.

In recent years, arguments have been made in favor of explicitly teaching strategies in order to develop learner autonomy. Rebecca Oxford (1990), a leading figure in the field of language learning strategies, argues that **strategies are essential for developing communicative competence**, and that learners who have developed appropriate learning strategies have greater self-confidence and learn more effectively. In *Expressions*, the learning process is focused on strategies in terms of:

- explicit goals;
- principles of active learning;
- inductive and deductive learning opportunities;
- learning strategy preference surveys;
- consolidation self-review and self-reflection opportunities;
- personalized word-building sections.

Inductive vs. Deductive Learning

Two particularly important strategies are *inductive* and *deductive* learning. Deductive learning is a process of adding to knowledge by working from principles to examples. When teachers provide grammatical rules or the meaning of vocabulary items, they are teaching deductively. When they involve learners in figuring out the rules and principles themselves, learners are functioning inductively.

There is **a place for both deductive and inductive teaching in the language classroom**. The proportion of time devoted to each will depend on a variety of factors, including learners' attitudes and cognitive styles, the teacher's preferences, and the goals of the instructional

Introduction

process. I am biased towards inductive learning in my own classrooms, because I believe it forces learners to process the language more deeply, which ultimately leads to more effective learning. In *Expressions*, there are ample opportunities for both deductive and inductive learning.

Personalization

Another key strategy is personalization. In personalized learning, learners are given space to bring their own experiences, attitudes, and feelings into the learning process. **Learning is thus made more meaningful and real**, and learners are able to make systematic connections between their own lives and the life of the classroom. When learning is personalized, content is processed more deeply, and learner independence and autonomy are fostered. Each unit of *Expressions* invites the learner to relate the content of the unit to their own life, interests, and feelings.

Form and Meaning

Of the many issues in our field, that of focus on form and focus on meaning has probably been one of the most widely discussed. These days, most applied linguists argue that both are important, and that they are in fact two sides of a single coin, and not two opposing issues. However, that does not (or should not) mean a return to presenting grammar out of context, nor of confronting learners with decontextualized, sentence-level structures that they are expected to memorize and internalize through repetition and manipulation. We need to dramatize for our learners the fact that **effective language use involves achieving harmony between form and function**. We need to show them that different forms will enable them to express different meaning in different contexts.

In *Expressions*, each unit provides an explicit focus on form. However, before the form-focused activities, learners will have encountered the forms within their communicative context. This makes it easier for learners to see the connection between form and function.

Authenticity

Language data can be authentic, simulated, or non-authentic. **Authentic data** are samples of spoken and written language that have not been specifically written for the purposes of language teaching. They come into being as two or more individuals engage in genuine communication. **Simulated data** are specially written, but are crafted in such a way as to appear authentic. **Non-authentic data** are those spoken and written texts, and other samples of language that have been specially written for the classroom.

When I started teaching, authentic data existed in the real world, and non-authentic data existed in the classroom. Non-authentic data were meant to provide learners with examples of target grammar and vocabulary in texts that were simple enough to enable learners to understand and process the language. As such, they are a valuable resource for learners, particularly in the early stages of learning.

However, in addition to non-authentic data, it is also beneficial for learners to work with simulated and authentic data. In such data, **learners encounter target language items in the kinds of contexts where they naturally occur**. If they never get to listen to or read authentic texts in the supportive atmosphere of the classroom, if they are fed an exclusive diet of contrived dialogs and listening/reading texts, the challenge of functioning effectively in genuine communication outside the classroom will be that much greater.

In recent years, a great deal has been said about 'authenticity.' The concept has been criticized by those who point out that as soon as you record a conversation (for example) and take the recording into the classroom, you are 'deauthenticating' it. Getting learners to eavesdrop on a conversation rather than take part in it places them in a different role from the conversational participants. Having them listen and then fill in a table or chart is a pedagogical artifact—this is not something that one typically does outside the classroom. However, classrooms are not the same as the world outside of them, and they are not the same for very good reasons. Classrooms provide supportive environments for learners to develop the enabling skills (fluency, grammatical accuracy, knowledge of vocabulary and so on) that will allow them to communicate effectively outside the classroom. In *Expressions*, learners will encounter a rich array of data to facilitate their learning experience.

References

Nunan, D. 1999. *Second Language Teaching and Learning*. Boston: Heinle & Heinle/Thomson Learning.

Oxford, R. 1990. *Language Learning Strategies: What Every Teacher Should Know*. Boston: Heinle & Heinle/Thomson Learning.

For a more detailed discussion of these and other related topics, see the above, and other professional development titles, in our collection at: www.heinle.com

Expressions Components

The *Expressions* series is a complete language learning course, with a range of interrelated components specially designed with the needs of both language learners and teachers in mind.

Student Book

The *Expressions* student book contains 16 units per level, as well as language summaries, useful classroom expressions, and learner preference questionnaires. Details on unit format are included on pages x–xi of the teacher's annotated edition.

Workbook

Each level of *Expressions* includes a workbook, containing 16 units, all of which are closely tied to their corresponding student book units in terms of language and contexts. Each 4-page unit is divided into the following sections:

Working with Words: vocabulary
Looking at Language: structures
Reading and Thinking: reading
Showing What You Know: functions

The workbook is designed to provide learners with opportunities for additional practice on their own, though teachers may wish to incorporate its use into the classroom, depending on the situation. Teachers may also wish to use any of its sections for assessment in class.

Audio Program

The *Expressions* audio program consists of 2 audio tapes or 2 audio CDs per level for classroom use. The audio material for the *Start Talking, Listen In, Say It Right,* and *Talk Some More* sections of each unit are contained here. An important feature of the audio tapes is that they contain multiple recordings of passages that require more than one play in the student book tasks. This eliminates the need to rewind tapes in the classroom.

Website

The *Expressions* website offers two types of activities for learners: online quizzes and Internet search activities. The quizzes allow additional practice of the language and topics presented in each unit, and are designed so learners may submit their answers and receive their scores automatically. The quizzes also allow teachers to receive an email containing the learner's score, if desired.

The Internet search activities are task-based, and build on the content in the *Read On* section of the student books. Here, learners are guided to search for related information on the Internet, allowing them to personalize their learning with authentic reading content.

Teachers may ask learners to access these sites in class, in a computer lab, on their own at home, or wherever they have Internet access. The uses for the online activities vary from self-access practice to learner assessment. Teachers are encouraged to visit the *Expressions* website (http://expressions.heinle.com) to check for additional content for both learners and teachers, which will be added periodically.

Assessment Package

The *Expressions* assessment package includes a diagnostic placement test that teachers can use to determine the appropriate entry level of their learners into the series. The package also features a mid-term and final exam for each level of the series, oral communication exams, and a quiz for each unit in the student book. Tests come with complete instructions, answer keys, tapescripts, and audio tapes. Contact your local Heinle & Heinle/Thomson Learning representative or bookseller for more information on ordering the assessment package.

Teacher's Annotated Edition

The teacher's annotated edition is designed to function not only as a storehouse of answer keys and tapescripts, but also as a teacher training tool. In addition to step-by-step instructions for each student book unit, teachers can find a variety of additional tools to help them effectively plan and implement the lessons in *Expressions*.

These include:

Challenge & Support sections: These are additional suggestions for adjusting the level of particular tasks in the student book in order to give more challenge or more support to learners who need it.

Pronunciation: This section, marked with the ⊙ icon offers teachers a phonetic transcription of names that appear in different sections of the student book, as an additional reference. The transcriptions are written in the International Phonetic Alphabet (IPA) system, and a guide to the symbols appears on the following page.

Expressions Components

Mid-unit Assessment: A checklist is provided to assess learners' progress, allowing teachers to determine whether certain areas should be reviewed before learners proceed with more creative tasks.

Extension Activities: Instructions for a group extension activity follows each *Read On* section in the teacher's annotated edition. These are optional tasks that teachers may wish to use as a follow-on to *Read On,* or in other parts of the unit.

Cultural Notes: These also follow the *Read On* activities in the teacher's annotated edition, and provide cultural background for topics related to the *Read On* passages for teachers' reference. These may be used as a point of discussion or further research for the learners.

International Phonetic Alphabet (IPA)

Vowels			Consonants		
Symbol	Key Word	Pronunciation	Symbol	Key Word	Pronunciation
/ɑ/	hot	/hɑt/	/b/	boy	/bɔɪ/
	far	/fɑr/	/d/	day	/deɪ/
/æ/	cat	/kæt/	/dʒ/	just	/dʒʌst/
/aɪ/	fine	/faɪn/	/f/	face	/feɪs/
/aʊ/	house	/haʊs/	/g/	get	/gɛt/
/ɛ/	bed	/bɛd/	/h/	hat	/hæt/
/eɪ/	name	/neɪm/	/k/	car	/kɑr/
/i/	need	/nid/	/l/	light	/laɪt/
/ɪ/	sit	/sɪt/	/m/	my	/maɪ/
/oʊ/	go	/goʊ/	/n/	nine	/naɪn/
/ʊ/	book	/bʊk/	/ŋ/	sing	/sɪŋ/
/u/	boot	/but/	/p/	pen	/pɛn/
/ɔ/	dog	/dɔg/	/r/	right	/raɪt/
	four	/fɔr/	/s/	see	/si/
/ɔɪ/	toy	/tɔɪ/	/t/	tea	/ti/
/ʌ/	cup	/kʌp/	/tʃ/	cheap	/tʃip/
/ɜr/	bird	/bɜrd/	/v/	vote	/voʊt/
/ə/	about	/əbaʊt/	/w/	west	/wɛst/
/æ/	after	/æftər/	/y/	yes	/yɛs/
/ð/	they	/ðeɪ/	/z/	zoo	/zu/
/θ/	think	/θɪŋk/			
/ʃ/	shoe	/ʃu/			
/ʒ/	vision	/vɪʒən/			

Each unit in the student book consists of 8 pages, as well as a half-page *Language Summary* at the back of the book. Check the teacher's annotated edition for a variety of extension activities and additional materials to augment their use.

Unit Goals

Each unit begins with a title and unit goals. It is important to point out the goals of the unit and make sure that learners understand what they are aiming to accomplish. Teachers may also wish to refer learners' attention back to these at the end of each unit, giving learners a chance for reflection on what they've achieved.

Get Ready

Get Ready starts each unit by involving learners in a schema-building exercise that introduces the initial vocabulary, language and context for the unit. This is done through a variety of matching, identifying, brainstorming, and classifying tasks.

Start Talking

In *Start Talking*, learners practice a model conversation built on the context introduced in *Get Ready*. Although the conversations have been recorded for the teacher's convenience, use of the audio material is at the teacher's discretion. It is intended that the learners first listen to the conversation while reading along silently. Learners then practice the conversation aloud, first in its original form, and then substituting information introduced in *Get Ready*, and sometimes adding their own personal information.

Listen In

The tasks in this section allow learners to develop listening skills by practicing a variety of listening strategies (such as listening for main idea, for specific information, or for inference). It is important to note that learners are not expected to understand every word; success is determined by successful completion of the featured tasks. After a short pre-listening exercise (in most units), learners listen to the passage once and practice one of these strategies. Learners then hear the same passage a second time, this time focusing on a slightly more complex listening strategy. Teaching listening in this way helps learners achieve their goals, while systematically building their ability to understand spoken English.

Try This

Each unit contains 2–3 of these optional follow-on tasks, found in the *Listen In, Say It Right,* and *Work In Pairs* sections of the student book. Teachers may decide to use them as a means of encouraging learners to venture beyond their current level of comprehension or proficiency.

Say It Right

This section focuses learners' attention on aspects of the pronunciation, intonation, stress and rhythm of spoken English, in order to develop both their speaking and listening skills. Examples are taken directly from the context of the unit, and include consciousness-raising activities (where learners 'notice' rules about pronunciation) as well as practice opportunities.

Focus In

This section deals explicitly with the target structures of each unit. Structural exponents are presented in chart form, taken directly from the context of the unit. Teachers may wish to present the structures in an inductive or deductive fashion (as mentioned on page vi), depending on their situation. Reproductive tasks which follow the presentation allow learners to practice manipulating forms, while drawing their attention to the context of their use. These often also include a communicative aspect, where learners practice the forms in context with a partner.

Talk Some More

Talk Some More provides a longer, second model conversation for the unit, directly linked in context to the first one in *Start Talking*. Together, these conversations contextualize the language featured in *Focus In*. Here, learners are asked to manipulate the conversation through sequencing or fill-in activities before listening to and practicing the conversation as is. They are then asked to practice the conversation using the information that appears in earlier parts of the unit, and then to practice again using their own information.

Spotlight

This feature highlights a linguistic point from *Talk Some More*, usually in the form of explaining an element of spoken discourse, a common term or abbreviation, or commonly-used alternative expressions.

Student Book Unit Format

Work In Pairs

This section centers around an information-gap activity, where Students A and B work on separate pages to share information based on linguistic or visual prompts. The language required to successfully accomplish this task is based on that featured in all sections up to this point in the unit. This is the juncture where learners get their first chance to move slightly beyond formulaic and reproductive use of language, albeit in a 'safe' environment. For additional suggestions on how to manipulate pair and group work tasks, see pages xii–xiii.

Express Yourself

This contextually-linked section features pair- and group-based tasks that allow learners both to personalize and expand upon the language they've worked on throughout the unit. In *Express Yourself*, the focus is on developing fluency, usually through surveys, interviews, discussions and role plays.

Think About It

Think About It provides learners with a short cross-cultural passage, which usually examines a sociocultural aspect of spoken English, such as expressions linked to particular cultural situations, or explanations of particular customs common in English-speaking cultures. By comparing their own cultural situation with the information presented, learners may develop a deeper awareness of some of these issues. Each of these is followed by questions that may be used as a springboard for further discussion or research.

Write About It

This section presents a short realia-based example of a type of writing linked to the context of the unit. Using the piece as a model, learners practice creating their own texts, using their own information in many cases. You may wish to expand upon this section by having learners share their writing and doing peer correction.

Read On

Read On presents learners with reading passages of a variety of text types, linked contextually with the theme of each unit. The vocabulary and structural load of the passages purposely move beyond the scope of the production-oriented exponents presented in the unit. It is intended for learners to focus on the development of

reading strategies, instead of trying to understand every single word presented. Strategy-based tasks, as well as discussion questions, accompany each reading passage. A variety of pre-reading, reading, and post-reading activities, as well as extension activities, are also presented in the teacher's pages of this edition.

Review

Each unit culminates with a page that allows learners to reflect upon what they've learned. The exercises focus on vocabulary and grammar, though these are also linked to the context of the unit. Teachers may wish to assign this section for homework, do the exercises in class, or use the pages for assessment. At the end of each review page, learners are invited to go to the *Expressions* website for further practice.

Language Summaries

The *Language Summaries* at the back of the book consolidate the key language points presented in each unit. Teachers may wish to direct learners' attention to these sections as a general review, or as a quick reference for fluency activities. The *Word Builder* feature asks learners to note key vocabulary they'd like to remember, enabling them to utilize an important strategy for vocabulary retention.

A Note on Recycling

Research in second language acquisition has shown that not all learners acquire pieces of language at the same pace, or in the same order. In the student book, the tasks are designed to give learners numerous chances to recycle language in a variety of ways within the context of each unit. The *Expressions* workbook and website give additional opportunities for learners not only to recycle the language and context from the student book, but also to personalize the contexts for the own situation.

The *Expressions* syllabus is also designed in such a way that many of the key vocabulary, structures and functions are recycled in different units and contexts, both within each level of the series, as well as across all three. More detailed information on recycled language points can be found in the scope and sequence of each student book.

Pair and Group Work Ideas

Expressions features a variety of pair and group work tasks. These not only facilitate real communication between learners—they also provide learners with the maximum number of opportunities for practice in the classroom. When used effectively, these can also take some of the burden off the teacher in large classroom situations, where it may be impossible to speak with every learner one-on-one. Below are some guidelines for consideration in the implementation of these tasks.

Getting learners to use English

Many teachers have commented that one possible drawback of pair and group work tasks is that their learners quickly revert to their first language when they are unsure about what to do. These types of tasks may be different from what many learners are used to, and teachers may need to spend some time training them in the following ways in order to reduce this problem:

- Make sure that learners know what they are supposed to do (as much as possible).
- Anticipate and pre-teach the types of language that learners may need to accomplish a task which falls outside the realm of regular dialog creation, e.g., if learners need to be able to ask their partner *What answer do you have for number 5?*
- Pre-teach other useful expressions such as *Can you repeat that? Can you spell that? I don't understand,* and so on. (Several of these expressions can be found on page 6 of the student book.)

Modeling the task

Tasks often fall apart because students are unsure what they should be doing. It is important that the teacher:

- makes the instructions clear;
- models the task with a student (if necessary);
- checks that learners understand what they should be doing through comprehension questions.

Grouping learners

There are numerous ways in which students can be paired or grouped:

- *Pair up a learner with a person sitting at the same desk, or at the next desk:* This minimizes disruption to the class, and allows tasks to be set up quickly and efficiently. It also allows learners to become increasingly familiar with one another over time.
- *Peer teaching:* Match a 'more-able' with a 'less-able' student. The more-able student will help the less-able student (providing them with an additional challenge).

- *Pair students of the same ability:* This allows the teacher to 'tailor' a task to the appropriate level of ability, as well as being less threatening to the less-able learners (than if they were paired with a more-able student all the time).
- *Students select their own partners:* This is a way to encourage learner autonomy in the classroom. This might come after the class has 'bonded.'
- *Change pairings:* If time allows, have the pairs change and practice with a different partner. The second time, they may be more comfortable with the material.

Physical considerations

According to the classroom dynamics, as well as the physical and spatial restrictions within your classroom, you may wish to set up pair work tasks in different ways.

- *Sitting down, face-to-face:* Restrictions on movement may require all tasks to take place sitting down. If so, encourage eye contact by requiring students to sit face to face.
- *Back to back:* For example, if the task is a telephone conversation, have learners sit back to back. Make sure they do NOT make eye contact (like a real telephone conversation).
- *Standing up:* If possible, students should sometimes carry out tasks standing up. This varies the procedure, making it more interesting. This may not be suitable for tasks requiring a lot of writing.

On-task

At this stage of the language learning process, students should be given the opportunity for freer, less guided practice. It is important to create a classroom environment that allows students to feel comfortable, encourages them to speak in English, and facilitates thoughtful and creative language use.

Monitoring

While monitoring learners, teachers need to decide when to correct, and when to hold back from correcting. Over-correction may lead to learners' constantly focusing only on their accuracy, which may keep some learners from attempting to use language creatively for fear of making errors. However, there are times when correcting during the monitoring stage may be appropriate, depending on your learners' situation. Other aspects of this freer practice stage should include the following:

Pair and Group Work Ideas

- Encourage non-verbal communication, such as the use of gestures and facial expressions.
- Remind partners to make eye contact as they communicate, especially when they are more comfortable with the material and one another.

Wrap up

The wrap-up stage allows the teacher to provide useful feedback, make corrections, and bring the whole class together, giving closure to the task. Some tasks may be more suitable for this type of closure than others.

Wrap-up demonstration

- Select pairs to come to the front of the class and demonstrate the task.
- Select carefully, giving equal opportunity to all abilities (on-task monitoring may give a sense of whom to select).
- Correction should be done after the demonstration, by the whole class, with the teacher adding comments at the end.

Corrections

Write errors on the board and go over them as a class. Alternatively, give the students a few minutes in pairs to correct them together, then correct as a class (eliciting correct answers). This could be done as a quiz, with one point awarded for each correct answer. It is a good idea not to identify the source of the errors, as this may lead to damaged confidence.

Closure

If the teacher is confident that the task has been completed successfully (i.e., the target language has been used with sufficient accuracy, and the task's non-linguistic 'product' has been achieved), then there is closure. If not, there are a number of options:

- The class completes the task one more time (in different pairs).
- The teacher selects a different, but similar, task for the class.
- The teacher identifies students requiring remedial work, and provides additional practice (workbook, extension activities, and so on).

Modifying Tasks for Mixed-Ability Classes

Throughout the teacher's notes pages of the *Expressions* teacher's annotated edition, a number of suggestions have been provided for teachers to modify the level of challenge of individual tasks in the student book. These are marked *Support* (for making tasks less challenging), or *Challenge* (for making tasks more challenging). Teachers may sometimes wish to use these to modify a task for the whole class, and other times may wish to use them with particular groups of learners, or with individuals. It is hoped that through the use of this feature, teachers may build a repertoire of techniques that will help them better cope with the reality of catering to mixed-ability classes. Ideas for task modification include the following types of suggestions:

Support
- present language in context
- present familiar structures
- use familiar content
- give visual or non-verbal support
- present or elicit familiar vocabulary
- link concepts to learners' own knowledge
- use activities related directly to the text
- play listening passages several times
- practice only parts of a conversation
- reinforce conversation with similar situations
- practice conversation with book open
- require no justification for language choices
- augment theme with no further language

Challenge
- present language in isolation
- present unfamiliar structures
- use unfamiliar content
- give no visual or non-verbal support
- present or elicit unfamiliar vocabulary
- introduce unfamiliar concepts/situations
- use activities related indirectly to the text
- play listening passages only once
- ask learners to extend a conversation
- expand conversation with unrelated situations
- practice conversation with book closed
- require justification for language choices
- augment theme with further language

Getting Started with Expressions

Learner Preference Questionnaires

Research has indicated that second language learners who are aware of the processes underlying their learning, and who seek to use appropriate learning strategies, learn more effectively.

In addition to identifying learner needs before or early into a course, it is also useful to elicit learners' preferred learning activities. Learner preferences can have a significant effect on classroom dynamics, as well as on the use of materials and supplements. One way to assess learners' preferences is to administer a questionnaire. Each *Expressions* student book includes two types of questionnaire, one at the beginning and one at the end of the book (on pages 7 and 144).

The first questionnaire begins by asking learners to rate their preferences for learning by skill area. Then learners are asked to rate how much they like to engage in certain language learning activities both in and out of class. This will help introduce learners to certain types of activities they will encounter throughout the series, as well as raise learners' awareness about out-of-class activities that they may never have thought about exploiting.

The second questionnaire asks learners to list what they enjoyed about using *Expressions,* both in terms of skill areas and task types. Following this, learners are given the chance to assess their answers from the first questionnaire, so that they can compare whether any of their learning preferences have changed through their experience of learning with *Expressions*. They may find that their preferences are exactly the same, or they may find that some, or even many, have changed. In any event, this exercise not only makes them aware of a range of learning activities, it also allows them to adjust their own learning activities according to individual preferences, thereby taking more responsibility for their own learning.

Teachers may wish to collect the data from their learners' responses to these questionnaires in order to form a deeper understanding of their preferences and needs, allowing for better classroom planning and curriculum implementation. This may also allow teachers to gather a broad impression of English ability within the class.

Note: In the event that the content of the first questionnaire is too difficult for lower-level learners, teachers may want to consider translating it into the learners' first language in order to facilitate the collection of responses.

Useful Classroom Expressions

Another tool for getting started in the classroom is the *Useful Classroom Expressions* list on page 6 of the student book. These expressions can help learners to get (and stay) on task, negotiate meaning, and confirm information—all important things for effective use of classroom time.

Teachers may want to refer learners back to this page whenever there is an opportunity to use any of these expressions, as constant reinforcement may be necessary to get learners to use them on a regular basis. Through frequent practice, learners will hopefully begin to use the expressions not only with the teacher, but also when speaking to their classmates in pair and group work tasks.

Photocopiable First Day Activity

On the following page, a photocopiable first day activity has been provided for teachers who wish to start learners off with a class task that: (a) gets them talking right away, and (b) helps learners get to know one another. This type of activity can help make learners feel more at ease when they actually start working on activities in the student book.

Many of the questions in the chart have blanks so that teachers may personalize them for their own situation. Teachers may wish to make several photocopies of the chart first, and use these as master copies to create different versions to use with different classes. Teachers may wish to include names of local foods, places, activities and so on. Teachers may also wish to pre-teach the questions, and possible answers, before having learners do the activity.

The chart can be used to play classroom bingo in a variety of ways. Learners can either fill in answers and names to get four boxes in a row (horizontally, vertically or diagonally), or even fill up the entire chart.

More information on learner preferences and learner autonomy can be found in David Nunan's *Second Language Teaching and Learning* (©1999 Heinle & Heinle/ Thomson Learning).

Photocopiable First Day Activity

Ask your classmates questions. Write the person's answer. Then write the person's name.

Do you live in _____?	Is this your first English class?	Do you like to eat _____?	When's your birthday?
Answer: _____ **Name:** _____	**Answer:** _____ **Name:** _____	**Answer:** _____ **Name:** _____	**Answer:** _____ **Name:** _____
Do you like to go _____?	Do you like to go to _____?	Can you _____ _____?	Do you like _____ _____?
Answer: _____ **Name:** _____	**Answer:** _____ **Name:** _____	**Answer:** _____ **Name:** _____	**Answer:** _____ **Name:** _____
Can you _____ _____?	Do you like English?	Can you say _____ in English?	Do you use the Internet?
Answer: _____ **Name:** _____	**Answer:** _____ **Name:** _____	**Answer:** _____ **Name:** _____	**Answer:** _____ **Name:** _____
Do you like to travel?	What kind of _____ do you like?	What do you do in your free time?	Do you like _____?
Answer: _____ **Name:** _____	**Answer:** _____ **Name:** _____	**Answer:** _____ **Name:** _____	**Answer:** _____ **Name:** _____

Scope and sequence

UNIT	Title	Goals	Structures	Listening
1 Page 8	Are you Dr. Lowe?	• Introducing yourself • Practicing greetings • Asking who people are	• Questions and answers with *am/is/are*	• Expressions of introduction
2 Page 16	Is that your family?	• Talking about your family • Asking about families	• *This/that/these/those*	• Family terms
3 Page 24	Do you know Amy?	• Asking about appearance • Describing others	• Questions and answers with *do/does*	• Identifying people
4 Page 32	Where are you from?	• Asking and answering questions about where people are from	• *Is/Are* and *Do/Does*	• Where people are from
5 Page 40	Make yourself at home.	• Welcoming someone • Offering, accepting and refusing	• *Would* and *may*	• Hospitality
6 Page 48	How much is this sweater?	• Asking about and stating prices • Paying for goods	• *How much* and *How many*	• Shopping and prices
7 Page 56	Is there a pool?	• Asking for and identifying locations in a building • Giving directions	• *On/next to/between*	• Hotel facilities/locations
8 Page 64	First, you turn it on.	• Describing procedures • Narrating a sequence	• Sequencing words	• Instructions
9 Page 72	I get up early.	• Describing routines and schedules • Telling time	• Questions with *What + do*	• Time/daily routines
10 Page 80	I'd like a hamburger.	• Ordering food and drink • Asking for additional information	• *Would like* and *Will have*	• Fast food types
11 Page 88	Do you want to see a movie?	• Inviting • Making excuses	• *I'm ___-ing* and *I have to*	• Film genres/making excuses
12 Page 96	What's the weather like?	• Talking about the weather • Making suggestions	• *Let's* and *going to*	• Weather forecasts
13 Page 104	What can we get him?	• Talking about what people like • Talking about gift giving	• *Let's/How about...?* and *like*	• Hobbies/suggesting gifts
14 Page 112	We should go to the beach.	• Making suggestions • Voicing objections	• *Can* and *should*	• Choosing vacation destinations
15 Page 120	What's she like?	• Describing people and jobs • Using degrees of description	• Adverbs of degree + adjectives	• Jobs and character types
16 Page 128	I lost my cell phone.	• Talking about what you did • Asking about past events	• Simple past	• Talking about your day

Pronunciation	Writing	Reading	Recycling
• Question and statement intonation	• Making a business card	• Changing fashions in names • *Think before you read*	
• Pronouncing *th*	• Writing about your family	• Unusually large families • *Reading actively*	• Possessive adjectives • Asking who people are
• Reduced speech in sounds connecting words	• A letter to a pen pal	• Image consultants • *Inferring vocabulary*	• *Do you...?* • Questions/statements with *is/are*
• Syllable stress	• Filling in a form	• Different places with the same name • *Inferring content*	• Yes/no questions • Introducing yourself
• Pronouncing *c* as /s/ or /k/	• Writing a party invitation	• Visiting people at home • *Scanning*	• Practicing greetings
• Rising intonation for confirmation	• Writing a small ad	• Retro fashions • *Looking for main ideas*	• *It's/they're* • *This/that* • Accepting
• Stress for information	• Writing directions to your classroom	• Services • *Scanning*	• Questions using *where...?* • Imperatives
• Pronouncing /s/ and /sh/	• Writing instructions	• How does it work? • *Identifying reference words*	• Prepositions *in, on* • Giving instructions
• Intonation to transform statements into questions	• Writing a daily schedule	• An unusual daily routine • *Inferring content*	• *What do/does...?* • Narrating a sequence
• Pronouncing /s/ and /z/	• Writing a recipe	• The origins of fast foods • *Scanning*	• *Would* • Offering • Asking about/stating prices
• Intonation to show surprise	• Writing and replying to invitations	• On-line movies • *Identifying reference words*	• *Which* • *Want*
• Stress for information cues	• Writing a weather forecast	• Polar bear clubs • *Skimming*	• *What's...?/it's...* • Time expressions
• Pronouncing *What's* and *what does* in reduced speech	• Writing a thank you note	• Different gift-giving customs • *Reading actively*	• *Let's* • *...ing* for future • Making suggestions
• Pronouncing *can* and *can't*	• Writing a travel brochure	• All-American roads • *Inferring content*	• *Going to* + verb for future • Expressing opinions
• Question and statement intonation	• Describing people in your class	• Suitable business partners • *Inferring vocabulary*	• *What's...like?* • Describing others
• Vowel sounds	• Writing a diary entry	• The Unclaimed Baggage Store • *Identifying reference words*	• Sequencing words • Describing routines • Time expressions

Useful Classroom Expressions

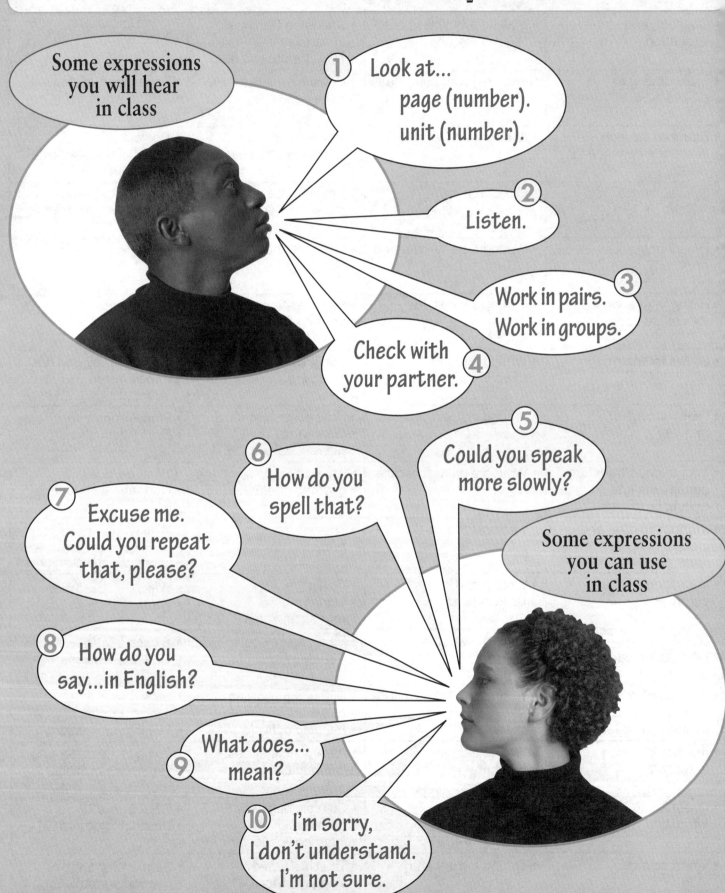

How do you like to learn?

A Preferences

○ **Which do you like? Put these in order (1–6).**

_____ Speaking	_____ Reading	_____ Grammar
_____ Listening	_____ Writing	_____ Vocabulary

B In class, I like...

○ **Check (✔) the boxes.**

	Not at all	A little	A lot	Not sure
doing role plays				
playing language games				
listening to tapes				
watching videos				
doing pair work				
doing group work				
studying grammar				
listening to the teacher				
writing things down				

C Out of class, I like...

○ **Check (✔) the boxes.**

	Not at all	A little	A lot	Not sure
talking with native English speakers				
watching English TV/movies				
reading English newspapers/books				
studying by myself				
writing letters/a diary in English				
doing homework				
studying from textbooks				
learning English from the Internet				

Check your ideas with a partner. Now you're ready to start *Expressions 1*.

Goals

○ **Introducing yourself**　　○ **Practicing greetings**　　○ **Asking who people are**

Are you Dr. Lowe?

1 Get Ready

A Look at the people. Write the number of the response in the correct place in the picture.

> 1. Nice to meet you, Rick.
> 2. Yes, I am.
> 3. No, I'm not. I'm Dr. Harris.

B Look at these personal titles. Which can be used for men? Which can be used for women? Which can be used for both? Fill in the chart.

(Dr.)　(Ms.)　(Prof.)

(Mrs.)　(Mr.)

Men	Women	Both
Mr.	Mrs.	Dr.
	Ms.	Prof.

2 Start Talking

A Look at the conversation and listen.

Ron: Are you Pat?
Mary: No, I'm not. I'm Mary.
Ron: Nice to meet you, Mary. I'm Ron.

Pair work **B** Practice with a partner. Use your own name. Then change partners and practice again.

Unit 1: Are you Dr. Lowe?

Goals
➤ **Introducing yourself**   ➤ **Practicing greetings**   ➤ **Asking who people are**

Workbook: pages 2–5

1 Get Ready

Task A

 Give students some typical first and family names. Have them decide which are which.

❶ Refer students to the picture on page 8. Read the sentences to the class. Have students think about which sentence belongs in each speech bubble.

❷ Have students write the numbers of the responses in the correct places.

❸ Have students check with a partner. Elicit answers from students.

Task B

❶ Have students write the titles in the correct columns.

❷ Go over answers.

2 Start Talking

Task A

❶ Have students read the conversation.

❷ Play the tape while students listen to the conversation.

Tapescript

M: Are you Pat?
W: No, I'm not. I'm Mary.
M: Nice to meet you, Mary. I'm Ron.

 Rewind the tape and have students repeat the conversation after the tape.

Task B

❶ Have them practice the conversation in pairs, using their own names.

❷ Have students swap partners and do the pair work again. Either have them practice with books open or closed.

 Write the names from Get Ready and Start Talking on pieces of paper. Give one to each student. Have students introduce themselves to each other, using the name on their paper.

3 Listen In

Task A

❶ Read the six expressions to the class. Ask the students which of the expressions is a question/ an answer/neither.

❷ Ask students to guess what might be the first expression they hear.

❸ Play the tape. Have students check the expressions each time they hear them.

❹ Go over answers.

Task B

❶ Read the six names to the class. Ask the students to say which are first names and which are family names.

❷ Play the tape. Have students write the number of the conversation in which they hear each name.

❸ Elicit answers from students.

 challenge ········ Have students practice the conversations using their own names.

TRY THIS! The answer is *Nice to meet you, too*. Repeat listening as necessary.

Tapescript

1. **M1:** Excuse me.
   W1: Yes?
   M1: Are you Melinda?
   W1: Why, yes, I am.
   M1: Nice to meet you. I'm Bill.
   W1: Nice to meet you, Bill.

2. **W2:** Excuse me, are you Mr. Mendoza?
   M2: Yes, I am.
   W2: Oh, great. There's a telephone call for you.

3. **W3:** Excuse me.
   M3: Yes?
   W3: Are you Larry Stevens?
   M3: No, I'm not.
   W3: Oh, sorry. What's your name?
   M3: Larry Sanders.
   W3: Nice to meet you, Mr. Sanders.

4. **M4:** Hello.
   W4: Hi.
   M4: Are you, uh, Tina Jones?
   W4: No, I'm not.
   M4: Oh, sorry.
   W4: Don't mention it.

4 Say It Right

Task A

❶ Play the tape and have students listen to the example.

 support ········ Model the intonations and have students repeat after you.

Task B

❶ Discuss rising and falling intonation with the students. (Rising intonation indicates a question. Falling intonation indicates a statement.)

❷ Play the tape. Have them listen to the names and mark the intonation.

❸ Play the tape again. Have them check their answers.

Task C

❶ Have students listen again and practice.

 challenge ········ Have students practice the dialogs using their own names.

Tapescript

M1: Are you Susan?
W1: No, I'm not.

M2: Excuse me.
W2: Yes?
M2: Are you Melinda?
W2: Yes, I am.

M3: I'm Bill.
W3: Nice to meet you.

3 Listen In

A How many times do you hear each expression? Check (✔) the expressions every time you hear them.

✔✔✔   Excuse me.   ✔✔✔✔   Are you...?

✔✔   Yes, I am.   ✔✔   No, I'm not.

✔✔✔   Nice to meet you.   ✔   What's your name?

B Listen again and number the names you hear (1–4).

1   Bill   1   Melinda

2   Mr. Mendoza   3   Larry Stevens

3   Mr. Sanders   4   Tina Jones

4 Say It Right

Try this

What's the answer to *Nice to meet you?* Can you remember?

A Listen to the example.

B Is the intonation rising (↗) or falling (↘)? Listen and mark the intonation.

C Listen again and practice.

5 Focus In

A Look at the chart.

Questions and answers with *am/is/are*		
Are you Pat?	Yes, I **am**.	No, I**'m** not. I**'m** Peggy./My name**'s** Peggy.
Am I in the right class?	Yes, you **are**.	No, you **aren't**. You**'re** in Class B.
Is he Greg?	Yes, he **is**.	No, he **isn't**. He**'s** Paul./His name**'s** Paul.
Is she Melanie?	Yes, she **is**.	No, she **isn't**. She**'s** Ann./Her name**'s** Ann.
Are they sisters?	Yes, they **are**.	No, they **aren't**. They**'re** friends.

B Fill in the missing information.

1. A: <u>Are</u> you Pat?
   B: No, <u>I'm</u> not. <u>I'm</u> Lee.

2. A: <u>Are</u> you from the United States?
   B: No, <u>I'm</u> not. <u>I'm</u> from Canada.

3. A: <u>Is</u> Lucy your sister?
   B: No, she <u>isn't</u>. <u>She's</u> my friend.

4. A: <u>Is</u> she Stella?
   B: No, she <u>'s/is</u> Yasuko.

C Fill in the blanks in the conversations.

1. A: <u>Hi</u>
   B: Hi.
   A: <u>What's your name?</u>
   B: I'm Andy Peters.

2. A: <u>Excuse me?</u>
   B: Yes?
   A: <u>Are you Lucy?</u>
   B: No, <u>I'm</u> not. I'm Connie.

6 Talk Some More

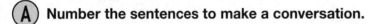

A Number the sentences to make a conversation.

Julie: <u>6</u> Julie Martin.
Julie: <u>4</u> Nice to meet you, Kevin.
Kevin: <u>3</u> I'm Kevin Tanner.
Julie: <u>2</u> Hi.
Kevin: <u>5</u> What's your name?
Kevin: <u>1</u> Hello.

B Check your answers.

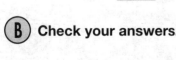

C Practice the conversation with a partner. Use your own name.

5 Focus In

Task A

❶ Go through the chart with the students. Point out correct use of contractions.

❷ Present more examples if necessary.

Task B

❶ Have students fill in the blanks.

❷ Have students check their answers together.

❸ Go over answers, giving more examples as necessary.

Task C

❶ Have students fill in the blanks.

❷ Have students check their answers together.

❸ Go over answers, giving more examples as necessary.

6 Talk Some More

Task A

❶ Have students number the sentences to make a conversation.

❷ Go through answers.

Tapescript

M: Hello.
W: Hi.
M: I'm Kevin Tanner.
W: Nice to meet you, Kevin.
M: What's your name?
W: Julie Martin.

Task B

❶ Have them compare answers with a partner.

❷ Play the tape and have students check their answers.

 Model the conversation again with students paying attention to intonation. Have them repeat the conversation using the correct intonation.

Task C

❶ Have students practice the conversation using their own information.

❷ Ask them to swap partners and do the exercise again.

❸ Ask the students to practice the conversation with their books closed.

 Write a similar conversation on a piece of paper. Make copies, and cut the conversation into sentence strips. Give a set of strips to each group of students. Have the groups put the strips in the correct order. Then, have students practice the conversation in pairs.

(SPOTLIGHT) Point out the difference between formal and informal usage. Give some examples of situations where greetings are used. Have students decide which greeting would be most suitable.

7 Work In Pairs

See pages xii-xiii for suggestions on pair work.

Task A

❶ Divide the class into pairs. Refer one student in each pair (Student B) to page 12.

❷ Have students write down the names of four famous people in the **You** section of the chart.

support ➤ ········ Model the exercise by asking a few students for the names they have written. Have them spell the names. Write the names on the board as they spell them.

❸ Have students ask their partners for information in order to fill in the **Your Partner** section of the chart.

> **Sample**
>
> **A:** What names do you have?
> **B:** Mariah Carey… Brad Pitt… Nelson Mandela… Jackie Chan…
> **A:** How do you spell 'Mariah?'
> **B:** M…A…R…

Task B

❶ Refer students to the photo and the target language in the speech bubbles. Ask a few students for names of the people in the picture. Have them spell the names. Write the names on the board as they spell them.

❷ Have students ask their partner for the missing names in order to fill in the blanks.

❸ Have them check their answers together at the end of the exercise.

challenge ➤ ········ Ask further questions such as *Is he Roger Walker?* or *Is she Carla Diaz?* Have students reply using correct sentences.

🔊 Edwin Sondhe: edwin sondi

> **Sample**
>
> **A:** Number two. What's his name?
> **B:** Edwin Sondhe.
> **A:** How do you spell that?
> **B:** E…D…W…

(**TRY THIS!**) Have students ask for and write each other's parents' names. Encourage students to ask their partner to repeat the spelling, if they are still unsure.

Work In Pairs — Student A

Student B: Use page 12

A Write the names of four famous people you know in the chart. Say and spell them for your partner. Then ask for your partner's four names and write them down.

You	Your Partner

B Ask your partner for the missing names. Fill in the blanks.

> Number four. What's his name?

> Roger Walker.

> How do you spell that?

BACK ROW: Lisa Maxwell, _Edwin Sondhe_, Carla Diaz, Roger Walker

FRONT ROW: _Stephen Lee_, Eric Simmons, _Susan Chen_

Try this

Ask for the names of your partner's parents.

Your partner's mother: _____

Your partner's father: _____

Work In Pairs (Student B)

Student A: Use page 11

A) Write the names of four famous people you know in the chart. Say and spell them for your partner. Then ask for your partner's four names and write them down.

You	Your Partner

B) Ask your partner for the missing names. Fill in the blanks.

BACK ROW: _Lisa Maxwell_ , Edwin Sondhe, _Carla Diaz_ , Roger Walker
FRONT ROW: Stephen Lee, _Eric Simmons_ , Susan Chen

 **Try this**

Ask for the names of your partner's parents.

Your partner's mother: _____

Your partner's father: _____

12   Unit 1

7 Work In Pairs

See p. T11 for suggested instructions for this task.

Mid-Unit Assessment

Once your students have finished Work In Pairs, they will have covered approximately half of this unit. How well are they accomplishing the unit goals at this stage? You may wish to assess their ability on the points below before beginning the fluency task Express Yourself. Check (✔) the appropriate space in the chart for each goal.

Can your students…	Yes, all can.	Yes, most can.	Maybe half can.	Only some can.
❶ introduce themselves? *e.g. I'm Peggy. My name's John.*				
❷ greet people? *e.g. Hi. Hello.*				
❸ ask who people are? *e.g. Are you Pat?*				
❹ use titles correctly? *e.g. Are you Dr. Lowe?*				
❺ use rising and falling question intonation correctly?				
❻ form questions and answers with *am/is/are?*				
❼ ask about spelling? *e.g. How do you spell that?*				
❽ spell people's names?				

If your students can already accomplish these fairly well, they're better prepared to expand their use of the target language in the tasks that follow. For those who are still having problems with particular items above, you may wish to direct them to the relevant areas of the unit on pages 8–12, to workbook pages 2–3, or to the online quiz on the *Expressions* website.

8 Express Yourself

Task A

❶ This activity can be done as a whole class or a small group, depending on size.

 ········ Put model language on the board if necessary, e.g. *Excuse me. What's your name?*, *How do you spell that?*, *Could you repeat that, please?*

❷ Have students ask questions and fill in the list with their classmates' names. Encourage language variety and politeness.

❸ Encourage students to ask their partner to repeat the spelling, if they are still unsure.

 ········ Ask them to collect other information such as parents' names or nicknames.

Task B

❶ Have students cover their lists.

❷ Have them look at each person and ask *Are you...?*, moving on if they get the answer *Yes, I am.*, or asking *What's your name?* if they get the answer *No, I'm not.*

9 Think About It

❶ Have students read the question and consider the answer. Offer any necessary language support.

❷ Discuss the question as a class. There may be different ways students communicate these points in their own culture. Note also non-verbal techniques and degrees of politeness.

❸ Elicit other possible situations where *Excuse me* might be used.

10 Write About It

Task A

❶ Ask students if business cards are common in their culture(s). Ask when and where they are used.

❷ Have students look at the two cards. Elicit what kind of information is presented.

Task B

❶ Have students design and complete their own card in the blank.

 ········ Put an example business card on the board for students to follow.

🔊 Lillian Arroche: lɪlɪən ɑroʃ

Express Yourself

(A) Ask for your classmates' names. Fill in the list.

Class List

(B) Cover your list. How many names can you remember?

Think About It

In English, when people:

- *want to call a server's attention*
- *want to ask a stranger a question*
- *accidentally step on someone's foot in a crowd*
- *want someone to move out of the way*

they usually say ***Excuse me***.

In what situations do you usually say ***Excuse me*** in your culture?

Write About It

(A) Look at the two business cards.

(B) Now make your own business card.

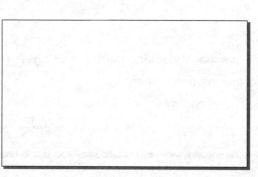

Lillian Arroche
International Sales Director
Online Education Inc.
238 Commonwealth Ave.
Boston, MA 02117
Tel: 617-555-7044 Fax: 617-555-7045
E-mail: lilliana@onlineed.com

Dr. Christopher Richie
Department of Humanities

Reading University
Whiteknights
Reading RU5 2BJ, U.K.
Tel: (44) 437 54890 Fax: (44) 437 54894
E-mail: c.richie@internet.com

Read On — Baby Names Over the Years

• Strategy: Think before you read

• What's your given name?
• Why were you named that?

How do parents choose the name of their baby?

In the United States, parents often give a baby the name of its father, mother or another family member. Some people just choose a name that's popular at that time. Two hundred years ago, 50% of boy babies in England were named William, John or Thomas, and 50% of girl babies were named Elizabeth, Mary or Anne. Some of these names are still popular, but other names are popular, too. Today, parents sometimes give their babies the names of famous athletes, film stars, characters from literature or TV shows.

Here are some of the most popular baby names over the years:

New York City, 1898
Girls: Mary, Catherine, Margaret, Ann(e), Rose, Marie, Ester, Sarah, Francis, Ida
Boys: John, William, Charles, George, Joseph, Edward, James, Louis, Francis, Samuel

New York City, 1964
Girls: Lisa, Deborah, Mary, Susan, Marie, Elizabeth, Donna, Barbara, Patricia, Ann(e), Theresa
Boys: Michael, John, Robert, David, Steven, Anthony, William, Joseph, Thomas, Christopher, Richard

New York City, 1999
Girls: Emily, Sarah, Brianna, Samantha, Hailey, Ashley, Kaitlyn, Madison, Hannah, Alexis
Boys: Jacob, Michael, Matthew, Nicholas, Christopher, Joshua, Austin, Tyler, Brandon, Joseph

Which names appear on more than one list? Write the names into the chart.

	Boys	Girls
1898	John, Joseph, William	Ann(e), Marie, Sarah, Mary
1964	Michael, Joseph, William, John, Christopher	Ann(e), Marie, Mary
1999	Michael, Joseph, Christopher	Sarah

Talk About It

○ What are some popular girls' names and boys' names among people your age?

○ How many names do you have? Do you know what they mean?

○ Do you have a nickname? Why do you have this name?

11 Read On

Before the Reading

1 Tell the class your given name. Explain why you think you were named that. Say whether you like your name or not. Then, ask the class these warm-up questions. Alternatively, have students first discuss them in pairs or in small groups.

What's your given name? Do you like your name? What other English names do you know?

2 List the English names you elicit from the students. Ask students to guess which are the most popular baby names in the U.S. today. Note their predictions on the board.

3 Refer students to page 14. Have students look at the title, heading and picture. Point out the list of 1999's popular names. Were the students' predictions correct? Refer students to the chart. Explain what information students should look for in order to fill in the chart. Go over the meaning of key words from the reading, e.g. *choose, parents, popular.*

During the Reading

1 Monitor students and offer language support where necessary.

2 Have students compare their answers with a partner.

Kaitlyn: ke̲i̲t̲lɪn, Brianna: bri̲ɑ̲nə, Hailey: he̲i̲li

After the Reading

1 Elicit names from the students for each row of the chart.

2 Go over the meaning of each of the Talk About It questions. Have students work in pairs, asking and answering the questions. Then discuss the questions as a class.

Optional questions:
Does your name have a meaning? Who chose it? Do you know other people with the same name?

Extension Activity

In groups, have students make lists of what they think are the three most common male and female names in the U.S. Note each group's predictions on the board. Compare the groups' guesses with the real answers (see below). Then, have each group make a list of famous people with those names. See which of the groups can make the longest list. (Most common names in U.S. 1990—male: 1. James; 2. John; 3. Robert; female: 1. Mary; 2. Patricia; 3. Linda.)

Cultural Note

Naming customs are not the same in all cultures. In some cultures, the mother and father name the baby; in others, the grandparents make the decision. In Greece, baby names are often decided by godparents (special friends chosen by the parents). Babies may be named after a friend, relative or a famous person. In the 1980s, many baby daughters were named Diana, after Diana, Princess of Wales. Religion can also play an important role; babies in Catholic countries, for example, are often named after saints. In some cultures, names are given which have special meanings, for example, Po Luk in Chinese means 'good' and 'joy.'

12 Vocabulary Review

Task A
❶ Have students search back through the unit for names—this could be done as a collaborative exercise if desired—and enter them into the correct columns.

❷ Check answers.

Task B
❶ Have students close their books. Say names from the list.

❷ Ask them to tell you if these are first names or family names.

❸ Ask them to spell the names.

 In pairs, have students test each other on the spellings of the names from the unit.

12 Grammar Review

Task A
❶ Have students unscramble the sentences.

❷ Have students exchange books and check each other's answers. Allow students to look back through the unit as necessary.

Task B
❶ Have students fill in the blanks.

❷ Have students exchange books and check each other's answers. Allow students to look back through the unit as necessary.

 Have students practice the conversation in pairs using their own information.

Log On

Have students do the online activities for this unit on the *Expressions* website: **http://expressions.heinle.com**

Language Summary

For a more detailed review of the language practiced in this unit, refer students to the **Language Summary on page 136**. Encourage them to add new vocabulary in the **Word Builder** section.

12 Review

1 Vocabulary Review

A Fill in the chart with the first names and family names you learned in this unit.

First names	Family names

B How many can you spell from memory?

What's your name?

2 Grammar Review

A Unscramble the sentences and write them correctly.

1. Are/Lowe/Dr./you _____ Are you Dr. Lowe?
2. No/not/I'm _____ No, I'm not.
3. What's/name/your _____ What's your name?
4. meet/to/you/Nice _____ Nice to meet you.
5. spell/do/you/How/that _____ How do you spell that?

B Fill in the blanks with the correct words.

A: Hi. _____Are_____ you Brenda?

B: No, I'_____m_____ not. My name _____'s/is_____ Anna.

A: Hello, Anna. I'_____m_____ Jerry.

B: Hi, Jerry. _____Are_____ you in this class?

A: Yes, I _____am_____.

3 Log On

Practice more with the language and topics you studied on the *Expressions* website:

http://expressions.heinle.com

Goals

○ *Talking about your family* ○ *Asking about families*

Is that your family?

1 Get Ready

A Look at the people. Write the numbers of all the family words possible for each person in the box, following the examples.

1. mother
2. father
3. son
4. daughter
5. brother
6. sister
7. husband
8. wife

Lisa: 1, 4, 8
Tim: 2, 7
John: 2, 7
Susan: 1, 8
Katie: 4, 6
Rick: 3, 5

B Look at the family picture, then read the sentences. Write *T* for true, or *F* for false.

1. __T__ Katie is Tim and Lisa's daughter.
2. __F__ Susan is John's mother.
3. __T__ Tim is Lisa's husband.

4. __F__ Katie is an only child.
5. __F__ John is Katie and Rick's father.
6. __T__ Rick and Katie are brother and sister.

2 Start Talking

A Look at the conversation and listen.

Hillary: Is that your family?
Lisa: Yes, it is. This is my husband.
Hillary: Are those your children?
Lisa: Yes. This is my son, and this is my daughter.

Pair work **B** Practice with a partner. Then look at the family in Get Ready. Imagine this is your family. Ask and answer questions about them.

Unit 2: Is that your family?

Workbook: pages 6–9

1 Get Ready

Task A

❶ Elicit any family terms including, and besides, those presented on page 16.

 ········ Read the vocabulary items and have students repeat.

❷ Have students look at the family portrait and think of which words can apply to each person. Have them write the numbers of the words in the appropriate boxes.

❸ Have them compare answers with a partner.

Task B

❶ Have students answer the true or false questions by referring to the numbered picture.

❷ Have them compare answers with a partner.

❸ Go through answers.

2 Start Talking

Task A

❶ Have students read the conversation.

❷ Play the tape while students listen to the conversation.

 ········ Rewind the tape and have students repeat the conversation after the tape.

Tapescript

W1: Is that your family?
W2: Yes, it is. This is my husband.
W1: Are those your children?
W2: Yes. This is my son, and this is my daughter.

Task B

❶ Have students practice the conversation in pairs.

❷ Have them practice using other family members from the picture.

❸ Have students swap partners and do the pair work again. Have them practice with books open or closed.

3 Listen In

Task A

❶ Elicit the family terms that relate to each of the pictures.

❷ In pairs, have them tell each other who they think is who.

❸ Elicit ideas from the students.

Task B

❶ Have students read through the vocabulary items.

❷ Play the tape. Have students listen and check the words they hear.

❸ Go over answers.

Task C

❶ Play the tape. Have students check the correct picture.

❷ Go over answers. Play tape again as necessary.

TRY THIS! The two ways are *Uh-huh* and *Sure*. Point out that these are informal.

Tapescript

M: Is that your family, Jill?

W: Uh-huh. This is my husband. And these are my children. How about you, Joe? Do you have a picture of your family?

M: Sure! Look, here they are. That's my mother, right there.

W: Oh, how nice. And, uh, is that your wife?

M: No, that's my sister. This is my wife. And these are my kids, of course. This is my son, Joey junior, and this is my daughter Laura.

4 Say It Right

Task A

❶ Refer students to the four sentences.

❷ Have them number the sentences according to the pictures.

Task B

❶ Play the tape and have students listen to the conversations and check their answers.

❷ Go over answers.

Task C

❶ Point out and model the pronunciation of /ð/ (th).

❷ Play the tape again. Have students practice the sentences.

challenge ⟶ ...... Extend to include *That* and *Those*.

Tapescript

A. **W1:** Cheryl, this is my father.
W2: Oh, nice to meet you. I've heard a lot about you...

B. **W3:** And this is my daughter—Jane.
M1: Hi, Jane. I'm Stuart.
W4: Nice to meet you.
M1: Same here.

C. **M2:** Oh, here she is.... This is my mother. Mom, this is Mr. Anderson, my boss.
W5: How do you do, Mr. Anderson?
M3: Please, call me Sam.

D. **M4:** ...And these are my children.
W6: Oh, they're so cute! And they look just like you!

A. **W1:** This is my father.

B. **W3:** This is my daughter.

C. **M2:** This is my mother.

D. **M4:** These are my children.

3 Listen In

A Look at the people in the three pictures. Who are the parents? Who are the sons and daughters? Tell your partner.

B Listen and check (✔) the words you hear.

_____ father	✔ mother	✔ husband	✔ wife	✔ children
_____ brother	✔ daughter	✔ sister	✔ son	_____ parents

C Which family is Joe talking about? Listen and check (✔) the correct picture above.

Try this
What are the two different ways of saying *yes* you heard? Can you remember?

4 Say It Right

A Write the number of the picture next to the correct sentence.

_2_ This is my daughter.
_1_ This is my father.
_4_ These are my children.
_3_ This is my mother.

B Listen to the conversations and check your answers.

C Listen again. Pay attention to the pronunciation of *this* and *these*. Practice the sentences.

Is that your family?   **17**

5 Focus In

A **Look at the chart.**

this/that/these/those		
Is **this** your family?	Yes, it is.	No, it isn't.
Is **that** your husband?	Yes, it is.	No, it isn't.
Are **these** your children?	Yes, they are.	No, they aren't.
Are **those** your sisters?	Yes, they are.	No, they aren't.

B **When do we use *this, that, these, those*? Check the spaces.
The first one has been done for you.**

	this	that	these	those
Only 1 person or thing	✔	✔		
2+ people or things			✔	✔
Close to the speaker	✔		✔	
Not close to the speaker		✔		✔

C **Work with a partner. Make up two sentences for each line below.**

1. Is __this/that__ your family?
2. Are __these/those__ your children?
3. Is __this/that__ your car?
4. Are __these/those__ your friends?
5. Susan, __this/that__ is my husband.
6. Are __these/those__ your keys?

6 Talk Some More

A **Write the words in the correct places.**

 I   you   have   do

Hillary: Do ___you___ have any
brothers or sisters?
Lisa: Yes, I ___do___. I ___have___
a brother and two sisters.
How about you?
Hillary: ___I___ have two sisters.

Spotlight
How about you?,
What about you? **and** *And you?*
have the same meaning.

B **Check your answers.**

 Pair work

C **Practice the conversation with a partner. Use information about your own family.**

5 Focus In

Task A

❶ Go through the chart with the students. Point out the concept of *close* and *not close* as determining choice of demonstrative.

❷ Present more examples if necessary.

 ⋯⋯ Use this as an opportunity to review pronunciation covered in Say It Right.

Task B

❶ Have students check the correct boxes in the chart.

❷ Have students check their answers together.

❸ Go over answers.

Task C

❶ Have students fill in the blanks.

❷ Have students check their answers together.

❸ Go over answers.

 ⋯⋯ Have students say each sentence to their partner. Their partner should give a suitable response.

6 Talk Some More

Task A

❶ Have students read the dialog and write the correct words in the spaces.

❷ Have students compare their answers with a partner.

Tapescript

W1: Do you have any brothers or sisters?
W2: Yes, I do. I have a brother and two sisters. How about you?
W1: I have two sisters.

Task B

❶ Play the tape and have students check their answers.

❷ Go over answers.

Task C

❶ Have students practice the conversation with a partner.

❷ Introduce negative sentences such as *No, I don't have any brothers or sisters.*, and *I have one sister, but I don't have any brothers.*

❸ Have them practice again using their own information, either with books open or closed.

(SPOTLIGHT) Use the extra rejoinders as a way of recycling the previous conversation.

7 Work In Pairs

See pages xii-xiii for suggestions on pair work.

Task A

❶ Draw your family tree on the board. Elicit vocabulary relating to your family.

 support ········ Review the meaning of any words students are unsure of.

❷ Pair students and refer student B to page 20.

❸ Have students draw their own family tree in the box provided.

❹ Put students in pairs and have them explain their family trees to each other. Do not ask them to draw their partner's family tree at this stage.

> **Sample**
>
> **A:** I have a father, a mother, two brothers and a sister. How about you?
> **B:** I have…

Task B/C

❶ Explain that the family they see in the photograph is their 'family.'

❷ Put model questions on the board such as *Are you married?*, *Do you have a wife/husband?* and *Do you have any children?*

❸ Have students take turns asking questions about the family in their partner's photograph.

❹ Have each student listen to their partner's descriptions and draw the family tree in the box provided.

❺ Have students check their answers together at the end of the exercise.

challenge ········ Go back to the original family tree description in Task A. This time have students draw each other's real family trees.

> **Sample**
>
> (Student B imagines he/she is one of the children in the picture on p. 20)
> **A:** Are you married?
> **B:** No, I'm not.
> **A:** Do you have any brothers or sisters?
> **B:** Yes, I have one brother.

TRY THIS! Have students write sentences either about their partner's fictitious family or their real one. Have them exchange books to check each other's sentences.

Work In Pairs Student A

A Draw your family tree in the space below. Describe your family to your partner.

My Family Tree

I have a father...

B Imagine you're one of the people in this family. Answer your partner's questions.

C Ask your partner questions. Draw your partner's family tree.

Try this

Make up two sentences about your partner's family.

1 _____

2 _____

Is that your family?   **19**

Work In Pairs Student B

Student A: Use page 19

A Draw your family tree in the space below. Describe your family to your partner.

My Family Tree

I have a father...

B Imagine you're one of the people in this family. Answer your partner's questions.

C Ask your partner questions. Draw your partner's family tree.

Try this

Make up two sentences about your partner's family.

1 _____

2 _____

Unit 2: Is that your family?

7 Work In Pairs

See p. T19 for suggested instructions for this task.

Mid-Unit Assessment

Once your students have finished Work In Pairs, they will have covered approximately half of this unit. How well are they accomplishing the unit goals at this stage? You may wish to assess their ability on the points below before beginning the fluency task Express Yourself. Check (✔) the appropriate space in the chart for each goal.

Can your students...	Yes, all can.	Yes, most can.	Maybe half can.	Only some can.
1 talk about their family? *e.g. This is my husband. I have two sisters.*	_____	_____	_____	_____
2 ask questions about families? *e.g. Is that your family? Do you have any children?*	_____	_____	_____	_____
3 use family vocabulary correctly? *(see Get Ready for list)*	_____	_____	_____	_____
4 pronounce /ð/ *(th)* correctly, as in *this* and *these*?	_____	_____	_____	_____
5 use *this, that, these, those* correctly?	_____	_____	_____	_____

If your students can already accomplish these fairly well, they're better prepared to expand their use of the target language in the tasks that follow. For those who are still having problems with particular items above, you may wish to direct them to the relevant areas of the unit on pages 16–20, to workbook pages 6–7, or to the online quiz on the *Expressions* website.

8 Express Yourself

Task A

1. Put students into small groups.

2. Go over the questions. Elicit the meaning of 'only child.'

3. Have them speak to as many people as possible. Encourage them to write several different names for each question. This exercise would best be done in a large space where students can mingle freely.

Task B

1. Have group members compare their results.

2. Have them write a name for each question.

3. Have them compare names to see who has the biggest family.

9 Think About It

1. Have the students read the information and consider the answers to the questions.

2. Discuss the questions as a class.

10 Write About It

Task A

1. Have students look at the photograph. Elicit the necessary family terms.

2. Have students read the description.

Task B

1. Have students look back to their family tree diagrams.

2. Have them write a description of their own families.

 ········· Have students write a description of another student's family.

8. Express Yourself

A Ask your classmates questions and write their names.

Find someone who...

Name

1. has a sister		
2. has two brothers		
3. has a brother and a sister		
4. has more than three brothers or sisters		
5. is an only child		
6. has one child		

Group work

B Check your answers.
Then answer these questions.

1. Who has the most brothers in your group?

2. Who has the most sisters in your group?

3. Who has the most children in your group?

Do you have any brothers or sisters?

9. Think About It

In some cultures, it is not polite to ask *Are you married?* when meeting for the first time, but in other cultures, it's OK.

• *How about in your culture? When can you usually ask the question* **Are you married?**

10. Write About It

A Look at the note and photo.

Here is a photo of my family. They live in Miami, Florida. These are my parents. This is my brother Edward, and my sister Mary.

B Go back to your own family tree in **Work In Pairs.** Then write about your own family.

Is that your family?   **21**

• **Strategy: Reading actively**

Read these statements.
Then read the article to mark them *True* or *False*.

	True	False
• The four girls and three boys were born very small.	✓	
• The family moved into a new house.	✓	
• The family called the president.		✓
• People gave the family many gifts.	✓	

At a time when most families are getting smaller, some families are getting much larger.

This is the story of one family.

On November 9, 1997, in Iowa, Bobbi McCaughey had seven babies. The four boys and three girls were born very small. They all stayed in the hospital for many weeks. The president called to congratulate Bobbi and her husband Kenny.

For your information

- **2 babies = twins**
- **3 babies = triplets**
- **4 babies = quadruplets**
- **5 babies = quintuplets**
- **6 babies = sextuplets**
- **7 babies = septuplets**

The family also received a lot of presents. They were given a large new house, a van, diapers, baby care products, food and money. For eight months, volunteers helped the family. Mom and Dad joined with popular singers and made a CD of baby songs. Sales from this CD, called *Sweet Dreams*, have helped the family with the high cost of taking care of seven children.

In 1997, there were born in the United States:
- 104,137 sets of twins
- 6,148 sets of triplets
- 510 sets of quadruplets
- 79 sets of quintuplets or larger numbers of babies

Talk About It

- Are you a twin or are there any twins in your family?
- Do you know any twins (or triplets, etc.)? Who?
- Do you know any stories of famous twins? Who?

11 Read On

Before the Reading

1. Ask the class these warm-up questions. Alternatively, have students first discuss them in pairs or in small groups.

   How many people are there in your family? How many members does a 'big' family have?

2. Write these words on the board: *babies, President, hospital, congratulate, family, seven, present.* Explain that all these words are from the Read On passage. Elicit the meaning of each word, and help with any words they don't know. In groups, have students predict the topic of the passage. Call on groups to give their predictions, and note them on the board.

3. Have students open their books to p. 22. Refer them to the title, heading and picture. Do the students still feel their predictions are correct? Write the four statements from page 22 on the board and go over the meaning of each. Explain that students need to read the passage to decide whether each statement is true or false.

During the Reading

1. Monitor and offer language support where necessary.

2. Have students compare their answers with a partner.

   🕐 Scotsboro: s̲k̲o̲t̲s̲b̲o̲r̲ə

After the Reading

1. Elicit answers from the students for each statement. Write *T* or *F* next to the statements on the board as you go through them.

2. Go over the meaning of each of the Talk About It questions. Have students work in pairs, asking and answering the questions. Then discuss the questions as a class.

   Optional questions:
   What do you think 'identical twins' means? How about 'conjoined twins?'

   Note: Non-identical twins are referred to as 'fraternal twins.'

Extension Activity

In groups, have students brainstorm a list of famous families, or famous siblings (in their own culture, or others). Note each group's list on the board. Elicit why these people are famous. Some examples from the U.S. include: the Kennedys (politicians), the Wright brothers (aviation pioneers), the Carpenters (musicians), and the Judds (country-western singers).

Cultural Note

There have been many cases of famous twins over the years. For example, Romulus and Remus, a pair of twins, allegedly founded the city of Rome in 753 BC. An extremely rare form of identical twins, which occurs about once in every 200 twin births, is that of conjoined twins. In this case, the two babies are connected to each other when they are born. The most famous case was that of Eng and Chang Bunker, who were born joined together at the chest. They became successful businessmen and ranchers in North Carolina and eventually died, within hours of each other, in 1874 at age 62. The Bunker twins were born in Siam (now Thailand), which is why conjoined twins are sometimes called 'Siamese twins.'

12 Vocabulary Review

Task A

1 Have students search back through the unit for family terms—this could be done as a collaborative exercise if desired—and enter them into the correct columns.

2 Elicit suggestions from students and review as a class.

Task B

1 Have students tell a partner.

2 Turn this into a whole class session and encourage discussion. Find out who has the biggest/smallest family, the most brothers, sisters, aunts, uncles, etc.

12 Grammar Review

Task A

1 Have students complete the task.

2 Allow students to look back through the unit to check their answers.

Task B

1 Have students write sentences about their own family.

2 Have students read their sentences to a partner.

 ········ Have students practice asking the questions in 'A' in pairs.

Log On

Have students do the online activities for this unit on the *Expressions* website: **http://expressions.heinle.com**

Language Summary

For a more detailed review of the language practiced in this unit, refer students to the **Language Summary on page 136**. Encourage them to add new vocabulary in the **Word Builder** section.

1 Vocabulary Review

A Fill in the chart with the family words you learned in this unit.

Men	Women

B How many of these people are there in your family?

2 Grammar Review

A Are these sentences correct? If not, write them correctly in the space.

	Correct	Incorrect	
1. Is these your husband?		✔	Is this your husband?
2. Is that your family?	✔		
3. Is those your sisters?		✔	Are those your sisters?
4. Are you have any brothers?		✔	Do you have any brothers?
5. Do you have any children?	✔		

B Make sentences about your family using the words shown.

1. brother/brothers _____

2. sister/sisters _____

3. married _____

4. children _____

3 Log On

Practice more with the language and topics you studied on the *Expressions* website:

http://expressions.heinle.com

Goals
○ Asking about appearance   ○ Describing others

Do you know Amy?

1 Get Ready

A Look at the people and read the words. Write the number of the words in the correct place in the picture (1–10). Use each word once.

1. tall
2. glasses
3. young
4. middle-aged
5. blond hair
6. short hair
7. curly hair
8. large earrings
9. short
10. mustache

B Read the sentences. Write *T* for true, or *F* for false.

1. _F_ Sandra has short hair.
2. _T_ George has a mustache.
3. _T_ Kathi has earrings.
4. _T_ Amy is short.
5. _F_ Tony has curly hair.
6. _T_ Erik is tall.

2 Start Talking

A Look at the conversation and listen.

Erik: Do you know Amy?
Sandra: I don't know. What does she look like?
Erik: She's kind of short, and she has curly hair.
Sandra: Oh, yes. I know her.

Pair work **B** Practice the conversation.
Then practice again, using the information about the people in Get Ready.
Can you think of any other words to describe people?

Unit 3: Do you know Amy?

Goals
▶ Asking about appearance ▶ Describing others

Workbook: pages 10–13

1 Get Ready

Task A
❶ Elicit the meaning of the vocabulary items. Go over the pronunciation of each.

❷ Have students write the numbers in the correct place in the picture.

❸ Have students compare answers with a partner.

❹ Check answers as a class.

❺ Ask which of the vocabulary items use *is* and which use *has*. Elicit, and summarize on the board.

 ┄┄┄┄ Elicit other words to describe the people in the picture.

Task B
❶ Have students read the sentences and write *T* or *F* for each one.

❷ Have them check with a partner.

❸ Go over answers as a class.

 ┄┄┄┄ Have students work in pairs to make their own T/F quiz using as much of the vocabulary as they can.

2 Start Talking

Task A
❶ Have students read the conversation.

❷ Play the tape while students listen to the conversation.

 ┄┄┄┄ Rewind the tape and have students repeat the conversation after the tape.

Tapescript
M: Do you know Amy?
W: I don't know. What does she look like?
M: She's kind of short, and she has curly hair.
W: Oh, yes. I know her.

Task B
❶ Have them practice the conversation in pairs, using their own names.

❷ Have students swap partners and do the pair work again.

❸ Have them practice with books open or closed. Elicit other words to describe people, and list them on the board.

 ┄┄┄┄ Describe someone in the picture, or someone in the class. Have students tell you who it is.

③ Listen In

Task A

❶ Have students practice using the vocabulary items from Get Ready to describe the people in the picture.

❷ Do this as pair work or a whole class activity.

Task B

❶ Tell students that they will hear four dialogs. They will need to listen to who is being described as well as the description.

 ········· To prepare students for the listening, describe the people in the picture yourself. Have students follow your descriptions.

❷ Play the tape. Have them listen and match the name with the person being described.

❸ Go over answers.

Task C

❶ Play the tape. Have them listen again and check the names of the people the speakers know.

❷ Go over answers.

(**TRY THIS!**) Play the tape again, as necessary.

Answers: Brian—kind of short, short blond hair, cute smile, doesn't have glasses; Nina—tall with dark hair, large earrings; Michael—middle-aged, short, dark hair, glasses; Anne—young, wears glasses, long blond hair.

 ········· Ask what words or expressions could be used to describe the other people in the picture.

Tapescript

1. **W1:** Do you know Brian Morgan?
   M1: I'm not sure. What does he look like?
   W1: Well, he's kind of short, with short blond hair. And he has a cute smile.
   M1: Does he have glasses?
   W1: No, he doesn't.
   M1: No, I don't know him.

2. **W2:** Say, you know Nina Hansen, don't you, George?
   M2: I don't know. What does she look like?
   W2: Well, she's tall with dark hair.
   M2: Does she wear large earrings?
   W2: Yes, she does.
   M2: Oh, yeah. I know her.

3. **W3:** Do you know Michael Shea?
   M3: I'm not sure. What does he look like?
   W3: Well, he's middle-aged, and he has short, dark hair.
   M3: Does he have glasses?
   W3: He sure does!
   M3: Oh, yeah. I know him.

4. **M4:** Do you know Annie Jones?
   W4: Hmm... I'm not really sure. What does she look like?
   M4: She's young. And she wears glasses.
   W4: Does she have short, blond hair?
   M4: No, she has long, blond hair.
   W4: Oh, no. I don't know her.

---

④ Say It Right

Task A

❶ Explain how some sounds become reduced in rapid speech.

 ········· Read through the examples, both reduced and unreduced, before playing the tape.

❷ Play the tape and have students listen for the underlined sounds.

Task B

❶ Play the tape, pausing after each part of the conversation.

❷ Have students repeat after the tape.

(**TRY THIS!**) Monitor students' efforts to produce sentences like the examples. Have them exchange papers and mark the reductions before practicing with their partner.

Tapescript

1. **M:** What does she look like?
2. **M:** I don't know.
3. **M:** Is she tall?
4. **M:** Does he have glasses?
5. **M:** Yes, he does.

3 Listen In

A Look at the people below. Which words in Get Ready could you use to describe them?

B Who are they talking about? Listen and draw a line from the name to the correct person.

Brian Morgan

Nina Hansen ✔

Michael Shea ✔

Annie Jones

C Do the speakers *know* these people? Listen again and check (✔) the names of the people they know.

Try this

Which words did the speakers use to describe each person? Can you remember?

4 Say It Right

A Some sounds are not pronounced clearly in rapid speech. Listen and pay attention to the underlined letters.

1. *What does she look like?*

2. *I don't know.*

3. *Is she tall?*

4. *Does he have glasses?*

5. *Yes, he does.*

Try this

Make up two more examples of your own.
Then practice with a partner.

B Listen again and practice.

5 Focus In

A Look at the chart. When do we use *does/doesn't*? When do we use *do/don't*?

Questions and answers with *do/does*	
Do you know George?	Yes, I **do**.
Do they know your boss?	No, they **don't**.
Does he have glasses?	Yes, he **does**.
Does she wear earrings?	No, she **doesn't**.
Does he have curly hair?	No, he **doesn't**. He has straight hair.

B Match the questions and answers. Then practice them with a partner.

1. Do you know Lisa?   **a.** No, you don't.
2. Does she have long hair?   **b.** Yes, they do.
3. Do they wear glasses?   **c.** No, he doesn't.
4. Does he have curly hair?   **d.** Yes, I do.
5. Do I know him?   **e.** No, she doesn't.

C Fill in the missing information. Then ask your partner the questions.

1. __Do__ your parents wear glasses?
2. __Do__ you know my English teacher?
3. __Do__ you know my best friend?
4. __Does__ your best friend have curly hair?
5. __Does__ your best friend speak English?
6. __Do__ your sisters wear earrings?

6 Talk Some More

A Write the words in the correct places.

Simon: ____Do____ you know my friend Paul?
Wendy: I'm not sure. What does he ____look____ like?
Simon: He ____has____ blond, curly hair.
Wendy: ____Is____ he tall?
Simon: No, he ____isn't____. He's kind of average height.
Wendy: Does he ____have____ glasses?
Simon: Yes, he ____does____.
Wendy: Oh, yeah. I ____know____ him.

(isn't) (know) (do) (does)

(has) (is) (look) (have)

B Check your answers.

 Pair work

C Practice the conversation with a partner. Use your own information.

Spotlight
yeah = yes
in casual speech

26   Unit 3

Unit 3: Do you know Amy?

5 Focus In

Task A

❶ Go through the chart with students.

❷ Elicit when we use *do* and when we use *does*.

 ········· Present more examples as necessary, for students to grasp the rule.

Task B

❶ Have students match the questions and answers by drawing lines between them.

❷ Have them check with a partner.

❸ Have them practice asking and answering the questions in pairs.

Task C

❶ Have students fill in the blanks with *do* or *does*.

❷ Have them check their answers with a partner.

❸ Go over answers with the class.

6 Talk Some More

Task A

❶ Have students fill in the blanks with the words given.

❷ Offer help as necessary.

Task B

❶ Play the tape.

❷ Have students check their answers.

Task C

❶ Have students practice the conversation.

❷ Have them practice again, using their own friends' names.

 ········· Put extra vocabulary on the board as desired.

 ········· Have students continue, describing family members.

(SPOTLIGHT) Point out that *yeah* is much more informal and should not be used in very formal situations.

Tapescript

M: Do you know my friend Paul?
W: I'm not sure. What does he look like?
M: He has blond, curly hair.
W: Is he tall?
M: No, he isn't. He's kind of average height.
W: Does he have glasses?
M: Yes, he does.
W: Oh, yeah. I know him.

7 Work In Pairs

See pages xii-xiii for suggestions on pair work.

Task A

❶ Divide students into pairs. Refer Student B to page 28.

❷ Have them look at the picture.

support ⟩········ Elicit the necessary vocabulary items to describe the people in the picture.

❸ Have them read the statements to each other, answering true or false.

> **Sample**
>
> **A:** True or false? All three women have earrings.
> **B:** False. All three men have glasses.
> **A:** False. Two of the men…

Task B

❶ Explain that neither person in each pair has the complete information.

❷ Point out the prompt question in the speech bubble.

❸ Elicit the question type needed and note it on the board, e.g. *Is s/he...? Does s/he have...?* Note the ways of responding, too.

❹ Have them ask and answer questions, filling in the chart with the information they receive.

❺ Have students check their answers together.

> **Sample**
>
> **A:** What does Sally look like?
> **B:** She's kind of average height.
> **A:** Does she have long hair?
> **B:** Yes, she does. And she has earrings. How about Dave? What does he look like?
> **A:** He's tall and he has glasses.
> **B:** Does he have blond hair?
> **A:** No, he doesn't. He has short, black hair.

Task C

❶ Direct students' attention back to the picture.

❷ Have them work in pairs to correctly number the people in the chart.

❸ Go through answers with the class.

TRY THIS! Tell students that the famous people they choose can be from any country or walk of life. Have them compare their sentences with a partner. Monitor as necessary.

challenge ⟩········ Have students close their books and think of descriptions of famous people. One student describes the person and others guess who it is. This can be done as pair work or in groups.

Work In Pairs

Student A

Student B: Use page 28

A Look at the people.
Then read the statements to your
partner. Your partner will answer
'True' or 'False.'

1. All three women have earrings.

2. Two of the men have dark hair.

3. One of the women has short hair.

B Ask your partner questions.
Fill in the missing information.

*What does
Sally look like?*

		IS	HAS
Dave	4	tall	short, black hair/glasses
Sally	6	average height	long, curly hair/earrings
Richard	1	average height	short, brown hair
Patricia	5	short	long, black hair
Bruce	3	average height	blond hair/glasses
Jean	2	average height	short, black hair

C Look at the picture again. Write the number of the person next to the correct name.

Try this

Make up three sentences describing famous people.
Example: Tom Cruise is short and has dark brown hair.

1 _____

_____

2 _____

_____

3 _____

_____

▶ Share your sentences with your partner. Were any similar?

Work In Pairs (Student B)

A Look at the people.
Then read the statements to your
partner. Your partner will answer
'True' or 'False.'

1. All three men have glasses.

2. Two of the women have curly hair.

3. One of the men has blond hair.

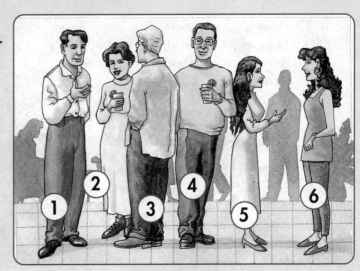

B Ask your partner questions.
Fill in the missing information.

*What does
Dave look like?*

		IS	HAS
Dave	4	tall	short, black hair/glasses
Sally	6	average height	long, curly hair/earrings
Richard	1	average height	short, brown hair
Patricia	5	short	long, black hair
Bruce	3	average height	blond hair/glasses
Jean	2	average height	short, black hair

C Look at the picture again. Write the number of the person next to the correct name.

Try this

Make up three sentences describing famous people.

Example: Tom Cruise is short and has dark brown hair.

1 _____

_____

2 _____

_____

3 _____

▶ **Share your sentences with your partner. Were any similar?**

7 Work In Pairs

See p. T27 for suggested instructions for this task.

Mid-Unit Assessment

Once your students have finished Work In Pairs, they will have covered approximately half of this unit. How well are they accomplishing the unit goals at this stage? You may wish to assess their ability on the points below before beginning the fluency task Express Yourself. Check (✔) the appropriate space in the chart for each goal.

Can your students...	Yes, all can.	Yes, most can.	Maybe half can.	Only some can.
1 ask about appearance? *e.g. What does she look like? Does he have glasses?*	_____	_____	_____	_____
2 use vocabulary to describe appearance correctly? *(see Get Ready for list)*	_____	_____	_____	_____
3 form sentences to describe appearance? *e.g. She has blond hair. He is short.*	_____	_____	_____	_____
4 understand and pronounce reduced sounds correctly in natural speech? *(see Say It Right for examples)*	_____	_____	_____	_____
5 form questions and answers using *do/does* and *don't/doesn't?*	_____	_____	_____	_____

If your students can already accomplish these fairly well, they're better prepared to expand their use of the target language in the tasks that follow. For those who are still having problems with particular items above, you may wish to direct them to the relevant areas of the unit on pages 24–28, to workbook pages 10–11, or to the online quiz on the *Expressions* website.

8 Express Yourself

Task A

support ▸ ········ Model this activity first by having students ask you questions until they guess the identity of the person you are thinking of.

1 Have students think of someone in the class, but keep the identity to themselves.

2 Divide students into groups.

Task B

support ▸ ········ Review the question forms needed, and note them on the board.

1 Explain that each person in the group will take turns being questioned.

2 Tell students not to answer questions which are formed incorrectly.

3 Have students do the activity. Monitor and offer support as necessary.

9 Think About It

1 Have the students read the information and consider the answers to the questions.

2 Discuss the questions as a class.

support ▸ ········ Have students make a list of polite conversation topics and write 1 or 2 questions for each topic.

10 Write About It

Task A

1 Have students read the letter.

2 Offer language support as necessary.

Task B

1 Have students write their own descriptions.

2 Check that no one has signed their letter, or identified themselves.

Task C

1 Mix up the papers.

2 Have each student read the paper they receive.

3 Have students stand up, walk around the room, and find the person on the paper. Encourage them to use English while they do this, e.g. *Excuse me, is this your letter?*

Express Yourself

(A) Think of a person in your class.
Don't tell anyone!

Group work

(B) Your classmates
will ask questions
and guess
the person.
Answer the
questions only
if they begin with
is or *does*.

Is he tall?

Yes, he is.

Think About It

In many cultures, it's OK to ask people certain questions but not others. In most cultures, people are interested in other people's age. In most English-speaking cultures, it's generally rude to ask a person's age. In your culture:

• *is it OK to ask adults their age?*
• *does it make a difference whether they're men or women?*
• *is it OK to ask children about their age?*

---

10 Write About It

(A) Read the following part of a letter to a pen pal.

(B) Write your own description to a pen pal on a
piece of paper. Don't write your name!

(C) Mix up the papers and take one. Read the
description and find the person.

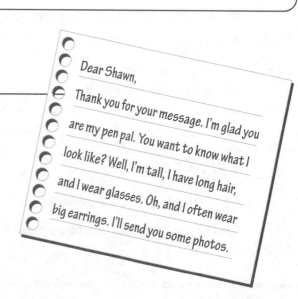

Dear Shawn,

Thank you for your message. I'm glad you are my pen pal. You want to know what I look like? Well, I'm tall, I have long hair, and I wear glasses. Oh, and I often wear big earrings. I'll send you some photos.

Read On Finding the Right Look

• *Strategy: Inferring vocabulary*

Is personal appearance really important?
Some companies want you to think so.

An 'image consulting company' can help you change your look. Just send them a photo of yourself, answer some questions about your job or your hobbies—and, of course, send money! They will send your picture back to you, together with ideas for new clothes, hairstyles, glasses, and jewelry that are right for you. They say they can help you plan a new look for work, for play, or even to find the perfect mate. They will even tell you where to shop!

The image consultants give women tips about makeup, and give men advice about their mustache or beard, if they have one. They teach you the best way to introduce yourself to other people. They also offer tips on what to say in job interviews, and how to act when eating out. By helping people change their style, they believe those people will feel better about themselves.

Look at the article again, and find words or phrases with the same meaning.
The first one has been done for you.

1. The way you look _____ personal appearance _____

2. Things you do in your free time ___ hobbies ___

3. The ideal husband or wife ___ the perfect mate ___

4. Hints ___ tips ___

5. Eating in a restaurant ___ eating out ___

Talk About It

○ Are there image consulting companies in your country?

○ Do you think these companies are a good idea? Why or why not?

11 Read On

Before the Reading

1. Bring in pictures (e.g. magazine covers) of famous people. Hold them up in turn, or place them all on the board. Ask the class these warm-up questions. Alternatively, have students first discuss them in pairs or in small groups. Note the students' responses on the board under each picture.

   Do you like the way these people look? Which person do you think has the best 'look?'

2. Write these words on the board: *image, consult, tips, advice, hairstyle, company, clothes, photo, send.* Elicit and discuss the meaning of each word. Explain that these words are all taken from the Read On passage. In groups, have the students predict the topic of the passage. Call on students to give their predictions and note them on the board.

3. Have students open their books to p. 30. Refer students to the title, heading and photos, and have them say whether they think their predictions were correct. Then, draw four columns on the board: *Yes, very important; Quite important; Not really important; Not important at all.* Point out the opening question in the heading: 'Is personal appearance really important?' Take a vote among the students in the class, and note the number of 'votes' under each column.

4. Write the phrases (1–5) from page 30 on the board. Explain that students need to find a word or words from the passage with the same meaning.

During the Reading

1. Monitor students and offer language support where necessary.

2. Have students compare their answers with a partner.

After the Reading

1. Elicit answers from the students. Write the correct words or phrases on the board.

2. Go over the meaning of each of the Talk About It questions. Have students work in pairs, asking and answering the questions. Then discuss the questions as a class.

   Optional questions:
   Who (in your country) has a good image, or 'look?' What kind of image would you like to have?

   Note: You may want to pre-teach some extra vocabulary, so that students can more effectively discuss these questions, e.g. *old-fashioned, smart, messy, fashionable, boring, strange, cool.*

Extension Activity

Bring in a large photo of someone (it could be a famous person, or someone you know). In groups, students have to create a new image for this person. They should give ideas on things like new clothes, hairstyle, makeup or mustache/beard. Have one person in each group label a picture of the 'new' person. Put the pictures on the board, and have the class discuss which is the best image for the person.

Cultural Note

In most English-speaking societies, it's considered polite to comment positively on someone's personal appearance, e.g. hairstyle, clothes. It's generally not acceptable to make negative comments, even between friends. Commenting on appearance is often used as an 'ice-breaker,' a way to start a conversation. For example, a woman might say to another woman, "Oh, I like your dress. Where did you buy it?"

12 Vocabulary Review

Task A

❶ Have students search back through the unit for relevant vocabulary—this could be done as a collaborative exercise if desired—and enter them into the correct columns.

❷ Elicit answers from students and review chart as a class.

Task B

❶ Have students use their own knowledge to list other words.

❷ Turn this into a whole class brainstorming session. Note student suggestions on the board.

12 Grammar Review

Task A

❶ Have students complete the task.

❷ Allow students to look back through the unit to check their answers.

Task B

❶ Have students write their own sentences. Monitor students and provide language support as necessary.

❷ Have students read their sentences to a partner.

 Have students practice asking *do/does* questions using vocabulary they have learned in this unit.

Log On

Have students do the online activities for this unit on the *Expressions* website: **http://expressions.heinle.com**

Language Summary

For a more detailed review of the language practiced in this unit, refer students to the **Language Summary on page 137**. Encourage them to add new vocabulary in the **Word Builder** section.

12 Review

1 Vocabulary Review

A Fill in the chart with words you learned in this unit.

Hair	Height	Age

B What other words are used to describe people's appearance? Note any others you remember.

Do you know Steve?

Well, he has sunglasses...

Hmm...What does he look like?

2 Grammar Review

A Fill in the blanks.

1. _Do_ you know Amy? Yes, I _do_ .
2. _Do_ they know your boss? No, they _don't_ .
3. _Does_ he have glasses? Yes, he _does_ .
4. _Does_ she wear earrings? No, she _doesn't_ .
5. _Does_ he have curly hair? No, he _doesn't_ . He has straight hair.

B Write questions or statements using the words below.

1. (know) _____
2. (hair) _____
3. (earrings) _____
4. (tall) _____

3 Log On

Practice more with the language and topics you studied on the *Expressions* website:

http://expressions.heinle.com

Goals

○ *Asking and answering questions about where people are from*

Where are you from?

1 Get Ready

A Look at the people.
Where are they from?
Write the number of the country
next to the correct people (1–6).

1. Brazil
2. Japan
3. Mexico
4. Taiwan
5. Canada
6. Korea

B Circle the cities. Underline the countries.
Which ones go together? Write them on a piece of paper.

Egypt Turkey Peru Istanbul Sydney Ireland
Lima Paris Cairo Australia France Dublin

2 Start Talking

A Look at the conversation and listen.

Stan: Where are you from?
Maria: Mexico. How about you?
Stan: Canada. Are you on vacation?
Maria: Yes, I am.

Pair work **B** Practice the conversation with a partner.
Then practice again, using different country names.

Unit 4: Where are you from?

Goals ➤ Asking and answering questions about where people are from

Workbook: pages 14–17

1 Get Ready

Task A

❶ Elicit country names that students know in English. List them on the board. Go over the pronunciation of the country names, including those listed in Get Ready.

❷ Refer students to the picture on page 32.

❸ Have students write the numbers in the correct place in the picture. Explain that two of the numbers can be used more than once.

❹ Have students compare answers with a partner.

❺ Check answers as a class by asking questions such as *Where is he from?* and *Where are they from?*

Task B

❶ Demonstrate the meaning of 'circle' and 'underline' on the board.

❷ Have students do the exercise, and check with a partner.

❸ Go over answers as a class.

 ········ For extra pronunciation practice, assign pairs/small groups a letter of the alphabet. Students must think of countries/cities beginning with that letter and practice saying them. Elicit suggestions and note them on the board. See which group can come up with the most suggestions.

2 Start Talking

Task A

❶ Let students read the conversation.

❷ Play the tape while students listen to the conversation.

 ········ Rewind the tape and have students repeat the conversation after the tape.

Task B

❶ Have students practice the conversation.

❷ Have them practice the conversation in pairs, using different countries and cities, either with their books open or closed.

Tapescript

M: Where are you from?
W: Mexico. How about you?
M: Canada. Are you on vacation?
W: Yes, I am.

3 Listen In

Task A

support ➤ •••••••• Go over the pronunciation of each of the names in 'A.'

❶ Play the tape. Have students listen to the three conversations and circle the names they hear.

❷ Go over answers.

Task B

❶ Have students write the four names in the chart. Explain that students will need to write a country name in the second cloumn, and *yes* or *no* in the third column. They can also add any other relevant information.

❷ Play the tape again. Have them listen and fill in the information.

❸ Go over answers.

(**TRY THIS!**) Play the tape again, as necessary. The woman says: *Oh, really?*

Tapescript

1. **W1:** And, so, where are you from, Steve?
   M1: I'm from Taiwan.
   W1: Oh, really? And, uh, are you on vacation here?
   M1: That's right.

2. **M2:** Who's that you were just talking to?
   W2: That's Tomoko.
   M2: Is she from Japan?
   W2: Yeah. Uh-huh. From Osaka.
   M2: Is she on vacation?
   W2: No, she isn't. She's a student.

3. **M3:** Hello. I'm John.
   W3: I'm Patricia.
   M3: Where are you from?
   W3: I'm from Mexico.
   M3: Are you here on vacation?
   W3: Yes, I am. How about you?
   M3: I'm on vacation, too.
   W3: Are you from the United States?
   M3: No, I'm not. I'm from Canada.

4 Say It Right

Task A

❶ Explain how words are broken into syllables, and how certain syllables are stressed.

support ➤ •••••••• Read through the examples slowly yourself before playing the tape.

❷ Have students match the countries with the same stress pattern.

❸ Have students compare their answers with a partner.

Task B

❶ Play the tape. Have students check their answers.

❷ Have students repeat after the tape, if necessary.

Task C

❶ Have students listen again and practice.

❷ Repeat the exercise using the city names from Get Ready.

(**TRY THIS!**) Pronounce the country names from Get Ready. Have students tell you which have the same stress patterns. (The stress patterns are: Ja<u>pan</u>, <u>E</u>gypt, <u>Tur</u>key, Pe<u>ru</u>, <u>I</u>reland, Aus<u>tra</u>lia.)

challenge ➤ •••••••• Elicit other country or city names and have students tell you which have the same stress pattern. Examples might include <u>Nor</u>way, <u>Ger</u>many, <u>Lon</u>don, Ber<u>lin</u>. Have students practice the correct pronunciation and stress patterns.

Tapescript

1. **M:** Are you from Mexico?
   M: He's from Canada.

2. **M:** She's from Brazil.
   M: They're from Taiwan.

3. **M:** Is she from Korea?
   M: We're from Malaysia.

4. **M:** He's from England.
   M: I'm from Sweden.

5. **M:** We're from Indonesia.
   M: Are they from Venezuela?

3 Listen In 🔊

A Listen and circle the names you hear. Then write them in the chart.

Anita   Paul   (Tomoko)   Winston
(Steve)   (John)   Anne   (Patricia)

B Where are they from? What are they doing? Listen again and fill in the chart.

Name	From?	On vacation?
Steve	Taiwan	yes
Tomoko	Osaka, Japan	no—student
John	Canada	yes
Patricia	Mexico	yes

Try this

What does the first woman say to show interest? Can you remember?

Where are you from?

4 Say It Right 🔊

A Which countries have the same stress pattern? Number them (1–5).

1. Mex • i • co   _3_ Ma • lay • sia
2. Bra • zil   _5_ Ven • e • zue • la
3. Ko • re • a   _1_ Can • a • da
4. Eng • land   _2_ Tai • wan
5. In • do • ne • sia   _4_ Swe • den

B Listen and check your answers.

Try this

Pronounce the names of the countries in Get Ready. Pay attention to the stress patterns.

C Listen again and practice.

Where are you from?   **33**

5 Focus In

A Look at the chart.

Is/Are and Do/Does

Where **are** you from?	**I'm** from Turkey.
Where **is** Amy from?	She**'s** from Canada.
Where **does** Jake come from?	He **comes** from Australia.
Where **do** Alec and Suzie live?	They **live** in San Francisco.

B Fill in the missing information.

1. Where ___is___ Sally from?
2. Where ___are___ Ric and Luc from?
3. Where ___does___ Hyo Soon live?

4. Where ___do___ you come from?
5. Where ___does___ Jake come from?
6. Where ___do___ Tomo and Saeko live?

C Draw lines to match the questions and answers.
Then practice with a partner using your own information.

1. What's your name?
2. Where are you from?
3. What do you do?
4. Are you on vacation?
5. Are you married?

a. I'm a doctor.
b. Yes, I am.
c. Yes, this is my husband.
d. Maria.
e. I'm from New York.

6 Talk Some More

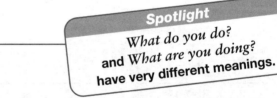

A Write the letter of the correct response in each blank to make a conversation.

Kelly: What's your name?
Maria: ___c___
Kelly: Where are you from?
Maria: ___d___
Kelly: Are you on vacation?
Maria: ___b___
Kelly: What do you do?
Maria: ___a___

a. I'm a student.
b. Yes, I am.
c. Maria.
d. I'm from Mexico.

B Check your answers.

C Practice the conversation with a partner. Use your own information.

5 Focus In

Task A

❶ Go through the chart with the students.

❷ Elicit when we use *is/are* and when we use *do/does*.

❸ Present more examples as necessary.

Task B

❶ Have students fill in the blanks with the correct words.

❷ Have them check with a partner.

❸ Have them practice asking and answering the questions using their own information.

Task C

❶ Have students match the questions and answers by drawing lines between them.

❷ Have them check their answers with a partner.

❸ Go over answers with the class.

❹ Have students ask each other the questions. Their partner should answer using real information about themselves.

6 Talk Some More

Task A

❶ Have students fill in the blanks with the letters given.

❷ Offer help as necessary.

Task B

❶ Play the tape.

❷ Have students check their answers.

Task C

❶ Have students practice the conversation.

❷ Have them practice again, using their own names, countries, etc. Brainstorm other possible questions and responses with the class.

 challenge ⟩ ········ Have students close their books, change partners, and continue practicing.

(SPOTLIGHT) Point out that *What do you do?* means *What is your job?*

Tapescript

W1: What's your name?
W2: Maria.
W1: Where are you from?
W2: I'm from Mexico.
W1: Are you on vacation?
W2: Yes, I am.
W1: What do you do?
W2: I'm a student.

7 Work In Pairs

See pages xii-xiii for suggestions on pair work.

Task A

❶ Divide students into pairs. Refer Student B to page 36.

❷ Have them look at the picture.

❸ Elicit suggestions from the students. Introduce any useful vocabulary, e.g. *tourists, immigration, airport.*

Task B

❶ Explain that neither person in the pair has the complete information.

❷ Have them fill in as much information as they can using the information on their page.

🔊 Gina Oliveira: <u>dʒinə ɔliveɪrə</u>

Task C

support ········ Note any useful question forms on the board, e.g. *What's _____'s family name? Is _____ a student?* Also, elicit any question forms students already know for clarifying, e.g. *How do you spell that?* and *Can you repeat that, please?*

❶ Have them ask and answer questions, filling in the chart with the information they receive.

❷ Have them check their answers together.

❸ Go through answers with the class.

> **Sample**
>
> **A:** Is Mary Stewart on vacation from Australia?
> **B:** Yes, she is. Is Gina Oliveira a student from Brazil?
> **A:** Yes, she is. Is…

TRY THIS! Have students write full sentences based on their now complete information about the three women, then compare with a partner.

Work In Pairs Student A

Student B: Use page 36

A Look at the women in the picture. Where do you think they are?

B Look at the information. Then fill in the chart with as much information as you can about the three women's names, where they are from, and what they're doing.

- *Mary is from Australia.*
- *Ms. Lee isn't from Australia or Brazil.*
- *Gina isn't from Taiwan or Australia.*
- *Ms. Oliveira is from Brazil.*

Name	From?	Doing what?
Mary Stewart	Australia	on vacation
Jenny Lee	Taiwan	student
Gina Oliveira	Brazil	student

C Read your information to your partner. Listen to your partner's information. Finish the chart. Ask your partner questions to check your answers.

Try this

Write sentences about the three women.

1 _____

2 _____

3 _____

Work In Pairs — Student B

Student A: Use page 35

A Look at the women in the picture. Where do you think they are?

B Look at the information. Then fill in the chart with as much information as you can about the three women's names, where they are from, and what they're doing.

- *Ms. Stewart isn't from Taiwan or Brazil.*
- *Jenny is from Taiwan.*
- *Mary is on vacation.*
- *Two of the people are students.*

Name	From?	Doing what?
Mary Stewart	Australia	on vacation
Jenny Lee	Taiwan	student
Gina Oliveira	Brazil	student

C Read your information to your partner. Listen to your partner's information. Finish the chart. Ask your partner questions to check your answers.

Try this

Write sentences about the three women.

1 _____

2 _____

3 _____

7 Work In Pairs

See p. T35 for suggested instructions for this task.

Mid-Unit Assessment

Once your students have finished Work In Pairs, they will have covered approximately half of this unit. How well are they accomplishing the unit goals at this stage? You may wish to assess their ability on the points below before beginning the fluency task Express Yourself. Check (✔) the appropriate space in the chart for each goal.

Can your students…	Yes, all can.	Yes, most can.	Maybe half can.	Only some can.
1 ask about where people are from? *e.g. Where are you from? Where does Jake come from?*	_____	_____	_____	_____
2 talk about where people are from? *e.g. I'm from Mexico. She's from Taiwan. They live in L.A.*	_____	_____	_____	_____
3 say the names of countries in English? *(see Get Ready for list)*	_____	_____	_____	_____
4 identify patterns of stressed syllables in words? *(see Say It Right for examples)*	_____	_____	_____	_____
5 use *is/are* and *do/does* correctly?	_____	_____	_____	_____

If your students can already accomplish these fairly well, they're better prepared to expand their use of the target language in the tasks that follow. For those who are still having problems with particular items above, you may wish to direct them to the relevant areas of the unit on pages 32–36, to workbook pages 14–15, or to the online quiz on the *Expressions* website.

8 Express Yourself

Task A

 Model this activity with students first by having them ask you questions until they guess the identity of the person you are thinking of.

1. Have students think of a famous person, but keep the identity to themselves.

2. Divide students into groups.

Task B

 Review the question forms needed, and note them on the board.

1. Explain that each person in the group will take turns being questioned.

2. Tell students not to answer questions which are incorrectly formed.

3. Have students do the activity. Monitor and offer support as necessary.

9 Think About It

1. Have the students read the information and consider the answers to the questions.

2. Discuss the questions as a class. Note the students' suggestions on the board under headings 'OK' and 'Not OK.'

 Have students use polite questions to interview each other. Students can be themselves or take on a new character, e.g. another classmate, famous person, etc.

10 Write About It

Task A

1. Have students read the hotel registration form.

2. Elicit the meaning of some of the more difficult words, such as registration, nationality, passport.

Task B

1. Have students fill in the blank registration form.

2. Tell them to make up passport numbers and dates of birth if they wish.

3. Have students check their partner's form.

Express Yourself

A Think of the name of a person from another country. It can be someone you know, someone you met before, or someone famous.

Where is he from?

Why is he famous?

What does he do?

Group work

B Work in groups. Take turns asking questions about each person. Ask as many questions as you can.

Think About It

When you meet a person for the first time, some questions are OK to ask and others may not be. Which questions do you think are OK?

- *Where are you from?*
- *How old are you?*

- *Do you have any children?*
- *How much money do you make?*

- *What's your name?*
- *What do you do?*

Does everyone in your class agree? What other questions are OK to ask in your culture? What questions are not OK?

Write About It

A Look at the hotel registration form.

HOTEL RICHMOND PLAZA

Guest Registration

Please fill in the following information.

Family Name ___Gallagher___

First Names ___Jeremy Spencer___

Nationality ___Australian___

Passport Number ___A3266790___

Date of Birth (M/D/Y) ___7/31/55___

Length of Stay ___4___ nights

Home Address ___31, Melville Street,___
___Concord West, NSW 25491,___
___Australia___

Thank You

HOTEL RICHMOND PLAZA

Guest Registration

Please fill in the following information.

Family Name _____

First Names _____

Nationality _____

Passport Number _____

Date of Birth (M/D/Y) _____

Length of Stay _____ nights

Home Address _____

_____

_____

Thank You

B Now fill in the form. Use your own information.

Where are you from?   **37**

I'm from Portland...but which one?

• *Strategy: Inferring content*

Portland is a popular name for cities in English-speaking countries. Which Portland is each person describing?

#1 My Portland is next to the Atlantic Ocean. It's a beautiful town. We have many homes from the 19th century. On weekends we like to hike or bike on trails by the waterfront or in nearby forests. Our most famous food is lobster. Our city was founded in 1786. Its name came from Portland, England. We love living here. You should come to visit us.

#2 My Portland is at a place where two rivers meet. Its nickname is the 'Bridge City' because we have eight bridges. On weekends we enjoy biking, jogging, or sailing. Nearby are mountains where we can ski in the winter. We are proud of our local salmon and wine. Our city was founded in 1845 and its name came from Portland, Maine. It's a great place to live, and we love visitors.

#3 My Portland is on a small island near the Atlantic Ocean. People have lived here for thousands of years. Our island is very green, and our beaches are sandy. Many people enjoy diving, windsurfing, sailing, and rock climbing here. Tourists like to visit our castles and churches and to drink tea in our tearooms. Portland is a very special place. Come see us!

Portland, Oregon — Portland, Maine

Portland, England

Write the number of the paragraph next to the correct place.

Portland, Oregon: Paragraph _____2_____
Portland, England: Paragraph _____3_____
Portland, Maine: Paragraph _____1_____

Now circle the vocabulary in the text that helped you decide.

Talk About It

- Which of these cities would you most like to visit? What would you like to do there?
- Have you ever visited a very interesting city?
- Which place have you always wanted to visit? Why?

11 Read On

Before the Reading

❶ Ask the class these warm-up questions. Alternatively, have students first discuss them in pairs or in small groups. Write the students' suggestions under three columns on the board: *nouns, adjectives, verbs*.

What nouns can you use to describe your hometown? What adjectives would you use? What things can you do there?

❷ Write these words at random on the board: *church, island, castle, ocean, bridges, rivers, forests, hike, bike, jog, sail, windsurf, sandy, famous, beautiful, local, special.* In groups, have students classify the words according to the three categories on the board. Call on students for their answers and note them under the columns on the board.

❸ Have students look at page 38. Refer them to the title of the reading, the headline, and the two maps, and have them say what they think the passage is about. Then, write the names of the three places on the board. Explain that students need to decide which passage describes each place. Next, they should circle the words that helped them decide.

During the Reading

❶ Monitor students and offer language support where necessary.

❷ Have students compare their answers with a partner.

After the Reading

❶ Elicit answers from the students for each place. Write the correct number next to each on the board. Have students call out the words that helped them decide, and note them next to each place.

❷ Go over the meaning of each of the Talk About It questions. Have students work in pairs, asking and answering the questions. Then, discuss the questions as a class.

Optional questions:
Portland, Oregon is called the 'Bridge City.' Do you know any nicknames for other cities?
Note: You could instead write a list of cities and their nicknames on the board (see Culture Note for suggestions) and have groups match them.

Extension Activity

Write some country names on the board (e.g. *France, United States, Japan, Hong Kong, Brazil, China, Italy, United Kingdom, Canada, Australia*). In groups, have students think of at least one famous person from each country and write a sentence about them (e.g. *Jackie Chan is from Hong Kong*). Have each group call out its sentences, and note the names under each country. See which group can come up with the most sentences.

Cultural Note

The article mentions that Portland, Oregon has a nickname: 'Bridge City.' Many other towns and cities around the world have nicknames. Some examples are: 'The Windy City' (Chicago), 'The Big Apple' (New York City), 'Old Smokey' (Edinburgh, Scotland), 'City of Angels' (Los Angeles) 'The Eternal City' (Rome, Italy), and 'City of Dreaming Spires' (Oxford, England). Las Vegas has several nicknames, including 'The City That Never Sleeps,' 'The City of Sin,' and 'Lost Wages.' Also, each state in the U.S. has its own nickname, e.g. 'The Sunshine State' (Florida), and 'The Lone Star State' (Texas).

12 Vocabulary Review

Task A

❶ Have students search back through the unit for country names—this could be done as a collaborative exercise if desired—and enter them into the correct columns.

❷ Check answers as a class. See if students can add any other countries to each column.

Task B

❶ Have students express their own opinion. Encourage them to give reasons for their choice. Turn this into a whole class session and encourage discussion.

 Have students talk about activities they would do, or particular cities they would visit, in their chosen country. Make sure they give reasons to support their views.

12 Grammar Review

Task A

❶ Have students complete the task.

❷ Allow students to look back through the unit to check their answers.

❸ Have students ask and answer the questions in pairs.

Task B

❶ Have students complete the task.

❷ Have students compare their answers then practice asking and answering the questions in pairs.

 Have students write a few statements about themselves. They can be true or false. Pair students and have Student A read statements to Student B, who should then supply the question. Student B should also decide if each statement is true or false. Pairs swap roles and repeat the activity.

Log On

Have students do the online activities for this unit on the *Expressions* website: **http://expressions.heinle.com**

Language Summary

For a more detailed review of the language practiced in this unit, refer students to the **Language Summary on page 137**. Encourage them to add new vocabulary in the **Word Builder** section.

12 Review

1 Vocabulary Review

A Fill in the names of the countries you learned in this unit.

Asia	The Americas	Others

B Which of these countries would you like to visit? Why?

Where are you from?

I'm from Atlantis.

2 Grammar Review

A Fill in the blanks.

1. Where __are__ you from?   __I'm__ from Mexico.
2. Where __is__ Laura from?   __She's__ from Scotland.
3. Where __is__ Steve from?   __He's__ from Taiwan.
4. What __do__ you __do__?   __I'm__ a teacher.
5. What __does__ Laura __do__?   __She's__ a student.
6. What __is__ John __doing__?   __He's__ on vacation.

B Circle the best response in each pair.

1. What do you do?   a. I'm from Paris.   (b.) I'm a student here.
2. Do you come from India?   (a.) Yes, I do.   b. Yes, I am.
3. Where are you from?   a. I am in California.   (b.) I come from California.
4. Is she a student?   (a.) No, she works here.   b. No, she doesn't.

3 Log On

Practice more with the language and topics you studied on the *Expressions* website:

http://expressions.heinle.com

Make yourself at home.

1 Get Ready

A Look at the words.
Are they names of food or drink?

1.	juice
2.	cookies
3.	tea
4.	coffee
5.	bread
6.	orange
7.	cola
8.	apple
9.	milk
10.	sandwich

Welcome. Come in and make yourself at home.

Thanks.

Your new apartment is really nice.

Thanks. I like it a lot, too.

Would you like some tea?

Yes, please.

B Write the missing information in the correct place in the pictures.

- *Thanks. I like it a lot, too.*
- *Yes, please.*
- *Thanks.*

2 Start Talking

A Look at the conversation in Get Ready and listen.

Pair work

B Practice the conversation with a partner. Offer other food and drink items.
Try using the following expressions:

- *Hi. Come in and have a seat.*
- *I really like your new place.*
- *Would you like something to drink?*

Unit 5: Make yourself at home.

Goals
➤ Welcoming someone ➤ Offering, accepting, and refusing

Workbook: pages 18–21

1 Get Ready

Task A
❶ Elicit food and drink words the students know. List them on the board.

❷ Go over the pronunciation of the vocabulary items on page 40.

❸ Have them decide which items relate to food, and which to drink. *Food: cookies, bread, orange, apple, sandwich. Drink: juice, tea, coffee, cola, milk.*
Note: In some forms of English, tea, orange and apple can be both food and drink.

Task B
❶ Have students read the sentences and write them in the correct places in the picture.

❷ Have students compare answers with a partner.

2 Start Talking

Task A
❶ Let students read through the conversation again.

❷ Play the tape. Have students check their answers in Get Ready, 'B,' while they listen to the conversation.

 Rewind the tape and have students repeat the conversation after the tape.

Task B
❶ Have students practice the conversation.

❷ Elicit ways to refuse politely, e.g. *No thanks.*, and *No, thank you.*

❸ Have students look at the three sentences at the bottom of page 40. Ask them to say in which part of the conversation each one would be suitable.

 Have students swap partners and practice the conversation again, using the different expressions given, and the various food and drink items in Get Ready.

> **Tapescript**
>
> **W1:** Welcome. Come in and make yourself at home.
> **W2:** Thanks.
>
> **W2:** Your new apartment is really nice.
> **W1:** Thanks. I like it a lot, too.
>
> **W1:** Would you like some tea?
> **W2:** Yes, please.

Unit 5: Make yourself at home.

3 Listen In

Task A

❶ Elicit vocabulary for rooms in a house.

❷ Have students try to identify the rooms in the picture.

❸ Have them check their answers with a partner.

Task B

❶ Review the meaning and pronunciation of the words listed.

❷ Play the tape. Have them listen and check the words they hear.

❸ Go over answers.

Task C

❶ Play the tape. Have students listen and number the pictures. The second picture is not used.

❷ Go over answers.

(**TRY THIS!**) Play the tape again, as necessary. The man says: *Wow.*

Tapescript

1. **M1:** Would you like some coffee or juice?
   M2: No, thank you. But may I just have a glass of water?
   M1: Sure.

2. **M1:** Hey, come and see the rest of the apartment.
   M2: OK.
   M1: This is the bedroom.
   M2: Wow. It's really big. And a nice view, too.
   M1: Yeah.

3. **M1:** So, that's about it.
   M2: It's great.
   M1: Mmm. Much better than my old place.
   M2: May I use your bathroom?
   M1: Of course. It's right over there.

4 Say It Right

Task A

❶ Explain how the letter 'C' in English can have the sound /k/ or /s/ depending on where it comes in a word, and the vowel sound which follows.

support ⟶ Give other examples before students do the exercise.

❷ Ask students to individually circle and underline the sounds.

❸ Have students compare their answers with a partner.

Task B

❶ Play the tape. Have students check their answers.

❷ Have students repeat after the tape, if necessary.

Task C

❶ Have students listen again and practice the dialog in pairs.

challenge ⟶ Have students, in groups, make a list of as many words as they can think of containing the letter 'C.' Ask them to categorize the words according to the 'C' sound. Have groups exchange papers to check each other's lists. Elicit words, and categorize them on the board. Some examples are: /s/ *city, face, rice;* /k/ *curly, culture, car.*

(**TRY THIS!**) Have students write two sentences and exchange them with a partner. The partner should identify which sounds are /s/ and which are /k/. Model some examples first on the board, if necessary.

Tapescript

1. **W:** Come in. Make yourself comfortable.
   M: Wow. This place is really nice.

2. **W:** Would you like some juice or coffee?
   M: Thanks. A cup of coffee sounds great.

3. **W:** How about some cookies?
   M: No, thanks. But can I have some water, please?
   W: Of course.

3 Listen In

(A) Look at the pictures below. Which rooms can you see in the man's home?

③

not used ✗

①

②

(B) Listen and check (✔) the words you hear.

_____ tea	___✔___ juice	_____ cookies	___✔___ bedroom	_____ kitchen
___✔___ coffee	___✔___ water	_____ cakes	_____ living room	___✔___ bathroom

(C) Listen again and write the number of the conversation above the correct picture (1–3).

Try this

What word does the second man use to show surprise? Can you remember?

4 Say It Right

(A) Sometimes the letter *c* sounds like /s/ and sometimes like /k/. Circle the ones that sound like /s/. Underline the ones that sound like /k/.

1. A: Come in. Make yourself comfortable.
   B: Wow. This place is really nice.

2. A: Would you like some juice or coffee?
   B: Thanks. A cup of coffee sounds great.

3. A: How about some cookies?
   B: No, thanks. But can I have some water, please?
   A: Of course.

Try this

Make up two more examples of your own. Exchange your sentences with your partner. Circle the /s/ sounds; underline the /k/ sounds.

(B) Listen and check your answers.

(C) Listen again and practice.

5 Focus In

A Look at the chart.

Would/may	
Would you like some coffee?	Yes, please.
Would you like some tea?	No, thanks. But **may** I have some water?
May I use your bathroom?	Of course. It's the second door on the right.
May I have some juice?	**Would** you like orange or apple?

B Change these sentences into polite offers.

1. Come in!   <u>Would you like to come in?</u>
2. Have some juice!   <u>Would you like some juice?</u>
3. I want some water!   <u>May I have some water?</u>
4. I want to use the bathroom!   <u>May I use the bathroom?</u>
5. I want some more!   <u>May I have some more?</u>

C Where would you hear these sentences? Write the number next to the correct place. (There may be more than one answer for some.)

1. May I help you?   <u>1/3/4</u> At a restaurant.
2. Take a look around.   <u>2</u> At a friend's house.
3. Please turn off your cell phone.   <u>1/2</u> At a store.
4. Would you like to order?   <u>1/3</u> At a movie theater.

6 Talk Some More

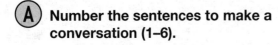

A Number the sentences to make a conversation (1–6).

Eric:	<u>6</u>	Thanks a lot.
Phoebe:	<u>5</u>	Sure. Here you are.
Eric:	<u>4</u>	May I have some coffee, please?
Eric:	<u>2</u>	Thanks. Nice place.
Phoebe:	<u>1</u>	Hi. Come in.
Phoebe:	<u>3</u>	Thanks. Would you like some tea or coffee?

Spotlight
Thanks a lot is stronger than Thanks.

B Check your answers.

Pair work **C** Practice the conversation. Then practice again offering different items.

5 Focus In

Task A

❶ Go through the chart with students.

❷ Elicit which are offers *(Would you...?)* and which are requests *(May I...?).*

 ········ Present more examples as necessary.

Task B

❶ Have students rewrite the sentences, according to the example.

❷ Have them check with a partner.

❸ Have them practice making the offers and requests.

Task C

❶ Have students write the number of the sentence next to the appropriate place(s).

❷ Have them check their answers with a partner.

❸ Go over answers with the class.

 ········ Have students practice role-playing short conversations for one or more of the places in the list.

6 Talk Some More

Task A

❶ Have students number the sentences to make a logical conversation.

❷ Offer help as necessary.

Task B

❶ Play the tape.

❷ Have students check their answers.

Task C

❶ Have students practice the conversation.

❷ Have them practice again, using different foods and drinks.

 ········ Write a similar conversation on a piece of paper. Make copies, and cut the conversation into sentence strips. Give a set of strips to each group of students. Have the students put the strips in the correct order. Then, have students practice the conversation in pairs.

(SPOTLIGHT) Point out that *Thanks a lot,* while stronger, is also informal. Tell students that *Thank you very much* is the more formal version of this expression.

> **Tapescript**
>
> **W:** Hi. Come in.
> **M:** Thanks. Nice place.
> **W:** Thanks. Would you like some tea or coffee?
> **M:** May I have some coffee, please?
> **W:** Sure. Here you are.
> **M:** Thanks a lot.

7 Work In Pairs

See pages xii-xiii for suggestions on pair work.

Task A

❶ Divide students into pairs. Refer Student B to page 44.

❷ Have them look at the pictures.

❸ Ask them to identify the food and drink in the pictures.

Sample

A: I can see orange juice. And some fruit.
B: And is that cola?
A: No, I think it's iced tea...

Task B

❶ Explain that neither person in the pair has any verbal information.

❷ Have students fill in the speech bubbles using their own ideas.

 ········ Elicit and write possible language for the speech bubbles on the board. Have students copy the sentences next to the correct photos.

❸ Monitor as necessary.

Task C

❶ Have students read the information to their partner and let him or her find the correct matching information.

❷ Monitor and assist as necessary.

❸ Have them write their conversation together.

❹ Have them practice the conversation. Have them reverse roles as well, if there is time.

Sample

A: 1–Would you like some iced tea or juice? 2–Would you like some fruit? 3–Hi. Come in.
B: 4–May I have some iced tea, please? 5–No, thank you. 6–Thanks. Nice place.
A: OK. I think 3 matches 6.
B: Yes. And 1 matches 4. And 2 matches 5...
A: OK, so let's do 3, 6, 1, 4, 2, 5...

(TRY THIS!) Allow students to practice the conversation as necessary; do not allow the activity to lose momentum. Give students the freedom to expand/lengthen their conversations using extra vocabulary and expressions they think of.

Work In Pairs (Student A)

A Look at the pictures below. What types of food or drink can you see? Check with your partner.

B Look at the pictures. Write what you think the host is saying in the speech bubbles.

Would you like some iced tea or juice?

Would you like some fruit?

Hi. Come in. Make yourself at home.

C Read the information to your partner. Ask your partner to tell you which picture (4–6) matches yours (1–3). Then write the conversation.

Host: _____

Guest: _____

Host: _____

Guest: _____

Host: _____

Guest: _____

Try this

Try the conversation again using the different foods and drinks from Get Ready.

Make yourself at home.

Work In Pairs   Student B

A Look at the pictures below. What types of food or drink can you see?
Check with your partner.

B Look at the pictures. Write what you think the guest is saying in the speech bubbles.

④ May I have some iced tea?

Thanks. Nice place.

No, thank you.

⑤

⑥

C Read the information to your partner. Ask your partner to tell you which picture
(1–3) matches yours (4–6). Then write the conversation.

Host: _____

Guest: _____

Host: _____

Guest: _____

Host: _____

Guest: _____

Try this

Try the conversation again using the different foods and drinks
from Get Ready.

Unit 5: Make yourself at home.

7 Work In Pairs

See p. T43 for suggested instructions for this task.

Mid-Unit Assessment

Once your students have finished Work In Pairs, they will have covered approximately half of this unit. How well are they accomplishing the unit goals at this stage? You may wish to assess their ability on the points below before beginning the fluency task Express Yourself. Check (✔) the appropriate space in the chart for each goal.

Can your students…	Yes, all can.	Yes, most can.	Maybe half can.	Only some can.
❶ welcome someone in their home? *e.g. Welcome. Come in. Make yourself comfortable.*	_____	_____	_____	_____
❷ offer food and drink to guests? *e.g. Would you like some tea?*	_____	_____	_____	_____
❸ accept food and drink? *e.g. Yes, please. That sounds great.*	_____	_____	_____	_____
❹ refuse food and drink? *e.g. No thanks.*	_____	_____	_____	_____
❺ make requests? *e.g. May I have some tea?*	_____	_____	_____	_____
❻ say the names of food and drink items? *(see Get Ready for list)*	_____	_____	_____	_____
❼ recognize and form the correct pronunciation of 'C' in words? *(see Say It Right for examples)*	_____	_____	_____	_____
❽ use *would* and *may* correctly in questions?	_____	_____	_____	_____

If your students can already accomplish these fairly well, they're better prepared to expand their use of the target language in the tasks that follow. For those who are still having problems with particular items above, you may wish to direct them to the relevant areas of the unit on pages 40–44, to workbook pages 18–19, or to the online quiz on the *Expressions* website.

T44

8 Express Yourself

Task A

❶ Have students refer to page 40 and make a list of items they would offer a visitor to their home.

 ········ Brainstorm other items as a class, if desired. List them on the board.

❷ Check spellings and *a/some* usage as in *a sandwich/some fruit.*

Task B

❶ Have students offer their classmates the items they listed. Urge them to use all the items on their list and ask as many classmates as they can.

❷ Tell them they are free to accept or refuse, but they should do so politely.

 ········ Have students, in groups, discuss which items offered were the most and least popular.

9 Think About It

❶ Have the students read the information and consider the answers to the questions.

❷ Discuss the questions as a class.

 ········ Have students work in groups to make a list of things that guests should/shouldn't do in their culture(s). For example, a guest should take off their shoes, they shouldn't arrive late, etc. Then have groups check each other's lists. Do they agree?

10 Write About It

Task A

❶ Have students read the invitation.

❷ Offer language support as necessary.

Task B

❶ Have students write their own invitations, using different times and dates.

❷ Have them pass it to several different students.

❸ Have students reply to the invitations they received.

 ········ Have students politely refuse invitations which clash with any that they have already accepted. If there is time, have students write invitations for different events or parties.

8 Express Yourself

A How many food and drink items can you remember from Get Ready?
Write at least four in the space.

○ _____
○ _____
○ _____
○ _____
○ _____
○ _____

B Offer your classmates the items on your list.
Write their first names next to the items they accept.
Write a different name for each item.

9 *Think About It*

When you visit someone's home for the first time, do you like to look around? If so, you're not unusual. Most people love to see how others live.

• How about in your culture? Is it OK to ask your host to show you around? Why/why not?

10 Write About It

A Look at the housewarming invitation and the reply.

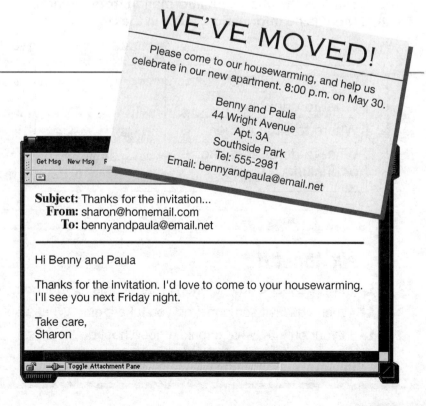

WE'VE MOVED!

Please come to our housewarming, and help us celebrate in our new apartment. 8:00 p.m. on May 30.

Benny and Paula
44 Wright Avenue
Apt. 3A
Southside Park
Tel: 555-2981
Email: bennyandpaula@email.net

Subject: Thanks for the invitation...
From: sharon@homemail.com
To: bennyandpaula@email.net

Hi Benny and Paula

Thanks for the invitation. I'd love to come to your housewarming. I'll see you next Friday night.

Take care,
Sharon

B Make up your own housewarming invitation. Pass it to several students. Write replies to the ones you receive.

Make yourself at home.

11 Read On   Good Guests and Good Hosts

How would you make your guests feel at home?

Angela Ascanio, Venezuela _____

Venezuelans usually invite only close friends or relatives to our homes. At home, we always offer guests a cup of strong, black coffee. Visitors usually bring a gift, like flowers. At meals we sit on chairs around a table. We eat with knives and forks, though many people just use the fork. After guests finish eating, they put the knife and fork in the center of their plate.

Jariya Anukulsupart, Thailand _____

We don't tell our dinner guests what time to arrive. In the city we sit on chairs around a table, but in the countryside we sit on mats on the floor. We hold our spoon in our right hand and our fork in our left. We push food onto the spoon with the fork. We drink water or beer with our meal. When we finish, we put our fork and spoon together on the plate.

Mohammed Al-Swailem, Saudi Arabia _____

In Saudi Arabia we have a special room for visitors. We usually sit on cushions on the floor. When a guest visits, we serve strong coffee or sweet mint tea. We never serve alcohol. When guests finish drinking, they cover the cup with their hand. When they finish eating, the host must offer more food, but the guests should politely say no. My father generally invites only men to visit him. My mother invites only women. A man must not bring a gift for the wife of the house, but he may bring gifts for the children.

**Complete the chart with information from the article.
If there is no information, put X in the box.**

	Venezuela	Thailand	Saudi Arabia
What gift to bring...	flowers	X	gifts for children
What to drink...	coffee	water/beer with meal	coffee/mint tea
Where to sit at dinner...	around the table	mats on the floor	cushions on the floor
What to do after eating or drinking...	put knife and fork in center of plate	put spoon and fork together on plate	cover cup with hand refuse more food

---

Talk About It _____

- In your culture, do you often invite people to your home?
- When you visit someone, do you take a gift? What would you take?
- In your culture, what should a good host do?

Unit 5: Make yourself at home.

11 Read On

Before the Reading

❶ Ask the class the following warm-up questions. Alternatively, have students first discuss them in pairs or in small groups.

What food do you serve when guests come to your house? What drinks?

❷ Explain that students are going to read a piece about visiting someone's home for dinner. Write these verbs on the board: *serve, bring, visit, offer, invite, eat, sit, arrive, drink, finish*. Draw three columns, and label them: *Guest, Host, Both*. In groups, have students decide which things a guest would do, which a host would do, and which both might do. Then, have students decide the order in which the things would happen. Elicit suggestions and note them on the board.

❸ Have students open their books to page 46. Refer the students to the title of the reading, the headline, and the three flags. Ask students to say what they think the passage is about, and which three countries the article refers to. If necessary, explain where these three countries are. You may want to explain the meaning of *make someone feel at home* (= to make someone comfortable, as if they're in their own house).

❹ Draw the chart from page 46 on the board. Explain what information students will need to find in order to complete the chart. Explain that if there is no information, they should add an X.

During the Reading

❶ Monitor and offer language support where necessary.

❷ Have students compare their answers with a partner.

🌙 Ascanio: əsk<u>a</u>ny<u>ɔ</u>, Jariya Anukulsupart: dʒɑr<u>i</u>yɑ ɑn<u>uku</u>ns<u>upɑ</u>t,
Mohammed Al Swailem: mʌh<u>a</u>mʌd ɑl swa<u>ilɛ</u>m

After the Reading

❶ Elicit answers from the students. Write the correct information on the board.

❷ Go over the meaning of each of the *Talk About It* questions. Have students work in pairs, asking and answering the questions. Then discuss the questions as a class.

Optional questions:
Who would you like to invite to a dinner party at your house? (It can be someone you know or a famous person.) What food and drinks would you serve?

Extension Activity

Have students work in pairs. Explain that they will do a role-play: one person will be a host and the other will be a guest arriving for dinner. Elicit phrases from students that might be useful for the role-play and write them on the board. Have each pair write a dialog and then perform their role-play.

Cultural Note

In English-speaking countries, it's generally acceptable to take a gift when invited to someone's house for dinner. Common gifts include flowers, chocolates and drinks, or a gift from your own country. In some English-speaking societies, the host may say, "Oh, you shouldn't have!" on receiving a gift; this is a way of expressing thanks and is not meant literally!

T46

12 Vocabulary Review

Task A

❶ Have students search back through the unit for food and drink items—this could be done as a collaborative exercise if desired—and enter them into the correct columns.

❷ Go over answers as a class. Have students add any other items to the lists.

Task B

❶ Have students express their own opinion.

❷ Turn this into a whole class session and encourage discussion. Have students give reasons why they offer certain food and drink but don't offer other food and drink items.

12 Grammar Review

Task A

❶ Have students complete the task.

❷ Go through answers.

Task B

❶ Have students complete the task individually or in pairs.

❷ Go through answers.

 Have students practice the sentences in 'B' in pairs, accepting or refusing as appropriate. If there is time, have pairs put the sentences from 'A' into a mini-dialog and get them to role-play the situation.

Log On

Have students do the online activities for this unit on the **Expressions** website: **http://expressions.heinle.com**

Language Summary

For a more detailed review of the language practiced in this unit, refer students to the **Language Summary on page 138**. Encourage them to add new vocabulary in the **Word Builder** section.

12 Review

1 Vocabulary Review

A Fill in the chart with words you learned in this unit.

Hot drinks
_____
_____
_____
_____

Cold drinks
_____
_____
_____
_____

Food
_____
_____
_____
_____

B Which do you usually offer guests? Which don't you offer?

2 Grammar Review

A Fill in the blanks.

1. <u>Make</u> <u>yourself</u> at home.
2. <u>May</u> <u>I</u> use your bathroom?
3. <u>Would</u> <u>you</u> like some tea?
4. No, thanks. But <u>may</u> <u>I</u> have some water, please?
5. Is it OK if <u>I</u> <u>look</u> around?

B Write the correct sentences on the right.

1. your/may/use/I/telephone ___*May I use your telephone?*___
2. I/just/water/have/may/please ___*May I just have water, please?*___
3. like/sandwich/you/would/a ___*Would you like a sandwich?*___
4. apartment/wow!/this/nice/a/is ___*Wow! This is a nice apartment.*___
5. coffee/a/sounds/cup/great/of ___*A cup of coffee sounds great.*___

3 Log On

Practice more with the language and topics you studied on the *Expressions* website:

http://expressions.heinle.com

Goals

○ *Asking about and stating prices*   ○ *Paying for goods*

How much is this sweater?

1 Get Ready

A Look at the advertisement. Write the number of the item next to the correct picture.

1.	T-shirts
2.	sweaters
3.	shorts
4.	jeans
5.	shirts
6.	shoes
7.	dresses

SALE! SALE! SALE! SALE

$16 $7.99 $3.50 $8.60 $19.50 $29.99 $14

One Day Only!

B Look at the words. Are they used to describe colors or patterns? Which words can be used to describe the items in the ad?

1. blue	3. striped	5. brown	7. purple	9. checked
2. floral	4. green	6. yellow	8. red	10. white

2 Start Talking

A Look at the conversation and listen.

Eugene: I need a sweater.
Jill: Here are some sweaters
Eugene: How much are they?
Jill: $16.

Pair work **B** Practice the conversation with a partner.
Then practice again, using different items from the ad.

Unit 6: How much is this sweater?

Goals ➤ Asking about and stating prices   ➤ Paying for goods

Workbook: pages 22–25

1 Get Ready

Task A

❶ Elicit any clothing or color words the students know. List them on the board.

 ········ Go over the meaning and pronunciation of the items listed in Get Ready.

❷ Have students write the numbers in the correct places in the picture.

❸ Have students compare answers with a partner.

❹ Check answers as a class. Ask questions such as *What's $16?* and *What's $3.50?* to check student comprehension.

Task B

❶ Go through the vocabulary items for color and pattern.

❷ Have students decide which relate to colors and which describe patterns.

 ········ List this information on the board in two columns.

❸ Have students look at the picture and decide which words relate to which items.

❹ Have students compare with a partner.

❺ Go over answers with the class. Ask questions such as *What's blue?* and *What's striped?*

2 Start Talking

Task A

❶ Let students read the conversation.

❷ Play the tape while students listen to the conversation.

 ········ Rewind the tape and have students repeat the conversation after the tape.

> ### Tapescript
>
> **M:** I need a sweater.
> **W:** Here are some sweaters.
> **M:** How much are they?
> **W:** $16.

Task B

❶ Have students practice the conversation. Have them practice again, either with books open or closed.

challenge ········ Have students say which items can be preceded by 'a' and which require 'some' *(some shorts, some jeans, some shoes).* List the words under two columns on the board, and have students practice saying *I need some shoes, I need some shorts, etc.*

❸ Listen In

Task A

❶ Have students identify the colors and patterns of the items in the picture.

❷ Have them check their answers with a partner.

Task B

❶ Play the tape. Have them listen and circle the words they hear for each sentence.

❷ Go over answers.

Task C

❶ Play the tape. Have students listen and write the items next to the correct prices.

❷ Have them compare answers with a partner.

❸ Go over answers. (Some items and prices are not used).

 support ········ Pause the tape after each conversation to give students time to write.

TRY THIS! Play the tape again, as necessary. The woman says: *Great.*

Tapescript

M1: Can I help you?
W1: Oh, yeah. Um, how much are the shoes?
M1: The shoes? $22.99.
W1: Thanks.

W2: I need some T-shirts.
M2: Here are some.
W2: How much are they?
M2: $4.50 each. How many do you want?
W2: Three.

W3: What are you looking for?
W4: I need a new dress.
W3: Here are some.
W4: How much is the black dress?
W3: $40.
W4: Great.

M3: I'll take this sweater.
M4: OK. That'll be $16.00.
M3: Do you take personal checks?
M4: No, I'm sorry. We don't. Cash only.

❹ Say It Right

Task A

❶ Explain how rising intonation is used to check that we have heard something correctly.

 support ········ Give other examples yourself before students do the exercise.

challenge ········ Have students mark what they think will be rising and falling intonation before listening.

❷ Ask students to individually mark the intonation.

❸ Have students compare their predictions with a partner.

Tapescript

Example
W1: I need a sweater.
M1: A sweater?
W1: Yes.

1. **M2:** How much are the shoes?
   W2: The shoes? $22.99.

2. **W3:** I don't like that dress.
   M3: You don't?
   W3: No.

3. **M4:** Do you take personal checks?
   W4: Personal checks? No.

Task B

❶ Play the tape. Have students mark the intonation in the three conversations.

 support ········ Have students check their answers with a partner.

❷ Play the tape again and have students repeat each line using correct intonation.

Task C

❶ Have students listen again and practice the complete conversations in pairs.

(A) Look at the items in the picture below. What colors are they?

(B) Listen and circle the words you hear.

1. How much are the (shoes)/sweaters?
2. How much (are they)/is it?
3. How many do you need/(want)?

4. What are you looking (for)/at?
5. How much is the (black)/red dress?
6. Do you take (personal)/(traveler's) checks?

(C) Listen again and write the name of each item next to the correct price.

$22.99 _shoes_
$2.99 _not used_
$15.00 _not used_
$4.50 _T-shirts_

$14.00 _not used_
$40.00 _black dress_
$16.00 _sweaters_
$60.00 _not used_

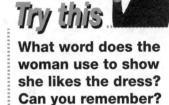

Try this

What word does the woman use to show she likes the dress? Can you remember?

4 Say It Right

(A) When we want to check if we heard something correctly, we can use rising (↗) intonation.

(B) Listen and mark the intonation in the three conversations.

(C) Listen again and practice.

5 Focus In

A Look at the chart.

How much/How many	
How much is the sweater?	It's $36.
How much are the shoes?	They're $48 a pair.
How many T-shirts are on the table?	One.
How many shorts do you need?	I need two pairs.

B Fill in the blanks with *how much/how many*.

1. _How many_ pairs of jeans do you want?
2. _How much_ is a new pair of shoes?
3. _How much_ are his pants?

4. _How many_ shirts does she have?
5. _How much_ does his sweater cost?

C Number the lines in order to make a conversation. Then practice with a partner.

_3_ A: They're on sale. Five dollars each.

_5_ A: How many do you want?

_1_ A: May I help you?

_2_ B: Yes, please. How much are the T-shirts?

_6_ B: Um, I'll take four.

_4_ B: Five dollars? Great. I want some blue ones.

6 Talk Some More

A Write the words in the correct spaces.

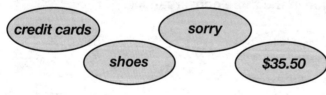
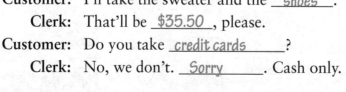

Customer: I'll take the sweater and the _shoes_ .
Clerk: That'll be _$35.50_ , please.
Customer: Do you take _credit cards_ ?
Clerk: No, we don't. _Sorry_ . Cash only.

> **Spotlight**
> When a price has dollars AND cents, people often say the numbers only. $35.50 can be said as:
> *Thirty-five dollars and fifty cents* or *Thirty-five fifty.*

B Check your answers.

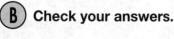

C Practice the conversation. Then practice again with different items and prices.

5 Focus In

Task A

1 Go through the chart with the students.

2 Elicit when *How much* and *How many* are used.

 ········ Present more examples as necessary.

Task B

1 Have students fill in the blanks.

2 Have them check with a partner.

3 Have them practice asking and answering the questions.

Task C

1 Have students number the lines of the conversation.

2 Have them check their answers with a partner.

3 Go over answers with the class.

4 Have students practice the conversation with a partner.

6 Talk Some More

Task A

1 Review pronunciation of the words with students.

2 Have students write the words in the blanks.

3 Offer help as necessary.

Tapescript

W: I'll take the sweater and the shoes.
M: That'll be $35.50 (thirty-five fifty), please.
W: Do you take credit cards?
M: No, we don't. Sorry. Cash only.

Task B

1 Play the tape.

2 Have students check their answers.

Task C

1 Have students practice the conversation.

2 Have them practice again, either with books open or closed, using different items and prices.

 ········ Have students, in pairs, write their own short dialog and role-play it in front of the class.

(SPOTLIGHT) Point out that *Thirty-five fifty* is also common. Write some similar prices on the board and have students practice saying them using the numbers only.

7 Work In Pairs

See pages xii-xiii for suggestions on pair work.

Task A

❶ Divide students into pairs. Refer Student B to page 52.

❷ Have them look at the pictures.

❸ Have them individually write descriptions of the items.

❹ Monitor as necessary, but do not allow them to look at each other's books.

❺ Have students read their list to their partner to compare.

Task B

❶ Explain that neither person in the pair has complete information.

❷ Write the questions on the board, if necessary.

 ········ Have them fill in the information by asking *How much is/are the...?*

❸ Monitor and provide language support as necessary.

> **Sample**
>
> **A:** How much are the blue jeans?
> **B:** They're fourteen fifty. How much is the green sweater?
> **A:** It's fifteen ninety-nine. How much...?

Task C

 ········ Refer students to Say It Right and Talk Some More and review the language in those sections.

❶ Have students work together to write a conversation.

❷ Monitor and assist as necessary.

❸ Have them practice the conversation. Have them reverse roles as well.

 ········ Have pairs role-play their conversation for the class.

Work In Pairs   Student A

(A) Look at the pictures. Write descriptions of the items, following the example.
Read your list to your partner to compare.

Example   a red and yellow checked shirt

- __a green sweater__
- __a pair of blue jeans__
- __a floral dress__

- __a striped T-shirt__
- __a pair of blue shorts__
- __a pair of brown shoes__

$10.95   SALE $4.99 $18.50

$15.99 $14.50 $17.25 $8.60

(B) Ask your partner for the missing prices. Write them on the price tags.
Listen to your partner's questions and answer them.

(C) Imagine you are a clerk. Make up a shopping conversation with your partner.
Take turns writing each line. Then practice the conversation.

Clerk:_____

Customer: _____

Clerk:_____

Customer: _____

Clerk:_____

Customer: _____

Clerk:_____

Customer: _____

A Look at the pictures. Write descriptions of the items, following the example. Read your list to your partner to compare.

> ***Example*** <u>a red and yellow checked shirt</u>
>
> - <u>a green sweater</u>
> - <u>a pair of blue jeans</u>
> - <u>a floral dress</u>
>
> - <u>a striped T-shirt</u>
> - <u>a pair of blue shorts</u>
> - <u>a pair of brown shoes</u>

B Ask your partner for the missing prices. Write them on the price tags. Listen to your partner's questions and answer them.

C Imagine you are a customer. Make up a shopping conversation with your partner. Take turns writing each line. Then practice the conversation.

Clerk: _____
Customer: _____
Clerk: _____
Customer: _____
Clerk: _____
Customer: _____
Clerk: _____
Customer: _____

Unit 6: How much is this sweater?

7 Work In Pairs

See p. T51 for suggested instructions for this task.

Mid-Unit Assessment

Once your students have finished Work In Pairs, they will have covered approximately half of this unit. How well are they accomplishing the unit goals at this stage? You may wish to assess their ability on the points below before beginning the fluency task Express Yourself. Check (✔) the appropriate space in the chart for each goal.

Can your students…	Yes, all can.	Yes, most can.	Maybe half can.	Only some can.
❶ ask about prices? *e.g. How much is this shirt?*	_____	_____	_____	_____
❷ state prices? *e.g. They're $25.*	_____	_____	_____	_____
❸ pay for goods? *e.g. Do you take credit cards?*	_____	_____	_____	_____
❹ say the names of clothing items? *(see Get Ready for list)*	_____	_____	_____	_____
❺ describe items of clothing? *e.g. A red and yellow checked shirt.*	_____	_____	_____	_____
❻ use rising intonation for clarification? *(see Say It Right for examples)*	_____	_____	_____	_____
❼ use *How much* and *How many* correctly in questions?	_____	_____	_____	_____

If your students can already accomplish these fairly well, they're better prepared to expand their use of the target language in the tasks that follow. For those who are still having problems with particular items above, you may wish to direct them to the relevant areas of the unit on pages 48–52, to workbook pages 22–23, or to the online quiz on the *Expressions* website.

8 Express Yourself

Task A

❶ Elicit some types of clothing (different from the ones in Express Yourself) and ask students to say how much they would normally pay for them.

❷ Have students list the prices they would normally pay for the items in the first column.

❸ Go over currencies represented in the class, if necessary. Monitor and assist with spelling and pronunciation.

Task B

❶ Have students interview three other classmates.

❷ Have them fill in the prices and practice buying the items.

❸ Monitor as necessary.

 On the board write, or elicit, some expressions which will be useful for the activity e.g.: *How much is the...?, Do you take credit cards?, OK. I'll take it., Here you are, etc.*

9 Think About It

❶ Have the students read the information and consider the answers to the questions. Discuss the questions as a class.

❷ Find out what other differences there are concerning shopping customs in different cultures.

10 Write About It

Task A

❶ Have students read the ads.

❷ Offer language support as necessary.

Task B

❶ Brainstorm a list of things which might be found in ads of this kind.

 Write the items on the board.

❷ Have students write their own ad. Encourage them to use different items and prices.

 Have students pin their ads on the classroom walls. Students then circle around the class and pick something they want to buy. Have students role-play buying and selling things.

8 Express Yourself

A Look at the items. How much do they usually cost where you live?
Write the prices in the 'My Price' list. (Use your own currency.)

	My Price	No. 1	No. 2	No. 3
jeans				
shirts				
shoes				
sweaters				
T-shirts				

B Ask three partners for their prices and fill in the lists.
Then choose the items you want to buy and practice paying.

9 *Think About It*

In some cultures, sales clerks closely follow customers who are shopping for clothes or other items. Some customers like this, but some don't.

• How about in your culture? How do customers feel about close attention from sales clerks?

10 Write About It

A Look at the advertisements.

For Sale
Whitewater washing machine.
Almost new. $550
Call Rick at 3954-7945

Best price! $350
Dining table and chairs
for immediate sale.
Al Lamond Tel: 555-0286

For Sale
2 tickets to Cassandra Wilson concert.
$35 each—or make me an offer.
Call Mary at 555-5497

Must Sell $275
King size water bed.
Only six months old.
Owner going overseas.
Contact Paul Rice
Fax: 555-3956

B Make an advertisement to sell something of your own. Write it on a piece of paper.

Good fashion never dies.

Many years after they went away, the 1970s came back into fashion. After more than twenty years, young people started to wear the clothes that their parents, aunts, and uncles loved at their age. In the United States, second-hand stores, called 'resale shops' or 'thrift shops,' sell the popular items of that era.

At these shops, men can buy bell-bottom jeans, polyester suits, wide neckties, and plaid pants. In addition to bell-bottom jeans, women can find mini-dresses, vinyl mini-skirts, and go-go boots with high platform soles. This look became so popular again that some companies designed new clothes copying the style of this era.

How much do these retro fashions cost at a resale shop? It's not too hard to find a mini-dress for as low as $12, $5–10 for a jacket, $5 for a skirt or a pair of long pants, and you might get a T-shirt, belt, or a tie for only $1! The new copies of these styles cost a lot more.

Check (✔) the main idea for each paragraph in each pair.

Paragraph 1

_____ Fashions of the 1970s are now sold only in second-hand stores.

___✔___ The styles of the 1970s became popular again many years later.

Paragraph 2

___✔___ There are many types of '70s items for sale for both men and women.

_____ Both men and women can wear bell-bottom jeans.

Paragraph 3

___✔___ The original items from the 1970s are sold for low prices.

_____ New clothes cost more than clothes from the 1970s.

Talk About It

○ What do young people in your country think about wearing second-hand clothing?

○ Which styles are popular with young people in your country?

○ Do you like to follow fashion trends? Why or why not?

11 Read On

Before the Reading

1 Ask the warm-up questions below to the class. Alternatively, have students discuss them first in pairs or in small groups. List the clothing vocabulary you elicit from the students on the board under two columns: *You* and *Your parents.*

What kind of clothes do you like to wear? What clothes do your parents like to wear?

2 List these words and phrases on the board: *parents, popular, shops, bell-bottom jeans, mini-skirts, neckties, belt, this look, popular, resale, retro, copies.* (Note: a 'retro fashion' is an old style of fashion that is now popular again.) Tell the class that all these phrases are from the Read On article in the book. Elicit meanings, have students predict the topic of the passage, and note the predictions on the board. Have students say whether they think the clothing items in the list are for men, women, or both. Ask if the students, or their parents, wear any of these items.

 Include other phrases from the passage, e.g. *vinyl, polyester suits, go-go boots, plaid pants.*

3 Have students look at page 54. Refer them to the title of the reading, the headline, and the photo. Ask if they think their predictions were correct. Then, write the three pairs of statements on the board, and go through the meaning of each. Explain that they need to read the article to decide the main idea of each paragraph.

During the Reading

1 Monitor and offer language support where necessary.

2 Have students compare their answers with a partner.

After the Reading

1 Call on students for answers and check each one on the board. Explain why each is correct (the other statement is a detail of the paragraph, not the main idea), if necessary.

2 Go over the meaning of each of the Talk About It questions. Have students work in pairs, asking and answering the questions. Then discuss the questions as a class.

Optional questions:
What kind of fashion do you think people will wear ten years from now? How about fifty years from now?

Extension Activity

Elicit some types of clothing and list them on the board. Have students decide a price for each, and note it next to each item. Have students work in pairs, and tell them they are going to do a role-play: one person will be a fashion store clerk, the other will be a customer. The customer is going to a party and has to buy some items to wear. Give the students a price limit, e.g. $200. Elicit phrases students think will be useful for the role-play, and note them on the board. Have each pair write, and then perform, their role-play.

Cultural Note

Each decade develops its own distinctive clothes styles. Fashion inspired by hippie culture influenced clothing fashion in the 1960s and early 1970s; punk styles heavily influenced styles in the 1970s and 1980s. The 1990s were perhaps most noted for grunge fashion, which originated in Seattle in the U.S. These clothing fashions can reemerge many years after going out of style, as it sometimes becomes very fashionable to wear clothes from a different era.

Unit 6: How much is this sweater?

12 Vocabulary Review

Task A

1. Have students search back through the unit for clothing items—this could be done as a collaborative exercise if desired—and enter them into the correct columns.

2. Check answers.

Task B

1. Have students express their own opinions.

2. Turn this into a whole class session and encourage discussion.

 challenge Have students think of some special occasions and write them on the board. Either as a group or in pairs, have students talk about what they would wear on those occasions.

12 Grammar Review

Task A

1. Have students complete the exercise. Allow students to look back through the unit to check their answers.

2. Go through answers.

Task B

1. Have students complete the exercise. Allow students to look back through the unit to check their answers.

2. Monitor as necessary. Answers may vary.

 challenge Have students practice asking the questions they have written. Their partner should answer using his/her own information.

Log On

Have students do the online activities for this unit on the *Expressions* website: **http://expressions.heinle.com**

Language Summary

For a more detailed review of the language practiced in this unit, refer students to the **Language Summary on page 138**. Encourage them to add new vocabulary in the **Word Builder** section.

1 Vocabulary Review

A Fill in the chart with words you learned in this unit.

Men's Clothes	Women's Clothes	Both

B Which of these items do you usually wear? Which do you never wear?

2 Grammar Review

How much are the T-shirts?

A Fill in the blanks.

1. How much ___are___ the T-shirts?
2. ___They're___ $4.50.
3. How many ___do___ you need?
4. How much ___is___ the red dress?
5. ___Do___ you take personal checks?

B Make up questions about shopping with the words shown.

1. (shoes) _____
2. (want) _____
3. (how many) _____
4. (credit cards) _____
5. (look for) _____

3 Log On

Practice more with the language and topics you studied on the *Expressions* website:

http://expressions.heinle.com

UNIT 7

Goals

○ *Asking for and identifying locations in buildings*   ○ *Giving directions*

Is there a pool?

1 Get Ready

A Write the number of the location in the correct place in the hotel.

1. pool
2. front desk
3. business center
4. newsstand
5. restaurant
6. laundry
7. health club
8. coffee shop

B Read the sentences.
Write *T* for true, or *F* for false.

1. __T__ The coffee shop is on the first floor.
2. __F__ The pool is on the second floor.
3. __T__ The health club is on the third floor.

4. __F__ The business center is next to the pool.
5. __T__ The pool is to the left of the health club.
6. __T__ The newsstand is between the front desk and the coffee shop.

2 Start Talking

A Look at the conversation and listen.

Guest: Excuse me.
Clerk: Yes, sir?
Guest: Is there a business center in this hotel?
Clerk: Yes, there is. It's on the second floor, next to the restaurant.

Pair work

B Practice the conversation with a partner.
Then practice again, using different hotel facilities.

Unit 7: Is there a pool?

Goals
➤ Asking for and identifying locations in buildings   ➤ Giving directions

Workbook: pages 26–29

1 Get Ready

Task A

❶ Ask students what facilities they would expect to find in a hotel. Elicit any words they know, list them on the board, and go over meaning and pronunciation.

❷ Have students write the numbers in the correct places in the picture.

❸ Have students compare answers with a partner.

❹ Check answers as a class.

 In groups, have students draw up a list of other places where the facilities might be found. (For example, a pool can be found in a sports center, a laundry can be found in a hospital, etc.) Have groups compare their lists. Elicit suggestions and go over as a class.

Task B

 Elicit alternative vocabulary items the students might be familiar with, such as *kiosk, laundromat, lobby, fitness center, café.*

❶ Have students answer *T* or *F* according to what they can see in the picture.

❷ Have students compare with a partner.

❸ Go over answers with the class.

2 Start Talking

Task A

❶ Let students read the conversation.

❷ Play the tape while students listen to the conversation.

 Rewind the tape and have students repeat the conversation after the tape.

> **Tapescript**
>
> **M1:** Excuse me.
> **M2:** Yes, sir?
> **M1:** Is there a business center in this hotel?
> **M2:** Yes, there is. It's on the second floor, next to the restaurant.

Task B

❶ Have students practice the conversation.

❷ Have them practice the conversation in pairs, either with books open or closed, using the different facilities in the picture.

 Introduce other location vocabulary, such as *ground floor, basement, top floor, roof,* and note them on the board. Have students say what they think each one means. Then, have students, in pairs, write a similar short dialog using vocabulary they have covered so far. If there is time, have pairs role-play their dialog for the class.

Unit 7: Is there a pool?

3 Listen In

Task A

❶ Have students try to identify the facilities suggested by the different pictures. Have them write the name of the facility in each space.

❷ Have them check their answers with a partner.

Task B

❶ Play the tape. Have students listen and write the number of the conversation in which they hear each facility mentioned.

❷ Go over answers.

Task C

❶ Have students read through the directions. Offer language support where necessary.

❷ Play the tape. Have students listen and write the number of the facility next to the directions.

❸ Have them compare with a partner.

❹ Go over answers.

 ········ Pause the tape after each conversation.

(TRY THIS!) Play the tape again, as necessary. The questions are:
And how do I get there?, How do I find it? and *And where's that, please?*

4 Say It Right

Task A

❶ Explain how stress is used in speech to highlight key words.

 ········ Give other examples yourself before students do the exercise.

❷ Ask students to listen to the examples.

Task B

❶ Tell the students that they will hear six sentences describing the location of facilities.

❷ Play the tape. Have students check the correct column.

❸ Have students compare their answers.

Task C

❶ Have students listen again and check their answers.

 ········ Write the sentences from the transcript on the board. In pairs, have students practice saying them, using different types of stress.

3 Listen In

A Look at the pictures below. Write the facility where you can find each one.

B Listen and write the number of the conversation (1–4) next to the facilities pictured below.

② pool	① restaurant	② health club
④ business center	③ newsstand	④ laundry

C Listen again and write the number of the conversation next to the directions.

__4__ Take the elevator to the second floor. Turn left, and you'll find it next to the business center.

__3__ Just go down those stairs right there and turn right.

__2__ Take the elevator to the third floor and turn left.

__1__ Go up the stairs and turn right.

Try this

Can you tell me how to get there?
You heard three questions with the same meaning. What are they? Can you remember?

4 Say It Right

A Important information in a sentence is sometimes stressed. Listen to the examples. What is more important—the facility or where it is?

B Listen and check (✔) the correct column in the chart.

C Listen again and check your answers.

	Facility	Where
Example 1	✔	
Example 2		✔
1.	✔	
2.		✔
3.		✔
4.	✔	
5.		✔
6.		✔

5 Focus In

A Look at the chart.

Prepositions: *on/next to/between*	
Is there a business center in this hotel?	Yes, there is. It's **on** the first/second/third floor. It's **next to** the fitness center. It's **between** the restaurant and the laundry.

B Fill in the blanks. Use *between*, *next to*, or *on*.

1. A: Is there a pool?
   B: Yes, there is. It's ___on___ the third floor, _next to_ the fitness center.
2. A: I'm looking for the business center.
   B: Oh, it's ___on___ the second floor _between_ the restaurant and the laundry.
3. A: Are there any places to eat?
   B: Yes, there are. There's a coffee shop ___on___ the first floor _next to_ the newsstand.
   And there's a restaurant ___on___ the second floor _next to_ the business center.

C Look at the hotel in Get Ready. Answer the questions.

1. Excuse me. Is there a business center in this hotel? __(answers on opposite page)__
2. Excuse me. Is there a laundry in this hotel? _____
3. Excuse me. Is there a newsstand in this hotel? _____
4. Excuse me. Is there a health club in this hotel? _____

6 Talk Some More

A Look at the hotel in Get Ready. Fill in the missing information.

Guest: _Excuse me._____

Clerk: Yes, ma'am?

Guest: _Is there a____ health club in this hotel?

Clerk: Yes, _there is_____.

Guest: How do I get there?

Clerk: Take the elevator to the third floor.
It's _next to the pool_____.

Spotlight

Ma'am is the polite way to address a woman. The polite way to address a man is *Sir*.

B Check your answers.

 Pair work

C Practice the conversation with a partner.
Then practice again using different facilities in Get Ready.

5 Focus In

Task A

❶ Go through the chart with students.

❷ Model the prepositions of location as required.

 ⋯⋯⋯ Present more examples as necessary.

Task B

❶ Have students fill in the blanks to complete the sentences.

❷ Have them check with a partner.

❸ Have them practice asking and answering the questions.

Task C

❶ Have students look back to Get Ready.

❷ Have them answer the questions, giving the floor number and the relative location.

❸ Have them check their answers with a partner.

❹ Go over answers with the class.
Answers:
1. Yes. It's on the second floor between the restaurant and the laundry.
2. Yes. It's on the second floor next to the business center.
3. Yes. It's on the first (this) floor between the front desk and the coffee shop.
4. Yes. It's on the third floor next to the pool.

6 Talk Some More

Task A

❶ Have students refer back to the hotel in Get Ready and fill in the blanks.

❷ Offer help as necessary.

Task B

❶ Play the tape.

❷ Have students check their answers.

Task C

❶ Have students practice the conversation.

❷ Have them practice again, either with books open or closed, using different facilities.

 ⋯⋯⋯ Have students role-play their dialog for the class.

(**SPOTLIGHT**) Point out that *Madam* is also used.

> **Tapescript**
>
> **W:** Excuse me.
> **M:** Yes, ma'am?
> **W:** Is there a health club in this hotel?
> **M:** Yes, there is.
> **W:** How do I get there?
> **M:** Take the elevator to the third floor. It's next to the pool.

Unit 7: Is there a pool?

7 Work In Pairs

See pages xii-xiii for suggestions on pair work.

Task A

1. Divide students into pairs. Refer Student B to page 60.

2. Have them look at the hotel pictures.

3. Point out the language prompt in the speech bubbles and have them ask about the facilities in each other's hotels.

4. Monitor as necessary, but do not allow students to see each other's books.

5. Go over answers before continuing.

> **Sample**
>
> **A:** Is there a business center in your hotel?
> **B:** Yes, there is. Is there a restaurant in your hotel?
> **A:** Yes, there is. Is there a laundry in your hotel?
> **B:** Yes, there is. Is there a swimming pool in your hotel?
> **A:** No, there isn't. Is there...?

Task B

1. Explain that the facilities are in different parts of each hotel.

2. Have students find the location of the facilities in their partner's hotel by asking *What's on the ____ floor?* or *Where's the...?* Students should mark where these facilities are on their own hotel picture.

support ⟶ .... Write the question forms on the board, if necessary.

3. Monitor and provide assistance as necessary.

4. Have students check their hotels together at the end of the exercise.

> **Sample**
>
> **A:** What's on the first floor?
> **B:** There's a business center, front desk, and a coffee shop. The coffee shop is to the right of the front desk, and the business center is to the left. On the second floor is a health club, between a restaurant and a newsstand.
> **A:** And, on the third floor?
> **B:** There are just rooms on the third floor...

Task C

1. Have students work together to write the sentences.

2. Monitor and assist as necessary.

3. Go over answers.

challenge ⟶ .... Have pairs or small groups design a hotel. Students then mingle and ask questions about each other's hotels.

(TRY THIS!) Have students write sentences and compare with a partner.

Work In Pairs   Student A

Student B: Use page 60

A Look at the hotel in the picture. Ask if your partner's hotel has the same facilities as yours. List the facilities in your partner's hotel.

swimming pool, front desk, health club,
coffee shop, newsstand, business center,
restaurant, laundry

B Where are the facilities in your partner's hotel? Are they the same as yours? Ask your partner. How many differences can you find? Mark the location of your partner's facilities on your picture.

Try this

Write sentences about the facilities in your building. Then compare them with your partner's.

Work In Pairs   Student B

Student A: Use page 59

A Look at the hotel in the picture. Ask if your partner's hotel has the same facilities as yours. List the facilities in your partner's hotel.

no swimming pool, business center,
coffee shop, health club, restaurant,
newsstand, front desk, laundry

B Where are the facilities in your partner's hotel?
Are they the same as yours? Ask your partner. How many differences can you find?
Mark the location of your partner's facilities on your picture.

Try this

Write sentences about the facilities in your building.
Then compare them with your partner's.

Unit 7: Is there a pool?

7 Work In Pairs

See p. T59 for suggested instructions for this task.

Mid-Unit Assessment

Once your students have finished Work In Pairs, they will have covered approximately half of this unit. How well are they accomplishing the unit goals at this stage? You may wish to assess their ability on the points below before beginning the fluency task Express Yourself. Check (✔) the appropriate space in the chart for each goal.

Can your students…	Yes, all can.	Yes, most can.	Maybe half can.	Only some can.
❶ ask for places in a building? *e.g. Is there a coffee shop in this hotel? Where's the pool?*	_____	_____	_____	_____
❷ identify locations? *e.g. It's on the second floor, next to the restaurant.*	_____	_____	_____	_____
❸ give directions? *e.g. Take the elevator to the third floor and turn right.*	_____	_____	_____	_____
❹ say the names of places in a hotel? *(see Get Ready for list)*	_____	_____	_____	_____
❺ use stress correctly to signify place or location? *(see Say It Right for examples)*	_____	_____	_____	_____
❻ use prepositions of location correctly?	_____	_____	_____	_____

If your students can already accomplish these fairly well, they're better prepared to expand their use of the target language in the tasks that follow. For those who are still having problems with particular items above, you may wish to direct them to the relevant areas of the unit on pages 56–60, to workbook pages 26–27, or to the online quiz on the *Expressions* website.

8 Express Yourself

Task A

❶ Have students individually check the facilities they would like.

❷ Monitor and assist as necessary.

 ⤑ Have students add any other facilities to the list that they would like. Share their ideas with the class.

Task B

❶ Have students ask their partner for his/her preferences and circle their choices.

❷ Monitor as necessary.

❸ Go over answers as a class to find out which facilities most students would like.

 ⤑ Have students give reasons why they would like certain facilities and not others.

9 Think About It

❶ Have students read the information and consider the answers to the questions.
Discuss the questions as a class.
Find out what other differences there are concerning writing addresses in their cultures.

🌐 Shinjuku: ʃɪndʒuku

 ⤑ Write an address on the board and get students to name the different parts of it, i.e., house number, street name, area, postal/zip code, etc.

10 Write About It

Task A

❶ Have students read the note.

❷ Offer language support as necessary.

Task B

❶ Go over any vocabulary specific to the building you are in, and note them on the board.

❷ Have students write their own note. Encourage them to be as clear as possible in their explanations.

 ⤑ Have students role-play giving the directions orally.

Express Yourself

(A) **What facilities would you like in a hotel? Check (✔) the right answer for you. Would you like a...**

_____ health club?   _____ business center?

_____ restaurant?   _____ pool?

_____ coffee shop?   _____ laundry?

Pair work (B) **Ask a partner and circle your partner's answers.**

 Think About It

Many cultures use street names and numbers in their addresses. Some cultures don't. For example, in a huge city like Tokyo, where there are few street names and numbers, people are very good at giving directions.

Well, you take the subway to Shinjuku Station. Take exit 28C, turn right and walk for three blocks. You will see a police box. Turn left and walk two more blocks. On your left, you will see a large blue building. Make another left and walk one more block. Right in front of you will be a small coffee shop called Coffee Time. I'll meet you there.

• What about in your culture? Are there numbered street addresses in your country? Are there street names? How do you usually give directions?

10 Write About It

(A) **Look at the note.**

Dear Bill,

We're meeting in the business center.

Take the elevator to the third floor.

Turn right and go to the end of the hall.

The business center is on the left.

(B) **A new student is joining your class. Write a note explaining how to get from the front door of the building to your classroom.**

• **Strategy: Scanning**

The phone book is a great way to find goods and services nearby.

Pet Hotel
- Dog & cat boarding
- Loving care
- House boarding available
- Cat roomettes
- Music and special lighting
- All breed dog grooming

- Pick up and delivery service
- Reservations requested
- Labrador Retriever puppies for sale

We never close!
68 Oakridge Road, 555-4546

SUDZ'S LAUNDROMAT

Drop off or self service

Clean and modern

Helpful attendants

Tan or watch big screen TV

Espresso / Beer / Mini Deli

Open 7 days a week
7 a.m. – 11 p.m.
3107 Monroe, 555-7896

CAMPING WORLD RV-PARK
- Pull-thrus & full hook-ups
- Tent sites
- Clean restrooms & showers
- Cable TV, phone
- Laundry

- Groceries
- Game rooms
- Exercise room
- Fishing
- Swimming pool

Open May through September
8 miles east on Highway 231, 555-3849

Wordsmith's
BOOK COMPANY & CAFE

New and used books

Over 100,000 titles

Readings by authors

Good coffee and tea

Tasty foods, tempting desserts

No one will hurry you

Open every day 10 a.m. – 10 p.m.
Courthouse Square, 555-2125

Where can you...? Check (✔) the boxes.

	Laundromat	Bookstore	RV-Park	Pet Hotel
Eat and drink	✔	✔		
Watch TV	✔		✔	
Buy a dog				✔
Get a tan	✔			

Which place is...? Check (✔) the boxes.

	Laundromat	Bookstore	RV-Park	Pet Hotel
Always open				✔
Outside of town			✔	
Open 5 months a year			✔	
Open 16 hours a day	✔			

Talk About It

◯ What surprises you about each business?

◯ Which business do you think will make a lot of money? Why?

◯ Which of the businesses do you have in your country? Do they make a lot of money?

11 Read On

Before the Reading

❶ Ask the class the warm-up questions below. Alternatively, have students discuss them first in pairs or in small groups. Elicit and write words on the board. Include the following items on the list: *pet hotel, bookstore, laundromat, campsite,* and elicit the meaning of each.

What public services do you know? Which do you use every day/week/month?

❷ In groups, have students decide where they would go for each service. Have each group read out its list. Note the suggestions under each place name.

❸ Refer students to page 62. Ask students where they think the four extracts have been taken from (a 'yellow pages' phone directory). Draw copies of the two charts on the board, and elicit the meaning of each item. Explain that students need to scan the article for information, and then check the correct spaces in the columns.

During the Reading

❶ Monitor and offer language support where necessary.

❷ Have students compare their answers with a partner.

After the Reading

❶ Elicit responses from students, and check the correct answers on the board. Ask students to read out the part where they found each piece of information.

❷ Go over the meaning of each of the Talk About It questions. (Possible responses to the first question are: the pet hotel has music and special lighting; the laundromat has a tanning facility; the campsite has an exercise room; the bookstore serves food and drinks.)

Optional questions:
How do you usually find services you need? In a phone directory? On the Internet? Through friends?

❸ Have students work in pairs, asking and answering the questions. Then discuss the questions as a class.

Extension Activity

Bring copies of a local 'yellow pages' directory. Write 6–8 types of stores or services on the board, e.g. *a health club, laundromat, coffee shop, swimming pool, hotel, French restaurant, clothes store, bookstore.* In groups, have students search their directory to find, and list, at least one example of each type of store or service. See which group can make the longest list.

Cultural Note

As market competition increases, service providers are having to offer a much wider range of services than before. One trend in recent years has been the emergence of large chains of bookstores, such as Borders and Barnes and Noble, which offer seating areas and coffee shops to attract customers. Competition comes not just from other retail stores, but also from service providers on the Internet, for example, Amazon.com.

12 Vocabulary Review

Task A

1 Have students search back through the unit for the facilities and their locations—this could be done as a collaborative exercise if desired—and enter them into the correct columns.

2 Check answers.

Task B

1 Have students express their own opinion.

2 Turn this into a whole class session and encourage discussion.

 challenge Have students describe the location of one of these facilities, e.g. swimming pool, health club, in their local neighborhood.

12 Grammar Review

Task A

1 Have students do the exercise. Allow them to look back through the unit to check their answers.

2 Go through answers.

Task B

1 Have students complete the exercise.

2 Have pairs exchange books and check each other's answers. Monitor and offer assistance if necessary.

 challenge Have students turn back to either Get Ready or Work In Pairs and ask and answer similar questions using the hotel pictures.

Log On

Have students do the online activities for this unit on the *Expressions* website: **http://expressions.heinle.com**

Language Summary

For a more detailed review of the language practiced in this unit, refer students to the **Language Summary on page 139**. Encourage them to add new vocabulary in the **Word Builder** section.

12 Review

1 Vocabulary Review

A Write the names of four facilities you learned in this unit.
Then write where they are in the hotel in Get Ready.

Facility	Where?

B In which other places could you also find these facilities?

2 Grammar Review

A Fill in the blanks.

1. The pool is ___on___ the second floor.
2. The laundry is next ___to___ the pool.
3. The business center is ___between___ the restaurant and the newsstand.
4. Take the elevator ___to___ the third floor.
5. Go ___up___ the stairs and turn right.

B Check (✔) the correct sentence in each pair.

1. ___✔___ The coffee shop is on the third floor.
   _____ The coffee shop is on third floor.
2. _____ Is the laundry on the four floor?
   ___✔___ Is the laundry on the fourth floor?
3. _____ The pool is next the health club.
   ___✔___ The pool is next to the health club.
4. _____ Take the elevator to the first floor and turn to right.
   ___✔___ Take the elevator to the first floor and turn right.

3 Log On

Practice more with the language and topics you studied on the *Expressions* website:

http://expressions.heinle.com

UNIT 8

Goals

○ *Describing procedures* ○ *Narrating a sequence*

First, you turn it on.

1 Get Ready

A Look at the words.
Write the number next
to the correct item (1–6).

1.	fax machine
2.	cassette player
3.	CD player
4.	answering machine
5.	computer
6.	VCR

B Answer the questions. Then compare your answers with a partner's.

1. Which machines use a tape? ___*cassette player, answering machine, VCR*___

2. Which machines use a disk? ___*CD player, computer*___

3. Which of these machines do you use often? _____

4. Which have you never used? _____

2 Start Talking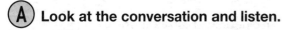

A Look at the conversation and listen.

> **Belinda:** Do you know how to use a computer?
> **Kate:** No, it looks difficult.
> **Belinda:** It's easy. First, you turn it on. Next, put in a disk. Then, you open a file. That's all.

Pair work

B Practice the conversation with a partner.
Then practice again, using the machines in Get Ready.

Unit 8: First, you turn it on.

Goals
➤ Describing procedures ➤ Narrating a sequence

Workbook: pages 30–33

1 Get Ready

Task A
❶ Ask students which machines they can find in an office, which in a home, which in both.

❷ Have students write the numbers in the correct places in the picture.

❸ Have students compare answers with a partner.

❹ Check answers as a class.

Task B
❶ Ask students to answer the questions individually.

❷ Have them compare their answers with a partner.

❸ Go over answers.
Note: For 3 and 4, answers may vary, depending on personal experience and levels of technological sophistication.

2 Start Talking

Task A
❶ Let students read the conversation.

❷ Play the tape while students listen to the conversation.

 ········ Rewind the tape and have students repeat the conversation after the tape.

Task B
❶ Have students practice the conversation. Have them practice the conversation in pairs, using the different machines from Get Ready.

 ········ Have them continue practicing with books closed.

Tapescript

W1: Do you know how to use a computer?
W2: No. It looks difficult.
W1: It's easy. First, you turn it on. Next, put in a disk. Then, you open a file. That's all.

Unit 8: First, you turn it on.

3 Listen In

Task A

❶ Go over the meaning of each instruction in the list.

 ⟶ Illustrate the instruction words by mime. Have students say the action each time.

❷ Have students work with a partner to answer the questions.

❸ Go over answers with the class.

Task B

❶ Play the tape. Have students listen and check the words they hear.

❷ Go over answers.

Task C

❶ Play the tape. Have students listen and number the items. VCR, answering machine and CD player are not used.

❷ Go over answers.

4 Say It Right

Task A

❶ Model the sounds by reading the two examples in the instructions to the class.

support ⟶ Give other examples yourself before students do the exercise. Make sure students can pronounce each sound and can differentiate between them aurally.

❷ Ask students to individually circle and underline the sounds.

❸ Have students compare their answers with a partner.

Task B

❶ Play the tape. Have students check their answers.

❷ Have students repeat after the tape, if necessary.

Task C

❶ Have students listen again and practice. Ask students what machine the instructions are for.

(TRY THIS!) The other words used are: *next, then, now.*

3 Listen In

(A) Look at the words. Which ones could you use to talk about a washing machine? Or a camera?

	1	2	3	4
plug in	✔		✔	
turn on	✔	✔		✔
open		✔	✔	
press			✔	✔
put in	✔	✔	✔	✔
click on		✔		
take out			✔	
turn off	✔		✔	

(B) Listen and check (✔) the words you hear in each conversation.

(C) Listen again. Which machine is each person giving instructions for? Number the items (1–4).

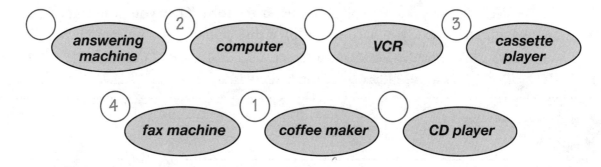

○ answering machine ② computer ○ VCR ③ cassette player

④ fax machine ① coffee maker ○ CD player

4 Say It Right

(A) Underline the words with the same sound as *s* in *cassette*. Circle the words with the same sound as *sh* in *shirt*.

First, make sure the cord is plugged in.
Next, press the *on* switch. Then you should push
this button. Now, sit back and enjoy the show.
That's all. It's simple.

Try this

We start the first instruction with the word *First*. What other words were used to start other instructions? Can you remember?

(B) Listen and check your answers.

(C) Listen again and practice.

5 Focus In

(A) Look at the chart.

Sequencing words	
Do you know how to use a VCR?	Yes, it's easy. **First**, you have to plug it in. **Next**, you need to press the *on* button. **Now**, you put in a tape. **Finally**, you press the *play* button.

(B) Write the number next to the correct response.

1. What do I do with the lid?   __5__ Click the button.
2. What should I do with the power cord? __4__ Just switch it on.
3. What do I have to do with the disk?   __2__ Plug it in.
4. How do I start the computer?   __3__ You have to put it in here.
5. How do I work the mouse?   __1__ You press it down.

(C) Underline the mistakes. Then write the instructions correctly.

"Well, first you have to plug on the power cord. They you need to turn in the computer. Next, you need to put off a disk. Finally, you have to click out the mouse."

"Well, first you have to plug in the power cord. Then you need to turn on the computer.
Next, you need to put in a disk. Finally, you have to click down the mouse."

6 Talk Some More

(A) Write the correct words in the correct spaces.

Jeff: I can't _turn on_ the VCR.
Sally: Well, first you need to _plug in_ the cord.
Jeff: Oh, OK.
Sally: Then you have to _press_ the *on* switch.
Jeff: All right.
Sally: Now, _put in_ the video tape.
Jeff: Uh-huh.
Sally: Finally, _press_ the *play* button.
Jeff: OK. Now what?
Sally: Now, _sit back_ and enjoy the show.

(B) Check your answers.

 Pair work

(C) Practice the conversation with a partner. Then practice again using different machines.

Unit 8: First, you turn it on.

5 Focus In

Task A
❶ Go through the chart with the students.

❷ Explain how instructions often use sequencers to signal the steps, along with imperative verbs.

 ⋯⋯⋯⋯ Present more examples as necessary.

Task B
❶ Have students number the responses.

❷ Have them check with a partner.

❸ Have them practice asking and answering the questions.

Task C
❶ Have students underline the mistakes.

❷ Have them write the correct instructions in full.

❸ Have them check their answers with a partner.

❹ Go over answers with the class.

6 Talk Some More

Task A
❶ Have students fill in the blanks.

❷ Offer help as necessary.

Task B
❶ Play the tape.

❷ Have students check their answers.

Tapescript

M: I can't turn on the VCR.
W: Well, first, you need to plug in the cord.
M: Oh, OK.
W: Then, you have to press the *on* switch.
M: All right.
W: Now, put in the video tape.
M: Uh-huh.
W: Finally, press the *play* button.
M: OK. Now what?
W: Now, sit back and enjoy the show.

Task C
❶ Have students practice the conversation.

 ⋯⋯⋯⋯ Elicit and note on the board any useful vocabulary and expressions needed for giving instructions for the other machines in the book.

❷ Have them practice again, using different machines. (e.g. from Get Ready or Listen In)

 ⋯⋯⋯⋯ Write necessary vocabulary on the board as students require it.

 ⋯⋯⋯⋯ Encourage students to close their books and use gestures. Model as necessary.

(SPOTLIGHT) Point out that *Uh-huh* is very informal. It's normally used to show that the listener is following what is being said.

Unit 8: First, you turn it on.

7 Work In Pairs

See pages xii-xiii for suggestions on pair work.

Task A

❶ Divide students into pairs. Refer Student B to page 68.

❷ Have them look at the pictures.

❸ Have them individually write the instructions above the relevant picture.

❹ Then have them sequence the instructions by writing the correct number in the circle on each picture.

❺ Monitor and assist as necessary.

Task B

❶ Explain that each partner has a different machine.

❷ Have them read the instructions to their partner in the correct order. Encourage them to go slowly, as one partner has to write the instructions.

❸ Monitor as necessary. Encourage students to use sequencers.

❹ Ask students to try and identify the machine they have been given instructions for.

❺ Have pairs check their answers.

❻ Make each student retell their partner's instructions from memory.

> **Sample**
>
> **A:** First, open the cover. Then, put in a CD. Next, close the cover. Finally, press the *play* button. What is it?
> **B:** Is it a CD player?
> **A:** Yes, it is.
> **B:** OK. First, put in the paper….

TRY THIS!
1. Have students think of a machine, but not tell their partner what it is.
2. Ask them to write a jumbled list of instructions for it in the box.
3. Monitor and assist as necessary.
4. Have them exchange books.
5. Each partner should now sequence the other's instructions.
6. Ask them to check their answers together.
7. Have them practice giving instructions to their partner.

Work In Pairs   Student A

A Write the correct instruction above each picture. Then use the circles to number the pictures in the correct order (1–4).

- put in a CD
- open the cover
- close the cover
- press the *play* button

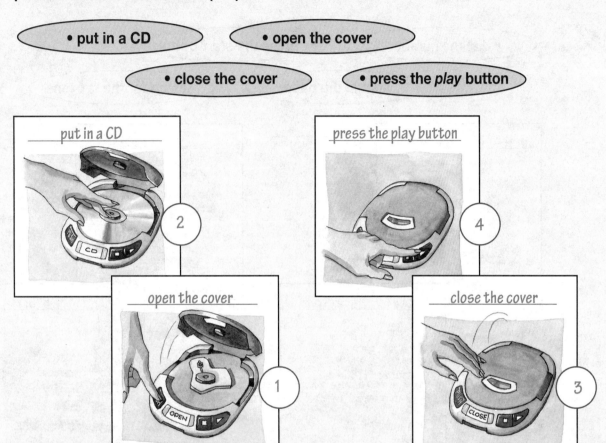

put in a CD
2

press the play button
4

open the cover
1

close the cover
3

B Read the instructions to your partner. Your partner will write them.
Then, ask your partner to tell you which machine you are describing.

Try this

Write some instructions in the wrong order. Put each instruction on a different line. Ask your partner to put your instructions in the correct order.

_____

_____

_____

_____

First, you turn it on.   **67**

(**A**) Write the correct instruction above each picture. Then use the circles to number the pictures in the correct order (1–4).

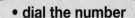

(• dial the number)   (• press the *start* button)

(• put in the paper)   (• listen for the fax tone)

<u>press the start button</u>

4

<u>dial the number</u>

2

<u>listen for the fax tone</u>

3

<u>put in the paper</u>

1

(**B**) Read the instructions to your partner. Your partner will write them. Then, ask your partner to tell you which machine you are describing.

Try this

Write some instructions in the wrong order. Put each instruction on a different line. Ask your partner to put your instructions in the correct order.

_____

_____

_____

_____

7 Work In Pairs

See p. T67 for suggested instructions for this task.

Mid-Unit Assessment

Once your students have finished Work In Pairs, they will have covered approximately half of this unit. How well are they accomplishing the unit goals at this stage? You may wish to assess their ability on the points below before beginning the fluency task Express Yourself. Check (✔) the appropriate space in the chart for each goal.

Can your students...	Yes, all can.	Yes, most can.	Maybe half can.	Only some can.
1 give simple instructions? *e.g. Turn it on. Open it.*	_____	_____	_____	_____
2 use sequencers? *e.g. First, next, then, finally*	_____	_____	_____	_____
3 say the names of different machines? *(see Get ready for list)*	_____	_____	_____	_____
4 ask how to operate a machine? *e.g. How do I use the VCR?*	_____	_____	_____	_____
5 use /s/ and /ʃ/ (sh) sounds correctly? *(see Say It Right for examples)*	_____	_____	_____	_____

If your students can already accomplish these fairly well, they're better prepared to expand their use of the target language in the tasks that follow. For those who are still having problems with particular items above, you may wish to direct them to the relevant areas of the unit on pages 64–68, to workbook pages 30–31, or to the online quiz on the *Expressions* website.

Unit 8: First, you turn it on.

8 Express Yourself

Task A

 Brainstorm the names of the machines as a class, and list them on the board. Model the activity by acting out how to use a machine, e.g. a coffee maker or a photocopier.

1. Have students silently choose one of the machines in the pictures.
2. Put the students in pairs.
3. Have them take turns to act out the sequence of instructions for their chosen machine. The other partner should say what is being done, and identify the machine.

Task B

1. Have students choose another machine.
2. Have them write instructions for it.

 Encourage groups to make their lists as detailed as possible. Have the other students listen to see if any steps have been missed out.

9 Think About It

1. Have the students read the information and consider the answers to the questions.
2. Discuss the questions as a class.
3. Find out the class' feelings about recorded messages (in any language).

 Brainstorm a list of things a caller to your school might want to know about. In groups, have students write some instructions that could be used in a recorded message for callers to the school.

10 Write About It

Task A

1. Have students read the instructions.
2. Offer language support as necessary.
3. Have students number the instructions.

Task B

1. Have students write out the instructions in the space provided.
2. Monitor and assist as necessary.

 Have students write instructions on how to use another machine that can be found in a public place, e.g. *vending machine, ticket machine,* etc. Have students read their instructions to a partner or to the class. Their partner/other students should try and guess the machine.

8 Express Yourself

Group work

A Choose one of the machines. Act out the instructions for using it. Let your partners say which machine you are using.

B Choose one of the machines in the pictures and write a list of instructions for it.

9 Think About It

Many companies use recorded phone messages as part of their customer service program. They can be very difficult to understand.

• Do you have a recorded message on your home telephone? What does it say?

> Thank you for calling Century Pizza.
> For restaurant locations, press 1.
> To hear our complete menu, press 2.
> For special promos, press 3.
> To place an order, press...

10 Write About It

A Look at the instructions. Number them in the correct order (1–8).

5	Wait.	1	Lift the handset.
3	Insert the phone card.	8	Finally, don't forget to take back the phone card!
2	Then listen for the dial tone.	7	Put down the handset.
6	Speak when someone answers.	4	Now punch in the phone number.

B Now write instructions on how to use a fax machine.

First, you turn it on.

Read On   How Does It Work?

• *Strategy: Identifying reference words*

Who needs an all-electric kitchen?
You can make an oven yourself, using the power of the sun.

Here's how you do it:

You'll need a tall, heavy cardboard box. Cut it as shown and then glue aluminum foil to one side of the cardboard.

Now put your oven in a sunny place, facing the sun. You'll need a large rock to hold up the front panel. If it's windy, you can hold the sides up with more rocks.

Put your food in a black cooking pot. Put the pot on the bottom piece of cardboard. Turn a clear glass bowl upside-down over it.

How does it work? The aluminum foil acts like a mirror. The sunlight hits the foil and reflects off of it. The five foil panels make the sunlight stronger and hotter. You don't have to plug it in or turn it on—the sun does everything for you.

What can you cook? Rice, soup, meat, vegetables—almost anything, but you'll need to double the cooking time. Try it!

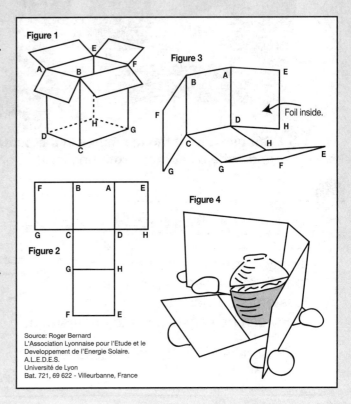

Source: Roger Bernard
L'Association Lyonnaise pour l'Etude et le
Developpement de l'Energie Solaire.
A.L.E.D.E.S.
Université de Lyon
Bat. 721, 69 622 - Villeurbanne, France

**Look at these sentences from the reading passage.
What does the word *it* mean in each one?**

1. How does *it* work?   The oven
2. Cut *it* as shown.   The cardboard box
3. Turn a clean glass bowl upside-down over *it*.   The cooking pot
4. ... and reflects off of *it*.   The foil
5. Try *it*!   Making the oven/solar cooking

Talk About It

◯ Can you cook? What can you cook?

◯ Have you ever cooked outside, maybe on a campfire? What did you make?

◯ Do you like to make things yourself? What did you make?

11 Read On

Before the Reading

1 Elicit cooking words, e.g. *cook, fry, oven, pan, boil, barbecue*, and list them on the board. Ask the class the following warm-up questions. Alternatively, have students first discuss them in pairs or small groups.

How do you usually cook your food? What kind of food do you cook in an oven?

2 Write these words on the board: *cardboard box, aluminum foil, large rock, front panel, vegetables, sun, glass bowl, pot, upside-down, mirror, soup.* Explain that the words are from the Read On passage. Elicit meanings, and help with words students don't know. In groups, have students predict the topic of the passage. Note their predictions on the board.

 Ask students to give reasons for their predictions.

3 Refer students to p. 70 and have them look at the title of the reading, the headline, and the illustration. Ask students whether they think their predictions were correct. On the board, write the 5 sentences. Explain that the students have to read the passage, and decide what *it* refers to in each sentence. Point out the example, where *it* refers to 'the oven.'

During the Reading

1 Monitor students and offer language support where necessary.

2 Have students compare their answers with a partner.

After the Reading

1 Elicit responses from students, and write correct answers on the board. Ask the students to point out where they found each sentence.

2 Go over the meaning of each of the Talk About It questions. Have students work in pairs, asking and answering the questions. Then discuss the questions as a class.

Optional questions:
Do you use anything that's solar-powered? What do you use?

Extension Activity

In groups, have students list the five most important inventions of the last 100 years, in order of importance (e.g., *the computer, airplane, TV, radio, space rocket, satellite, CD, mobile phone, karaoke machine*). Ask each group to report its list to the class, and note ideas on the board.

 Ask each group to give reasons for its choices.

Cultural Note

As more people are concerned about the impact of fossil fuels (coal, gas, oil) on the environment, the popularity of alternative energies like solar power is increasing. Solar-powered ovens are now sold in many places around the world. In the U.S., for example, you can buy a solar-powered oven for around $200. You can also buy solar-powered TVs, radios, even lanterns! Solar-powered machines are also becoming more efficient: the first solar-powered car, made in the late 1970s, took 48 hours to fully recharge, but today's solar cars take less than 4 hours.

Vocabulary Review

Task A

1. Have students search back through the unit for instruction verbs—this could be done as a collaborative exercise if desired—and enter them into the correct columns.

2. Check answers as a class.

challenge ········ Divide the class into pairs. One student is to name a machine or appliance and the other must explain how to use it in 4 basic steps. For higher level students increase this to 6 steps.

Grammar Review

Task A

1. Have students complete the exercise. Allow them to look back through the unit to check their answers.

2. Go through answers as a class.

Task B

1. Have students look back to Talk Some More, if necessary.

2. Go through answers.

challenge ········ Have students practice the instructions in pairs with their books closed.

Log On

Have students do the online activities for this unit on the *Expressions* website: **http://expressions.heinle.com**

Language Summary

For a more detailed review of the language practiced in this unit, refer students to the **Language Summary on page 139**. Encourage them to add new vocabulary in the **Word Builder** section.

12 Review

1 Vocabulary Review

A Which verbs in this unit can you use with *on*, *off*, *in* and *out*?

on	off	in	out

Do you know how to use the VCR?

Yes, it's easy.

2 Grammar Review

A Fill in the blanks.

1. Make sure the cord is plugged ____in____.
2. Then, you turn it ____on____.
3. When the song is finished, take ____out____ the cassette.
4. Click ____on____ the icon to open the file.
5. After you finish, make sure to turn it ____off____ again.

B Write instructions on how to operate a VCR using the words shown.

1. (plug in) _____
2. (press) _____
3. (put in) _____
4. (press) _____
5. (sit back) _____

3 Log On

Practice more with the language and topics you studied on the *Expressions* website:

http://expressions.heinle.com

I get up early.

1 Get Ready

A Match the activity with the picture.

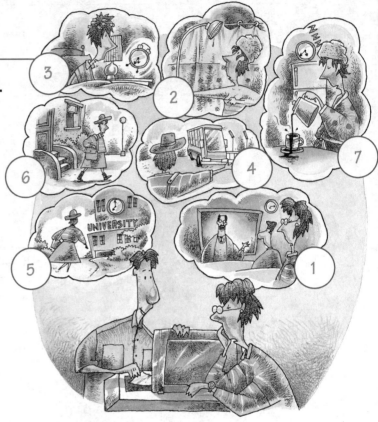

1.	start class
2.	take a shower
3.	get up
4.	catch the bus
5.	arrive at school
6.	leave home
7.	make coffee

B Circle the correct answer.

1. What is the opposite of *get up*?   (Go to bed) / Go to sleep
2. What is the opposite of *leave home*?   Be home / (Come home)
3. What is the opposite of *arrive at school*? Be at school / (Leave school)
4. What is the opposite of *class starts*?   (Class finishes) / Class stops

2 Start Talking

A Look at the conversation and listen.

Henry: You look tired.

Jane: I am. I'm really busy in the mornings.

Henry: Why?

Jane: Well, I get up at 5:30. I take a shower and make coffee. Then I leave home at 6:00 and catch the 6:15 bus. I have to arrive at school by 7:00. My Spanish class starts at 7:15.

Pair work ▶ **B** Practice with a partner.
Then practice again using information about your own daily schedule.

Unit 9: I get up early.

Goals ➤ Describing routines and schedules   ➤ Telling time

Workbook: pages 34–37

1 Get Ready

Task A

  ········ Ask students what time they do the activities in the picture.

① Go over the pronunciation and meaning of the vocabulary items.

② Have them individually match the activities with the correct picture.

③ Have them compare answers with a partner.

④ Go over answers.

Task B

① Have students circle the opposites.

② Have students compare answers with a partner.

③ Check answers as a class.

 ········ Elicit other ways to say some of these activities, such as *begin class, shower, take the bus, go to school,* and *leave the house.*

2 Start Talking

Task A

① Let students read the conversation.

② Play the tape while students listen to the conversation.

 ········ Rewind the tape and have students repeat the conversation after the tape.

Task B

① Have students practice the conversation.

 ········ Elicit other morning activities. Write them on the board. Examples might include *take a bath, have breakfast, exercise, listen to the radio, read the paper.*

② Have them practice the conversation in pairs, using information about their own routines.

Tapescript

M: You look tired.
W: I am. I'm really busy in the mornings.
M: Why?
W: Well, I get up at 5:30. I take a shower and make coffee. Then I have to leave home at 6:00 and catch the 6:15 bus. I have to arrive at school by 7:00. My Spanish class starts at 7:15.

3 Listen In

Task A

❶ Have students speculate about the possible times.

❷ Have them compare their answers with a partner.

Task B

❶ Play the tape. Have them listen and number the pictures.

❷ Go over answers.

Task C

❶ Play the tape. Have students listen and mark the times on the clocks.

 .... Pause the tape after each line of conversation.

❷ Go over answers. Were any of the students' predictions correct?

challenge .... Ask yes/no comprehension questions like *Does she catch the bus at 6:30?* and *Does she go to the gym after she meets her boyfriend?*

Tapescript

W1: What's the matter?
W2: Oh, I have a busy day. I have to get up at six.
W1: How come?
W2: Well, I have coffee at around 6:15, and then catch the bus at 6:30, so I can get to the gym by 7:00.
W1: Yeah. That is kind of early.
W2: After the gym I meet my boyfriend for breakfast at 8:15.
W1: What—downtown?
W2: Uh-huh—Lucontoni's. You know, that little...
W1: Oh, yeah. And what time do you go to work?
W2: I start work at 9:00. By that time I'm already tired!

4 Say It Right

Task A

❶ Review how rising intonation can echo a statement as well as turn it into a question.

support .... Give other examples yourself before students do the exercise.

❷ Have students listen and practice the intonations they hear.

Task B

❶ Play the tape.

❷ Ask students to individually circle the answers.

❸ Have students compare their answers with a partner.

Task C

❶ Play the tape again for students to check their answers.

❷ Pause the tape after each sentence to go over answers as a class.

TRY THIS! Play the tape again, as necessary. The words are *around* and *by.*

Tapescript

[i] **M:** Five o'clock. Five o'clock?
   M: Tired. Tired?
   M: By bus. By bus?
   M: Busy day. Busy day?
   M: Downtown. Downtown?

[ii] **W:** I get up around five o'clock.
   W: How do you feel?
   W: How do you get to work?
   W: I feel really tired.
   W: I have breakfast downtown with my boyfriend.

[iii] 1. **W:** I get up around five o'clock.
   M: Five o'clock?

   2. **W:** How do you feel?
   M: Tired.

   3. **W:** How do you get to work?
   M: By bus.

   4. **W:** I feel really tired.
   M: Busy day?

   5. **W:** I have breakfast downtown with my boyfriend.
   M: Downtown?

A Look at the activities in the pictures. What time do you think each one happened?

B Listen and number the pictures (1–6).

C What time did each activity happen? Listen again and mark the time on the clocks.

4 Say It Right

A Listen and practice the statement and question intonations.

1. *Five o'clock.*   *Five o'clock?*
2. *Tired.*   *Tired?*
3. *By bus.*   *By bus?*
4. *Busy day.*   *Busy day?*
5. *Downtown.*   *Downtown?*

Try this

I start work AT 9:00. Which two other words (instead of *at*) did you hear before the time in Listen In?
Can you remember?

B Listen and circle the best response to each statement you hear.

C Listen again and check your answers.

5 Focus In

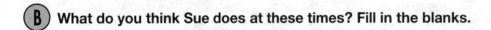

A Look at the chart.

Questions with *what + do*	
What do you **do** in the morning?	I **go** to school.
What time does Pete get up?	He **gets up** at around 5:30.
What does she **do** in the evenings?	She **watches** TV or reads a book.
What do they **do** on the weekends?	They **visit** their parents.

B What do you think Sue does at these times? Fill in the blanks.

Well, I generally ___get up___ at 6:30.
I _take a shower_ and then I have ___breakfast___ at around 7:30.
I _catch the bus_ at 8:15. It's a 45-minute trip, so I _get to school_
at around 9:00. I ___have lunch___ from 12:30–1:30,
and I ___get home___ at 5:00.

C Write five sentences about your own daily schedule.

1. _____
2. _____
3. _____
4. _____
5. _____

6 Talk Some More

Spotlight
How come? is the same as *Why?*, but it is very informal.

A Number the sentences to make a conversation.

Gina: __3__ Tired? What time do you get up?
Gina: __1__ What's the matter?
Jack: __4__ 5:30.
Jack: __2__ I'm tired.
Jack: __6__ I have an early morning computer class.
Gina: __5__ How come?

B Check your answers.

Pair work

C Practice the conversation using the activities on the list in Get Ready. Then practice again using information about your own daily schedule.

5 Focus In

Task A

1 Go through the chart with the students.

2 On the board, write questions using *What + do* and *What + does*, some of which contain errors. Ask students to say which are correct and which are incorrect, and the reasons why.

 ⋯⋯⋯ Have students rewrite the sentences correctly.

Task B

1 Have students fill in the blanks with the missing activities.

2 Have them check with a partner.

3 Have them practice asking and answering questions about Sue's daily schedule.

Task C

 ⋯⋯⋯ Write five sentences about your own daily schedule, without the times. Have students guess what time you do each activity.

1 Have students write 5 sentences with their own information.

2 Have them read their answers to a partner.

 ⋯⋯⋯ Have students respond to their partner's sentences by asking the correct question about their daily routine to match the answer.

6 Talk Some More

Task A

1 Have students number the sentences to make a logical conversation.

2 Offer help as necessary.

Task B

1 Play the tape.

2 Have students check their answers.

> **Tapescript**
>
> **W:** What's the matter?
> **M:** I'm tired.
> **W:** Tired? What time do you get up?
> **M:** 5:30.
> **W:** How come?
> **M:** I have an early morning computer class.

Task C

1 Have students practice the conversation.

2 Have them practice again, using different activities from the list in Get Ready or from their own schedules in Focus In.

 ⋯⋯⋯ In pairs, have students write a similar short dialog and role-play it in front of the class.

(SPOTLIGHT) Point out that *How come?* is informal.

7 Work In Pairs

See pages xii-xiii for suggestions on pair work.

Task A

❶ Divide students into pairs. Refer Student B to page 76.

❷ Have them look at the chart and think about the missing times. Have students make predictions, but don't let them see each other's books.

Task B

❶ Explain that neither person in the pair has complete information.

❷ Have them ask questions and fill in their charts.

❸ Monitor as necessary.

> **Sample**
>
> **A:** What time does Andrew get up?
> **B:** He gets up at five o'clock in the afternoon. What time does Matt get up?
> **A:** He gets up at six-thirty in the morning. What time does Matt have breakfast?
> **B:** He has breakfast at seven o'clock in the morning. How about Andrew…?
> **A:** He has breakfast at five-thirty in the afternoon. What time does Andrew…?

Task C

❶ Have students speculate about Andrew's work.

❷ Go over ideas with the class (jobs might include police officer, night manager, doctor, truck driver, bartender, server).

Task D

❶ Have students use their own ideas to fill in times for the new activities.

(TRY THIS!) Have each student ask their partner for the information in Task D. Have them write sentences to describe when Andrew/Matt does each activity.

 ⋯⋯ Have students call out their ideas and see if anyone has the exact same times. Have students give reasons for choosing those times.

Work In Pairs 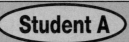 Student A

Student B: Use page 76

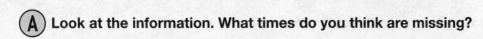

A Look at the information. What times do you think are missing?

	gets up	has breakfast	goes to work	comes home	has dinner	goes to bed
Matt	6:30 am	7:00 am	7:45 am	6:30 pm	7:00 pm	10:30 pm
Andrew	5:00 pm	5:30 pm	6:00 pm	5:15 am	6:30 am	10:00 am

B Ask your partner questions and fill in the missing information.

> What time do you get up?

> 10:30

C What kind of work do you think Andrew does?

D Make up some more times. What time do you think Matt...

takes a shower?   He takes a shower at _____

catches the bus?   He catches the bus at _____

gets to work?   He gets to work at _____

finishes work?   He finishes work at _____

Try this

Now ask your partner for the same information about Andrew.
Write four sentences about Andrew with the information.

_____

_____

_____

_____

Work In Pairs   Student B

A Look at the information. What times do you think are missing?

	gets up	has breakfast	goes to work	comes home	has dinner	goes to bed
Matt	6:30 am	7:00 am	7:45 am	6:30 pm	7:00 pm	10:30 pm
Andrew	5:00 pm	5:30 pm	6:00 pm	5:15 am	6:30 am	10:00 am

B Ask your partner questions and fill in the missing information.

C What kind of work do you think Andrew does?

D Make up some more times. What time do you think Andrew...

takes a shower?   He takes a shower at _____

catches the bus?   He catches the bus at _____

gets to work?   He gets to work at _____

finishes work?   He finishes work at _____

Try this

Now ask your partner for the same information about Matt. Write four sentences about Matt with the information.

_____

_____

_____

_____

7 Work In Pairs

See p. T75 for suggested instructions for this task.

Mid-Unit Assessment

Once your students have finished Work In Pairs, they will have covered approximately half of this unit. How well are they accomplishing the unit goals at this stage? You may wish to assess their ability on the points below before beginning the fluency task Express Yourself. Check (✔) the appropriate space in the chart for each goal.

Can your students...	Yes, all can.	Yes, most can.	Maybe half can.	Only some can.
1 describe routines and schedules? *e.g. I get up at 7:00. I take a shower and eat breakfast at 7:30.*	_____	_____	_____	_____
2 tell the time? *e.g. seven o'clock, seven thirty...*	_____	_____	_____	_____
3 ask for reasons? *e.g. Why? How come?*	_____	_____	_____	_____
4 say the names of daily routine activities? *(see Get Ready for list)*	_____	_____	_____	_____
5 use intonation to transform statements into questions?	_____	_____	_____	_____
6 form questions with *what* and *do*?	_____	_____	_____	_____

If your students can already accomplish these fairly well, they're better prepared to expand their use of the target language in the tasks that follow. For those who are still having problems with particular items above, you may wish to direct them to the relevant areas of the unit on pages 72–76, to workbook pages 34–35, or to the online quiz on the *Expressions* website.

8 Express Yourself

Task A

 ········· Write the target question form on the board: *What time do you...?*

1. Tell students they will survey three classmates. Have them stand and mingle for this activity.

2. Have them get answers from three different classmates for each question.

3. When they finish, have them share their information with a partner.

Task B

1. Ask a few students to say what they have found out.

2. Tell students to form groups.

3. Have them ask each other questions to find out the information for their group.

4. Elicit group answers. Find out answers for the whole class.

5. Tabulate on board, or turn into a discussion session as required.

9 Think About It

1. Have the students read the information and consider the answers to the questions.

2. Discuss the questions as a class. Find out whether a guest in someone's home should/ shouldn't arrive late and what they should say if they do.
   Note: You could take this opportunity to introduce/review what students should say if they are late for class.

10 Write About It

Task A

1. Have students read the daily planners.

2. Offer language support as necessary.

Task B

1. Have students write their own daily planners.

2. Monitor as necessary.

challenge ········· Have students ask and answer questions about their schedules, in pairs.

8 Express Yourself

A Survey three of your classmates. Find out what time they...

Group work

	Name 1	Name 2	Name 3
get up			
have breakfast			
leave home			
arrive at work or school			
have lunch			
go home			
have dinner			
go to bed			

B Share your information with the class. Then answer these questions.

1. Who gets up the earliest in your class? _____
2. Who gets up the latest? _____
3. Who goes to bed the earliest? _____
4. Who goes to bed the latest? _____

9 Think About It

In some cultures it's OK to arrive late for a social event. In other cultures it's important to be on time.

• How about in your culture? Do you have to apologize if you're late?

10 Write About It

Mon.	**Tue.**	**Wed.**
6:15 go jogging	12:00 meeting with Jerry	10:15 pick up photos
12:00 lunch with Sue	1:30 visit clinic	1:30 phone dentist
5:30 meet John at Regal theater	6:30 phone Jim Benson	6:45 cocktails with Jen
	8:00 meet Phil for drink	9:00 dinner with Julie

A Look at the daily planner.

B Now fill in your own daily schedule.

My Schedule

Mon.	Tue.	Wed.	Thu.	Fri.

Here's a daily routine with a difference...

Lee Weston, Wildlife Biologist, Alaska

I do a lot of work outdoors in the Alaskan mountains. Although it's summer, I have to take snowshoes and a lot of warm clothes. I also take a tent, food, and my backpack.

I sleep in the tent. In summer in Alaska it's always daylight. When I get up I put on warm clothes. I make some breakfast. Then I put on my snowshoes and start work. I'm studying birds. I walk for a certain distance, looking. Then I stand still, writing in my notebook. This goes on all day.

I carry a lot of things: my map, radio, drinking water, lunch and a gun. The gun is for bears. I don't have any bullets in the gun—just noisemakers. I've never used it yet.

It's slow, walking in snowshoes and carrying all that stuff. In early summer the mountain streams are very high with melting snow. Sometimes I have to walk through them. The water is very cold and fast.

For lunch I eat a sandwich, cheese and crackers, and chocolate. Definitely chocolate. Then I work till late at night. I make some dinner and look over my notes. I go to sleep in the daylight, just as I got up.

What can you understand from Lee's story? Underline the place in the story where you found the information.

	True	False
• Lee sleeps under the stars.		✔
• She walks in the snow.	✔	
• She likes chocolate.	✔	
• The bears give her a lot of trouble.		✔
• A stream is like a little river.	✔	

Talk About It

- Have you ever camped in a very cold place in the mountains? Talk about it.
- Lee loves her work. What do you think she likes about it?
- Do you like working indoors or outdoors? Why?

Unit 9: I get up early.

11 Read On

Before the Reading

1. Ask the class these warm-up questions. Alternatively, have students first discuss them in pairs or small groups. List the words you elicit, under two columns: 'Indoor jobs' and 'Outdoor jobs.'

   What are some outdoor and indoor jobs? Which of these do you think are interesting jobs?

2. Write these verb and noun phrases in two separate columns on the board: *sleep in, put on, carry, make, eat, write in; a tent, a notebook, chocolates, dinner, a backpack, snowshoes.* Explain that the words are from the Read On passage. In groups, have students match each verb with a noun, e.g. *put on snowshoes.* Elicit answers from students and note them on the board. Then, have each group predict what they think the passage is about.

 Ask students to give reasons for their predictions.

3. Refer students to page 78. Ask students whether they think their predictions were correct. On the board, write the 5 sentences from page 78. Explain that the students have to read the passage and check whether each sentence is true or false.

During the Reading

1. Monitor students and offer language support where necessary.

2. Have students compare their answers with a partner.

After the Reading

1. Elicit responses from students, and check the correct answers on the board. Ask the students to read out the sentence where they found each answer.

2. Go over the meaning of each of the Talk About It questions. Have students work in pairs, asking and answering the questions. Then discuss the questions as a class.

   Optional questions:
   What things do you use each day at work (or school)? What's the most useful thing you use to do your job?

Extension Activity

Divide students into groups and tell them they are going on a camping trip. Each group has to decide 5 things they will eat or drink on the trip, 5 things they will wear, and 5 other things they will take. Have each group report their choices to the class.

 Ask each group to give reasons for their choices.

Cultural Note

Many Americans who are fed up with the stress of their big-city routines are turning to outdoor lifestyles instead. Some decide to quit their job for a full-time occupation working outdoors. Others use their vacation time to sample the outdoor life. One way is to take a vacation on a cowboy ranch. There are several ranches across the American West that will allow you to experience the lifestyle cowboys have enjoyed for more than one hundred years. Some of the ranches actually involve their guests in work on their grounds, while others are more like cowboy style resorts. Guests can enjoy horseback riding, hiking, fishing, spas, cowboy cuisine, strolling under the stars, and even join in a sing-along around a campfire. They can also take part in cowboy classes, where they learn to tie special knots, or how to rope cattle.

Unit 9: I get up early.

12 Vocabulary Review

Task A
1. Have students complete the exercise then search back through the unit for the correct answers.
2. Check answers.

Task B
1. Have students express their own opinion.
2. Turn this into a whole class session and encourage discussion.

12 Grammar Review

Task A
1. Have students complete both questions and answers.
2. Go through answers. Have students ask and answer the questions in pairs.

Task B
1. Have students unscamble the sentences and write the superfluous word at the end of the line.
2. Have students compare answers then go over the answers as a class.

 Have students write 3 or 4 questions about daily routines. Students should read their questions to a partner and their partner should answer the question using real information about themselves. Make a rule that questions already covered in the review tasks cannot be repeated.

Log On

Have students do the online activities for this unit on the *Expressions* website: **http://expressions.heinle.com**

Language Summary

For a more detailed review of the language practiced in this unit, refer students to the **Language Summary on page 140**. Encourage them to add new vocabulary in the **Word Builder** section.

12 Review

1 Vocabulary Review

A Fill in the blanks with verbs from this unit.

1. _take/have_ a shower.
2. _catch/take_ the bus.
3. ___go___ jogging.
4. _start/finish_ work.
5. _get/arrive_ home.
6. _have/eat_ breakfast/lunch/dinner.

B What time do you do these things?

I get up early.
How about you?

2 Grammar Review

A Fill in the blanks.
Then answer the questions with information about your own daily schedule.

1. What time _do you_ get up?

_____

2. What time _do you_ have breakfast?

_____

3. What time _do you_ start English class?

_____

4. What time _do you_ go to bed?

_____

B Write the correct sentences. Which word is not needed in each sentence?

1. (5:30/I/up/at/get/on) _I get up at 5:30._ (on)
2. (look/tired/you/matter) _You look tired._ (matter)
3. (school/he/at/7:00/busy/at/arrives) _He arrives at school at 7:00._ (busy)
4. (I'm/happy/oh/sorry/late) _Oh, sorry I'm late._ (happy)

3 Log On

Practice more with the language and topics you studied on the *Expressions* website:

http://expressions.heinle.com

Goals

○ *Ordering food and drink*   ○ *Asking for additional information*

I'd like a hamburger.

Get Ready

A Write the number next to the correct item (1–10).

1.	hamburger
2.	pizza
3.	fries
4.	salad
5.	chicken
6.	hot dog
7.	soda
8.	iced tea
9.	mustard
10.	ketchup

B How many toppings can you put on pizza? Make a list and then share it with your partner.

○ Cheese
○
○
○
○
○

Start Talking

A Look at the conversation and listen.

Server: Can I help you?

Maxine: I'd like a hamburger and a medium iced tea, please.

Server: Is that all?

Maxine: Yes, thanks.

Pair work

B Pair work. Practice the conversation with a partner. Practice again ordering different items from the menu.

Unit 10: I'd like a hamburger.

Goals
➤ Ordering food and drink ➤ Asking for additional information

Workbook: pages 38–41

1 Get Ready

Task A
❶ Go over the pronunciation and meaning of the vocabulary items.

❷ Have students write the numbers next to the correct items.

 Ask students what other kinds of items can be found in fast food restaurants.

Task B
❶ Have students work individually to write down as many toppings as possible.

❷ Have students compare answers with a partner.

❸ Check answers as a class. Possible answers are: *sauce, cheese, sausage, ham, tomatoes, pineapple, peppers, pepperoni, mushroom, olives, onion, anchovies, garlic.*

 Have students work in pairs to see who can come up with the most original pizza. Provide language support if necessary.

2 Start Talking

Task A
❶ Have students read the conversation.

❷ Play the tape while students listen to the conversation.

 Rewind the tape and have students repeat the conversation after the tape.

Tapescript

M: Can I help you?
W: I'd like a hamburger and a medium iced tea, please.
M: Is that all?
W: Yes. Thanks.

Task B
❶ Have students practice the conversation.

 Ask which words use *a* and which use *some*. Write them on the board in separate columns for reference.

❷ Have them practice the conversation in pairs, using the different food and drink items.

 Have them continue practicing using any other fast food items they know.

3 Listen In

Task A

❶ Elicit the meaning of 'regular.' ('Regular' is another word for 'medium.')

❷ Have students decide individually which items could be described as 'regular.'

❸ Have them check with a partner.

❹ Elicit suggestions from the students. Items most commonly described as 'regular' are: *hamburger, fries, pizza, hotdog, soda, coffee, iced tea, juice, salad.*

Task B

❶ Play the tape. Have students listen and check the words they hear.

❷ Go over answers.

Task C

❶ Play the tape. Have students listen and take the orders.

 ········ Pause the tape after each order to allow students time to write.

❷ Go over answers.

Tapescript

1. **W1:** Ready to order?
   M1: Uh-huh. I'd like a large pizza.
   W1: Anything to drink?
   M1: Um. A medium soda, please.
   W1: Is that all?
   M1: Uh-huh.

2. **W2:** Can I help you?
   M2: I'll have a six-piece bucket of chicken and a salad.
   W2: Small, medium or large for the salad?
   M2: Um, small, please.
   W2: Do you want any drinks?
   M2: No, thanks.

3. **W3:** All set?
   M3: A hot dog, please.
   W3: One hot dog coming up. Will that be all?
   M3: Do you have any mustard?
   W3: Sure. It's right there on the tray. Help yourself.
   M3: Thanks.

4. **M4:** Can I help you?
   W4: I'll have a hamburger please.
   M4: Regular or double?
   W4: Oh, uh, regular, please.
   M4: Anything to drink?
   W4: A large coffee.
   M4: OK. Will that be all?
   W4: Can I have some extra napkins?
   M4: Sure. Here you go.
   W4: Thanks.

4 Say It Right

Task A

❶ Explain how the letter 'S' in English can have the sound /s/ or /z/, depending on whether the preceding sound is unvoiced or voiced.

 ········ Give other examples yourself before students do the exercise.

❷ Ask students to say the words quietly to themselves and check the sound columns.

❸ Have students compare their answers with a partner.

Tapescript

[i] **M:** Do you want drinks?
   M: I'd like three hamburgers.
   M: How many hot dogs do you want?
   M: A large iced tea, thanks.
   M: Do you have extra napkins?

[ii] **M:** Drinks
   M: Hamburgers
   M: Hotdogs
   M: Thanks
   M: Napkins

Task B

❶ Play the tape. Have students check their answers.

❷ Have students repeat after the tape, if necessary.

Task C

❶ Have students listen again and practice.

 ········ Give other words, and ask students to tell you if 'S' has the /s/ or /z/ sound. Example words may include: *orders, salads, cups, chairs, seats, restaurants, pizzas.*

TRY THIS! Have students choose three words from Listen In and decide whether the plural forms end in /s/ or /z/.

3 Listen In

A Which items in the list could you describe using the word *regular*?

✔	hamburger	✔✔	hot dog	✔	mustard
	fries	✔	soda		ketchup
✔	chicken	✔	coffee		apple
✔	salad		iced tea		pie
✔	pizza		juice		ice cream

B Listen and check (✔) the words every time you hear them.

C Listen again and take the orders.

Pizza Palace
1 large pizza
_____
_____
1 medium soda
_____
_____

Chicken Bucket
1 (6-pc) bucket of chicken
_____
1 small salad
_____
_____

Harry's Hot Dogs
Order Form
1 hot dog

Burger Club
1 regular hamburger
_____
1 large coffee
_____

4 Say It Right

A Plural (two or more) things end with the letter *s*.
When we are speaking, sometimes the sound is /s/, sometimes the sound is /z/.
Do the words end in /s/ or /z/? Listen and check (✔) the correct column.

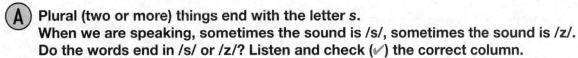

	/s/	/z/
drinks	✔	
hamburgers		✔
hot dogs		✔
thanks	✔	
napkins		✔

Try this
Choose three words from the list in Listen In.
Do the plural words end with /s/ or /z/?

B Listen and check your answers.

C Listen again and practice.

5 Focus In

A Look at the chart.

would like/will have	
Can I help you?	Yes, **I'd like** a cheeseburger please./No, thanks.
Would you like any ketchup and mustard on that?	**I'll have** some ketchup, but I don't want any mustard, thanks.
Would you like a drink?	Yes, **I'll have** an orange juice please.
What size **would you like**?	Small/Medium/Large, please.
Is that all?	Yes, thanks./No, **I'd also like** an iced tea, please.

B Put *some*, *any*, or *a/an* in the blanks. Then practice the conversations with a partner.

A: Can I help you?

B: I'd like ___a___ hamburger and ___some___ fries please.

A: Would you like ___any___ ketchup and mustard on your fries?

B: Yes, can I have ___some___ mustard, please? Thanks.

C Look at these food items. Fill in the blanks with *some*, *a* or *an*.

1. ___an___ apple
2. ___some___ mayonnaise
3. ___a___ hot dog
4. ___some___ chicken
5. ___some___ pizza
6. ___an___ ice cream cone

---

6 Talk Some More

A Number the sentences to make a conversation.

Mike: ___4___ Yes. And a soda, please.

Mike: ___2___ Yes. Can I have a hamburger, please?

Server: ___3___ Would you like ketchup and mustard on that?

Server: ___1___ Can I help you?

Mike: ___6___ Medium.

Server: ___5___ What size?

Spotlight
Always say *please* when you want someone to help you!

B Check your answers.

Pair work

C Practice the conversation with a partner.
Practice again using items from the list in Listen In.

5 Focus In

Task A

1 Go through the chart with the students.

2 Elicit which are offers and which are requests.

 ······· Present more examples as necessary, for students to grasp the rule.

Task B

 ······· Present more examples as necessary, for students to understand when to use *a* or *an*, and *some* and *any*.

1 Have students fill in the blanks.

2 Have them check with a partner.

3 Have them practice ordering using the dialog.

Task C

1 Have students fill in the blanks.

2 Have them check their answers with a partner.

3 Go over answers with the class.

 ······· Elicit more food and drink items and extend the exercise. If you think students are ready, elicit the use of *a/an* and *some/any* using non-food items.

6 Talk Some More

Task A

1 Have students number the sentences to make a logical conversation.

2 Offer help as necessary.

Task B

1 Play the tape.

2 Have students check their answers.

Task C

1 Have students practice the conversation.

2 Have them practice again, using different foods and drinks.

 ······· Brainstorm some other questions for students to practice, such as *Will that be for here or to go?*

(SPOTLIGHT) Point out to students the use of *please* in the dialog. Tell students that it is considered more polite and courteous to say *please* when asking for something.

Tapescript

W: Can I help you?
M: Yes. Can I have a hamburger, please?
W: Would you like ketchup and mustard on that?
M: Yes. And a soda, please.
W: What size?
M: Medium.

Unit 10: I'd like a hamburger.

7 Work In Pairs

See pages xii-xiii for suggestions on pair work.

Task A

❶ Divide students into pairs. Refer Student B to page 84.

❷ Have them look at the picture.

❸ Have students ask each other for the prices of the items on the menu.

support ┄┄┄ Write the question *How much is/are the...?* on the board.

> **Sample**
>
> **A:** How much is a double hamburger?
> **B:** A dollar twenty. How much is a regular hamburger?
> **A:** Seventy cents. How much is...?

Task B

❶ Explain that Student A is the customer, Student B the server.

❷ Model the conversation first with a student. You could also review the Talk Some More dialog as further preparation.

❸ Have them do the exercise, with Student B asking for choice of item size.

❹ Monitor as necessary.

> **Sample**
>
> **B:** Can I help you?
> **A:** Yes, can I have a cheeseburger, please?
> **B:** What size would you like?
> **A:** Double. And a hot dog with cheese, please.
> **B:** OK. Would you like a drink?
> **A:** No, thank you.
> **B:** Is that all?
> **A:** Yes, thanks.

Task C

❶ Have students swap roles and do the exercise again.

❷ Monitor and assist as necessary.

challenge ┄┄┄ If you think students are ready, have them practice the pronunication of numbers as they are spoken naturally. i.e.: *twennie* (twenty), *thirdy* (thirty), etc.

TRY THIS! Draw students' attention to the correct pronunciation of numbers, before they do the exercise.

Work In Pairs  Student A

Student B: Use page 84

A Ask your partner for the missing prices of the items on the menu. Write each price in the correct place.

Burger Wizard Menu

Hamburger	regular	.70	double	1.20
Cheeseburger	regular	.90	double	1.40
Hot dog	regular	.70	w/cheese	.90
Chicken	regular	.90	large	1.10
French fries	regular	.60	large	.80
Soft drinks	regular	.60	large	.80
Iced tea	regular	.50	large	.70

B Look at the menu and order food from your partner.

C Change roles. You are the server. Practice the conversation again with a new order. Write your partner's order.

Try this

Write down ten prices from the menu above. Say them to your partner and ask for the total. Is your partner's total correct? What is the total?

I'd like a hamburger.

7 Work In Pairs   Student B

A Ask your partner for the missing prices of the items on the menu.
Write each price in the correct place.

Burger Wizard Menu

Hamburger	regular	.70	double	1.20
Cheeseburger	regular	.90	double	1.40
Hot dog	regular	.70	w/cheese	.90
Chicken	regular	.90	large	1.10
French fries	regular	.60	large	.80
Soft drinks	regular	.60	large	.80
Iced tea	regular	.50	large	.70

B Imagine you are a server.
Practice taking your partner's order.
Write your partner's order on the order form.

C Now change roles.
Look at the menu
and order food
from your partner.

Is that all?

Burger Wizard Order Form

Try this

Write down ten prices from the menu above. Say them to your partner
and ask for the total. Is your partner's total correct? What is the total?

7 Work In Pairs

See p. T83 for suggested instructions for this task.

Mid-Unit Assessment

Once your students have finished Work In Pairs, they will have covered approximately half of this unit. How well are they accomplishing the unit goals at this stage? You may wish to assess their ability on the points below before beginning the fluency task Express Yourself. Check (✔) the appropriate space in the chart for each goal.

Can your students...	Yes, all can.	Yes, most can.	Maybe half can.	Only some can.
❶ order food and drink? *e.g. I'd like a hamburger and a medium iced tea, please.*	_____	_____	_____	_____
❷ ask for additional information? *e.g. What size? Would you like ketchup on that?*	_____	_____	_____	_____
❸ say the names of food and drink items? *(see Get Ready for list)*	_____	_____	_____	_____
❹ recognize and use /s/ and /z/ correctly in noun plural endings?	_____	_____	_____	_____
❺ use *would like* and *will have* correctly?	_____	_____	_____	_____

If your students can already accomplish these fairly well, they're better prepared to expand their use of the target language in the tasks that follow. For those who are still having problems with particular items above, you may wish to direct them to the relevant areas of the unit on pages 80–84, to workbook pages 38–39, or to the online quiz on the *Expressions* website.

8 Express Yourself

Task A

 Brainstorm restaurant types as a class. Elicit some menu items for each type of restaurant and write them on the board.

❶ Have students decide with a partner what kind of restaurant they are going to choose.

❷ Have students create a menu for their chosen restaurant type.

❸ Monitor and assist as necessary. Check *a/an*, *some/any* usage.

Task B

❶ Have students swap partners.

❷ Have them practice ordering and taking the orders.

❸ Have students practice in groups of 3. Two students are diners and one is the server.

 Ask students which items on offer were the most popular. You could also have a few pairs perform their conversation for the class.

9 Think About It

❶ Have the students read the information and consider the answers to the questions.

❷ Discuss the questions as a class.

❸ Ask what other 'rules' apply to restaurants in their countries.

10 Write About It

Task A

❶ Have students read the recipe.

❷ Offer language support as necessary.

Task B

❶ Have students write their own recipes.

❷ Monitor and provide language support as necessary.

 Have students read their recipes to a partner and see if their partner can guess what the recipe is for.

Express Yourself

Group work

A Choose a type of restaurant and create a menu with a partner. Don't forget to list the prices!

B Work with a different partner. Show your new partner the menu and take the order.

9 *Think About It*

In some cultures, people make special requests when ordering food in a restaurant. In other cultures, people order exactly what is on the menu.

• How about in your culture? Do people usually order extras?

10 Write About It

A Look at the recipe.

B Now write your own favorite recipe.

My Recipe

Recipe

STRAWBERRY SMOOTHIE

Ingredients:
• 10 fresh strawberries
• 1 glass milk
• 2 cups crushed ice

Procedure:
Put all ingredients in a blender. Blend together for 30 seconds. Serve in tall glasses.

I'd like a hamburger. **85**

Read On The Birth of the Burger

• *Strategy: Scanning*

Do you know the origins of these hamburger basics?

Cheese

Most historians believe that cheese originated in the Middle East more than six thousand years ago. The Romans were very good cheesemakers and made many kinds of it. Traders and soldiers spread the idea throughout Europe.

Bread

People began making bread around 12,000 years ago. Around 4,000 years ago the Egyptians began making 'modern' bread with wheat flour and with yeast.

Tomatoes

Early Nahuatl farmers in Mexico planted wild tomatoes for food, so long ago that we don't know when. The English word comes from the Nahuatl word *tomatl*. Travelers from Spain took tomatoes home with them in the 1500s.

Pickles

Cucumbers originated in India a long time ago. They were brought to the Tigris River valley in what is now Iraq. The early Iraqis began to pickle them around 2030 B.C. The Egyptians and Romans also enjoyed pickles.

Potatoes

Potatoes were first grown in the Andes Mountains of South America. Spanish travelers took them back home in the 16th century. From there, they spread to Europe and North America.

Write the names and the dates of the foods in the places where they originated. If the reading has no information, write *don't know*.

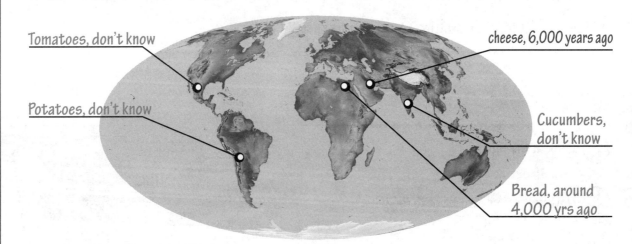

Tomatoes, don't know

Potatoes, don't know

cheese, 6,000 years ago

Cucumbers, don't know

Bread, around 4,000 yrs ago

Talk About It

○ What's your favorite fast food?

○ What international fast foods are popular where you live?

○ What fast foods from your country are popular in other countries?

Unit 10: I'd like a hamburger.

11 Read On

Before the Reading

1 Ask the class these warm-up questions. Alternatively, have students first discuss them in pairs or small groups.

What does 'fast food' mean? Do you like eating fast food? How often do you eat it?

2 List these food and place words on the board: *tomatoes, potatoes, cheese, cucumbers, bread; Middle East, India, South America, Egypt, Mexico.* In groups, have students predict where each food comes from. Then, call on students to give their answers and note them on the board.

 ······· Ask students also to guess how old each type of food is.

3 Refer students to page 86. Point out the example. Explain that they should read the passage, then write the names and dates in the correct spaces. If there is no answer, they should write *don't know.*

During the Reading

1 Monitor students and offer language support where necessary.

2 Have students compare their answers with a partner.

🌐 Nahuatl: nəhuɑtl, tomatl: təmɑtl

After the Reading

1 Elicit responses from students, and check correct answers on the board. Were their predictions correct? Ask students to read out the sentence where they found each piece of information.

2 Go over the meaning of each of the Talk About It questions. Have students work in pairs, asking and answering the questions. Then discuss the questions as a class.

Optional questions:
Where's the best place to go for a hamburger in your neighborhood? A sandwich? A pizza?

Extension Activity

Write these country names on the board: *France, Spain, Italy, United States, Korea, Japan, Mexico, Russia* (or, elicit 8–10 countries from the students). In groups, have students think of types of food or drink that each country is famous for. Ask groups to report their answers, and note them on the board. See which group can come up with the longest list. (Examples: *France, escargot; Spain, paella; Italy, spaghetti; United States, hot dog; Korea, kimchi; Japan, sashimi; Mexico, nachos; Russia, caviar.*) Have students say which of these foods they have/haven't tried, which foods they would like to try and which they wouldn't like to try. Have them give reasons why.

Cultural Note

The hamburger has an interesting history. The word comes from the seaport city of Hamburg, in Germany. Hamburg was the city from which many European immigrants to the U.S. departed. The original hamburger—a ground meat steak—was a popular food on the boats on the Hamburg-America line. Eventually, the hamburger took its modern form, and became one of the world's most popular foods.

12 Vocabulary Review

Task A

❶ Have students fill in the chart from memory.

❷ Have students look through the unit in pairs, or as a group, to check their answers.

Task B

❶ Have students express their own opinion.

❷ Turn this into a whole class session and encourage discussion.

 challenge ········ If students are ready, have them each write a list of fast food items/brands. Have them interview their classmates to find out which they eat, and how often.

12 Grammar Review

Task A

❶ Have students fill in the blanks.

❷ Have students look back through the unit to check their answers.

❸ Have students practice the dialog in pairs.

Task B

❶ Have students make sentences using the words shown.

❷ Have students read their sentences to a partner to check accuracy.

❸ Go through answers.

 challenge ········ Have students write their own conversation based in a fast food restaurant of their choice. Make sure students practice their conversation orally.

Log On

Have students do the online activities for this unit on the *Expressions* website: **http://expressions.heinle.com**

Language Summary

For a more detailed review of the language practiced in this unit, refer students to the **Language Summary on page 140**. Encourage them to add new vocabulary in the **Word Builder** section.

12 Review

1 Vocabulary Review

A Fill in the chart with words you learned in this unit.

Food	Drink	Size

B Which of the foods in the chart do you often eat?

2 Grammar Review

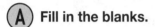

What size would you like?

Large, please.

A Fill in the blanks.

1. __Can__ __I__ help you?
2. __Can__ __I__ have a hot dog, please?
3. __Would__ __you__ like mustard and ketchup on that?
4. __Is__ __that__ all?
5. __I'd__ also like an iced tea, please.

B Make sentences using the words shown.

1. (hamburger/fries) _____
2. (regular/hot dog) _____
3. (like/mustard) _____
4. (size/like) _____
5. (salad/without) _____

3 Log On

Practice more with the language and topics you studied on the *Expressions* website:

http://expressions.heinle.com

I'd like a hamburger.

Goals

◯ *Inviting* ◯ *Making excuses*

Do you want to see a movie?

1 Get Ready

A Look at the picture.
What types of movies
can you see on the posters?
Write the number
in the correct place.

1.	science fiction
2.	comedy
3.	thriller
4.	drama
5.	action film

B Think of two real movie titles for each category below. Write them in the spaces.

1. science fiction _____
2. comedies _____
3. thrillers _____
4. dramas _____
5. action films _____

2 Start Talking

A Look at the conversation and listen.

Alice: Do you want to see a movie?

Rob: Which one?

Alice: How about *Arrival of the Visitors*?

Rob: Oh, no. I don't like science fiction.

Pair work

B Practice the conversation with a partner.
Then practice again using different movies.

Unit 11: Do you want to see a movie?

Goals ➤ Inviting ➤ Making excuses

Workbook: pages 42–45

1 Get Ready

Task A

 ········ Ask students about their favorite movies, when they were made, which country they're from, who stars in them, etc.

❶ Go over the pronunciation and meaning of the movie types.

❷ Have students individually number each film to match its correct category.

❸ Have them compare answers with a partner.

❹ Go over answers.

Task B

❶ Have students add two real movie titles to each category.

❷ Have students compare answers with a partner.

❸ Check answers as a class.

 ········ As students are reading out their movie titles, have other students say if they've seen the movies or not.

2 Start Talking

Task A

❶ Let students read the conversation.

❷ Play the tape while students listen to the conversation.

 ········ Rewind the tape and have students repeat the conversation after the tape.

Tapescript

W: Do you want to see a movie?
M: Which one?
W: How about *Arrival of the Visitors?*
M: Oh, no. I don't like science fiction.

Task B

❶ Have students practice the conversation.

❷ Have them practice the conversation in pairs, using the other films from Get Ready.

 ········ Elicit other film titles and have students continue practicing.

Unit 11: Do you want to see a movie?

3 Listen In

Task A

1 Have students identify the movie genres without looking back in their books.

2 Have them check their answers with a partner.

Task B

1 Play the tape. Have them listen and match the movie with the theater.

2 Go over answers.

Task C

1 Play the tape. Have students listen and write the number of each excuse in the correct box.

support ⸺ Pause the tape after each line of the conversation.

2 Go over answers.

Tapescript

1. M1: Sally?
W1: Hi, Dave.
M1: Say, do you want to go to the movies? There's a great thriller on at the Cineplex.
W1: I'm sorry, I can't. I have to work late tonight.

2. M2: I'm bored.
M3: Do you want to go to the movies? There's a fun kind of comedy on at the Lyric.
M2: Oh, I can't. I have to study for my exam tomorrow.
M3: You do? That's too bad.

3. W2: Hello. Can I speak to Jim, please?
M4: Speaking.
W2: Oh, Jim. Hi! It's Nina. Say, do you want to go to the movies? There's a new science fiction movie on at Movie World.
M4: I'm sorry, I can't. I'm going out with Judy tonight.
W2: Oh, well, maybe next time.

4. W3: Oh, look. That new drama with Teresa Hansen is finally out.
W4: Where?
W3: It's showing at the Ritz. Do you want to go?
W4: I'm sorry, I can't tonight. I'm going to the ball game.
W3: You are, huh? Well, maybe next time.

4 Say It Right

Task A

1 Review how rising intonation can echo a statement and indicate surprise.

support ⸺ Give other examples yourself before students do the exercise.

2 Have students listen and check the responses they hear that show surprise.

Task B

1 Play the tape.

2 Have students compare their answers with a partner.

support ⸺ Pause the tape after each sentence and correct line by line.

3 Give students the Listen In tapescript and have them practice the intonation in each conversation.

TRY THIS! Have students practice by writing statements which might have preceded the ones in the exercise. Monitor as necessary. Then have them practice their conversations, using the appropriate intonation.

Tapescript

M: You do? That's too bad.
M: You are, huh? Well, maybe next time.
M: You can't? Oh, that's too bad.
M: He is? I didn't know that.
M: She can't. She has to study.

3 Listen In

A Which types of movies can you see in the pictures below?

B Listen and match the theater with the type of movie.

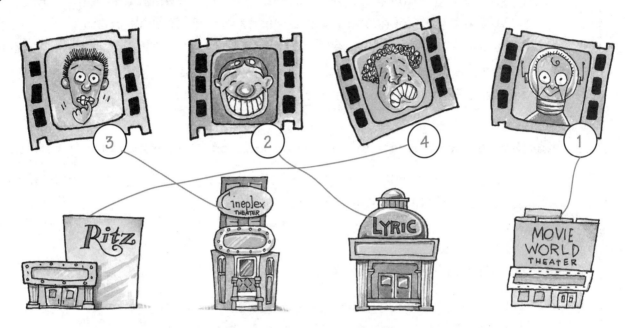

C Why can't the people go to the movies tonight?
Listen again and write the number of the excuse next to the correct movie.

1. I'm going out with Judy.   3. I have to work late.
2. I have to study.   4. I'm going to the ball game.

4 Say It Right

A Listen to the intonation and
check (✔) the responses that show surprise.

1. ___✔___ You do? That's too bad.
2. _____ You are, huh? Well, maybe next time.
3. ___✔___ You can't? Oh, that's too bad.
4. ___✔___ He is? I didn't know that.
5. _____ She can't. She has to study.

Try this

What statements do you think went before the surprise responses? Write them. Then practice making the statements and giving surprise responses with a partner.

B Listen again and practice.

5 Focus In

A Look at the chart.

I'm _____ing and I have to	
What **are** you **doing** tonight?	**I'm going** to the movies.
What **are** your friends **doing** this weekend?	**They're going** to the beach.
Do you want to see the new sci fi movie?	I can't. **I'm going** to a concert.
How about going on a picnic?	I can't. **I have to** study.
What's Pete up to this evening?	**He has to** work late.

B Number the sentences to make a conversation. Then practice with a partner.

___6___ I can't, Sally. I have to go to a meeting.   ___4___ Which one?

___5___ It's a thriller called *The Knife*.   ___1___ Hi, John.

___3___ Do you want to see a movie?   ___2___ Hi, Sally.

C Fill in the blanks using *have to* or _____*ing*.

1. I can't go to the ball game. I _have to finish_ (finish) my homework.
2. I _have to visit_ (visit) my sick aunt in the hospital.
3. They _have to work late_ (work late) tonight.
4. We _'re picking up_ (pick up) our parents and then _we're taking_ (take) them to dinner.
5. He _has to study_ (study) and then he _'s taking_ (take) his girlfriend to the movies.

6 Talk Some More

Spotlight
It's usually best to start your excuse with the word *Sorry*.

A Number the sentences to make a conversation (1–6).

Carol: ___6___ Oh, no. I forgot. I have to work late tonight.

Pete: ___3___ Do you want to go to a concert tonight?

Pete: ___5___ The Screamers.

Carol: ___2___ Hi, Pete.

Carol: ___4___ Who's playing?

Pete: ___1___ Hello, Carol.

B Check your answers.

 C Practice the conversation with a partner.
Then practice again using your own information.

5 Focus In

Task A

❶ Go through the chart with students.

❷ Exemplify *I'm ...ing* and *I have to*, pointing out that the former indicates a pleasurable activity, previously arranged, whereas the latter is used to talk about an obligation.

 .... Present more examples as necessary, for students to grasp the rule.

Task B

❶ Have students number the sentences to make a logical conversation.

❷ Have them check with a partner.

❸ Have them practice the conversation.

Task C

❶ Have students fill in the blanks with the correct verb forms.

❷ Have them check their answers with a partner.

❸ Go over answers with the class.

 .... Have students work in pairs to practice the sentences. Students should take turns making their own invitations or questions to elicit one of the responses in Task C.

6 Talk Some More

Task A

❶ Have students number the sentences to make a logical conversation.

❷ Offer help as necessary.

Task B

❶ Play the tape.

❷ Have students check their answers.

Task C

❶ Have students practice the conversation.

❷ Have them practice again, using different movies from Get Ready or their own information.

 .... Have students close their books and practice using different activities and different excuses.

(*SPOTLIGHT*) Emphasize the value of an apology when making an excuse.

> **Tapescript**
>
> **M:** Hello, Carol.
> **W:** Hi, Pete.
> **M:** Do you want to go to a concert tonight?
> **W:** Who's playing?
> **M:** The Screamers.
> **W:** Oh, no. I forgot. I have to work late tonight.

7 Work In Pairs

See pages xii-xiii for suggestions on pair work.

Task A

❶ Divide students into pairs. Refer Student B to page 92.

❷ Have them decide which activities relate to work.
(Answers may vary—the exam might be work related—but those involving the words *work, boss* and *meeting* are the likely answers.)

 ········ Have students think of 2 or 3 activities they already have planned for the weekend.

Task B

❶ Explain that neither person in the pair has the complete information.

❷ Have students ask questions to find what everybody is doing at the times indicated.

❸ Have students use the speech bubbles and sample dialog below.

❹ At the end of the exercise, have them check the schedules together and decide on a day and time that everyone can make to go and see a movie.

> **Sample**
>
> **B:** Do you want to see a movie?
> **A:** OK. How about Friday evening? Can Karen come?
> **B:** No, she has to clean her apartment. And Bob?
> **A:** He has to work late. How about Joan for Friday evening?
> **B:** Yes, she's free. What about Philip?
> **A:** Yes, he's free, too. How about Saturday afternoon? Is Bob free?
> **B:** No, he has to go to a meeting. What's Karen up to?
> **A:** She's free. What's Philip doing on Saturday?

Task C

❶ Have students change one aspect of each person's schedule, canceling or changing times to suit themselves. Make sure this is done individually.

❷ Repeat the exercise.

TRY THIS! Have students write Bob's excuses. Monitor for correct verb forms and sentence structure.

Work In Pairs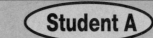

A Look at the activities in the chart.
Which are related to work and which are not?

	Friday Evening	Saturday Afternoon	Saturday Evening	Sunday Afternoon	Sunday Evening
Bob	work late	go to meeting	meet boss at airport	free	prepare for a meeting
Karen	clean apartment	free	visit aunt in hospital	go shopping	free
Philip	free	play tennis	free	study for exam	free
Joan	free	take car to garage	go to concert	bake cookies	free

B You and your partner want to go and see a movie with your friends.
Ask questions and decide the best time to go.

C Change one thing about each person's schedule. Do the exercise again.

Try this

Why can't Bob go to the movies on Friday, Saturday and Sunday evenings?
Write his excuses.

● Because_____

● Because_____

● Because_____

Work In Pairs   Student B

A Look at the activities in the chart.
Which are related to work and which are not?

	Friday Evening	Saturday Afternoon	Saturday Evening	Sunday Afternoon	Sunday Evening
Bob	work late	go to meeting	meet boss at airport	free	prepare for a meeting
Karen	clean apartment	free	visit aunt in hospital	go shopping	free
Philip	free	play tennis	free	study for exam	free
Joan	free	take car to garage	go to concert	bake cookies	free

How about Friday evening for Karen?

She has to clean her apartment.

B You and your partner want to go and
see a movie with your friends.
Ask questions and decide the best time to go.

C Change one thing about each person's schedule. Do the exercise again.

Try this

Why can't Bob go to the movies on Friday, Saturday and Sunday evenings?
Write his excuses.

O Because_____

O Because_____

O Because_____

Unit 11: Do you want to see a movie?

7 Work In Pairs

See p. T91 for suggested instructions for this task.

Mid-Unit Assessment

Once your students have finished Work In Pairs, they will have covered approximately half of this unit. How well are they accomplishing the unit goals at this stage? You may wish to assess their ability on the points below before beginning the fluency task Express Yourself. Check (✔) the appropriate space in the chart for each goal.

Can your students…	Yes, all can.	Yes, most can.	Maybe half can.	Only some can.
1 extend invitations? *e.g. Do you want to see a movie tonight?*	_____	_____	_____	_____
2 make excuses? *e.g. I'm going to a concert. I have to work late.*	_____	_____	_____	_____
3 say the names of movie types? *(see Get Ready for list)*	_____	_____	_____	_____
4 recognize and use intonation that shows surprise?	_____	_____	_____	_____
5 use *I'm ___ing* and *I have to* correctly?	_____	_____	_____	_____

If your students can already accomplish these fairly well, they're better prepared to expand their use of the target language in the tasks that follow. For those who are still having problems with particular items above, you may wish to direct them to the relevant areas of the unit on pages 88–92, to workbook pages 42–43, or to the online quiz on the *Expressions* website.

8 Express Yourself

Task A

1 Have students fill in the chart with real, or imaginary, activities.

2 Monitor and provide language support as necessary.

Task B

1 Tell students to form groups.

2 Have them work together to find mutually convenient times to go and see a movie.

3 Tell them they can change their schedules if they wish, but should not disappoint others.

4 Monitor as necessary during the activity.

5 Go over arrangements with the class, asking each group for details of their arrangements.

9 Think About It

1 Have the students read the information and consider the answers to the questions. Discuss the questions as a class.

2 Find out about how and when excuses are made in the students' culture(s). What constitutes a 'good' excuse?

10 Write About It

Task A

1 Have students read the emails.

2 Offer language support as necessary.

Task B

1 Have students write their own invitations.

2 Monitor as necessary.

3 Have them pass their invitations around to several students.

4 Have them accept or reject the ones they receive, but insist on a good excuse being given.

 .... Have students refuse invitations which clash with one previously accepted.

8 Express Yourself

A Make a note of the things you have to do this week. Leave two spaces free.

	Monday	Tuesday	Wednesday	Thursday	Friday
Afternoon					
Evening					

Group work

B Talk to your partners and arrange a time to see a movie. You might need to change your schedule.

9 *Think About It*

In English-speaking cultures, if someone invites you out but you can't go, you should give a reason why. If you're doing something you *want to* do, you say *I'm...* If it's something you *don't want to* do, you say *I have to...*

• How about in your culture? Do you give reasons? What do you say?

10 Write About It

A Look at the invitation and the replies.

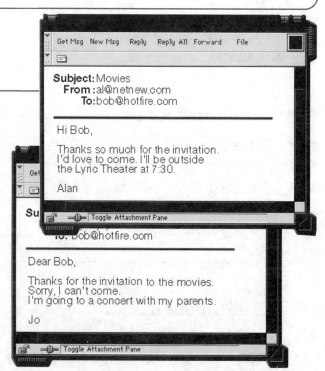

Subject: Movies
From: al@netnew.com
To: bob@hotfire.com

Hi Bob,

Thanks so much for the invitation. I'd love to come. I'll be outside the Lyric Theater at 7:30.

Alan

Subject: Movies
From: bob@hotfire.com
To: jojo@joynet.com
al@netnew.com

Dear Alan and Jo,

Do you want to come to the movies tomorrow night? There's a new science fiction movie showing at the Lyric Theater.

Bob

Su...
...ob@hotfire.com

Dear Bob,

Thanks for the invitation to the movies. Sorry, I can't come. I'm going to a concert with my parents.

Jo

B Now write your own invitation to a movie or a concert on a piece of paper and pass it to several students. They will write a note accepting or rejecting the invitation.

• *Strategy: Inferring vocabulary*

What's the latest thing in movies? It's called digital filmmaking, or desktop filmmaking.

All you need is a digital camcorder, a computer, and some special software. These cost about US$6,000. After you have the equipment, you can make a full-length movie for less than US$1,000.

Think about it. You can tell your own story. Use the camcorder to shoot in your house, in your favorite park, on a bus. When you finish, you can look at your 'takes' immediately on the computer. Edit them any way you like. Keep the best ones, 'cut' the bad ones.

This is the way of the future. Homemade movies are hot right now. Do you want to check it out? Do a web search for 'desktop filmmaking,' or 'digital filmmaking.' You can learn how to do it and where to buy the equipment.

What could be more fun than getting together with a bunch of friends and making your own movie?

Find a word or expression in the text that means the same as

1. a video camera	(1 word)	*camcorder*
2. the things that you need	(1 word)	*equipment*
3. choose the best 'shots' for the movie	(1 word)	*edit*
4. popular	(1 word)	*hot*
5. look at it	(3 words)	*check it out*

Talk About It

○ What's your favorite movie? What do you like about it?

○ Do you like the idea of independent, homemade movies? Why or why not?

○ Where would be a good place to make a video? Why?

11 Read On

Before the Reading

❶ Ask the class these warm-up questions. Alternatively, have students first discuss them in pairs or small groups.

Do you like watching movies? What people/things would you need to make a movie?

❷ Elicit vocabulary from students in answer to the second question and note on the board, e.g. *cameras, actors, director, location, money.* Ask students how much they think it would cost to make a movie.

❸ Refer students to page 94. Have them look at the title of the reading, the headline, and the photos, and ask what they think the passage is about. Write the five definitions on the board, and explain that the students have to read the passage to find words or phrases with the same meaning.

During the Reading

❶ Monitor and offer language support where necessary.

❷ Have students compare their answers with a partner.

After the Reading

❶ Elicit responses from students, and write the correct answers on the board. Ask students to read out the sentence where they found each piece of information.

❷ Go over the meaning of each of the Talk About It questions. Have students work in pairs, asking and answering the questions. Then discuss the questions as a class.

Optional questions:
Some movies can now be viewed on the Internet. Would you watch a movie in this way? Why or why not?

Extension Activity

Have students work in small groups. Tell them they are going to make a homemade movie. Each group has $1,000 (they already have the necessary equipment). They need to decide the type and title of the movie, the location and who would star in it. They should also decide how the money will be spent. (Each group could also create a poster for their movie.) Have each group present its movie ideas to the class. Take a vote of which movie would be the most successful.

Cultural Note

Computer technology is having an enormous impact on the way in which movies are being created and promoted. Many animated movies are now created entirely through computer technology. Whereas big budget pictures from major studios like *Titanic* and *Star Wars* may cost up to US$200 million each, the availability of desktop filmmaking technology now means that anyone can create a movie for a fraction of that cost.

12 Vocabulary Review

Task A

1 Have students unscramble the anagrams.

 ⋯⋯⋯ Write each anagram in circular formation on the board—this often helps students to crack them.

2 Check answers.

Task B

1 Have students express their own opinion.

2 Turn this into a whole class session and encourage discussion.

 ⋯⋯⋯ Have students talk about types of movies they *don't* like and give reasons why. How many students share the same opinion? How many have opposing opinions?

12 Grammar Review

Task A

1 Have students complete both answers.

2 Monitor for correct verb forms, depending on the nature of the excuse.

3 Go through answers. Have students ask and answer the questions.

Task B

1 Have students work on the conversation in pairs.

2 Have them look back through the unit to check their answers.

3 Go through answers. Allow students their own creative freedom with this. The answer on page 95 is a model only. Students' answers do not have to follow this exactly.

4 Have students practice the conversation in pairs.

 ⋯⋯⋯ Have students make their own conversation and practice it in pairs.

Log On

Have students do the online activities for this unit on the *Expressions* website: **http://expressions.heinle.com**

Language Summary

For a more detailed review of the language practiced in this unit, refer students to the **Language Summary on page 141**. Encourage them to add new vocabulary in the **Word Builder** section.

12 Review

1 Vocabulary Review

(A) Unscramble the words to make film types.

1. INOCAT   _action_
2. AMRAD   _drama_
3. RITHRELL   _thriller_
4. MEYDOC   _comedy_
5. RORRHO   _horror_

(B) What are *your* favorite types of movies?

2 Grammar Review

(A) Fill in the blanks with the correct excuses.

1. Do you want to see a movie?   I'm sorry, _I have to do my homework_ (do my homework).

   I'm sorry, _I'm going to a concert_ (go to a concert).

2. Do you want to go out tonight?   I'm sorry, _I'm meeting my friend_ (meet my friend).

   I'm sorry, _I have to wash my car_ (wash my car).

3. How about going out for lunch?   I'm sorry, _I have to finish this report_ (finish this report).

   I'm sorry, _I'm going on a picnic_ (go on a picnic).

(B) Make a conversation using the words shown.

hello/Bob/Susan/want/concert/who/the Boston Pops/sorry/work late tonight

Hello, Bob? This is Susan.

Oh, hi Susan. How are you?

Good thanks. Do you want to go to a concert tonight?

Well, who's playing?

The Boston Pops.

Oh, I'm sorry. I have to work late tonight.

3 Log On

Practice more with the language and topics you studied on the *Expressions* website:

http://expressions.heinle.com

Goals

○ *Talking about the weather*   ○ *Making suggestions*

What's the weather like?

1 Get Ready

A Write the number of the adjectives next to the correct picture.

1.	hot
2.	snowy
3.	cold
4.	sunny
5.	rainy
6.	cloudy
7.	fine

B What are the opposites? Write each one in the correct space.

(cold) (wet) (low) (cool) (rainy) (cloudy)

1. hot _cold_
2. warm _cool_
3. sunny _rainy_
4. fine _cloudy_
5. high _low_
6. dry _wet_

2 Start Talking

A Look at the conversation and listen.

Murray: What's the weather like there?
Sue: It's hot and sunny.
Murray: Oh, really? It's cold and snowy here.

 Pair work **B** Practice the conversation with a partner. Practice again using different adjectives.

96

Unit 12: What's the weather like?

Goals ➤ Talking about the weather   ➤ Making suggestions

Workbook: pages 46–49

❶ Get Ready

Task A
 ······· Ask students about the seasons in their country/ies, and the weather they usually expect in each season. Provide vocabulary as necessary.

❶ Go over the pronunciation and meaning of the vocabulary items.

❷ Have them write the number of the correct weather words in the circles provided.

Task B

❶ Have students work individually to write down the opposites.

❷ Have students compare answers with a partner.

❸ Check answers as a class.

 ······· Brainstorm other weather vocabulary, such as *windy, stormy, cool, warm, breezy*.

❷ Start Talking

Task A

❶ Let students read the conversation.

❷ Play the tape while students listen to the conversation.

 ······· Rewind the tape and have students repeat the conversation after the tape.

> **Tapescript**
>
> **M:** What's the weather like there?
> **W:** It's hot and sunny.
> **M:** Oh, really? It's cold and snowy here.

Task B

❶ Have students practice the conversation.

❷ Have them practice the conversation in pairs, then using different pictures from Get Ready.

 ······· Have them continue practicing with books closed, and describe today's weather in your area.

3 Listen In

Task A

❶ Ask students what information they usually hear on a weather forecast. Provide vocabulary.

❷ Have students decide individually on the vocabulary items they might hear.

❸ Have them check their answers with a partner.

❹ Go over answers with the class.
Note: *Next year* and *last month* are unlikely to be heard in a weather forecast. The other expressions all feature in the listening.

Task B

❶ Play the tape. Have students listen and circle *yes* or *no*.

❷ Go over answers.

Task C

❶ Play the tape. Have students listen and check the words they hear.

support ········ Pause the tape after each weather report, rewind and play again.

❷ Go over answers.

Tapescript

1. M1: ...Good morning from the Channel 3 Weather Center. It's fine and sunny outside right now. However, this afternoon it will be cloudy and a little bit rainy. Temperatures will be...

2. W1: ...This forecast is brought to you by Weatherwall Airconditioning. Later today it will be be hot and sunny, with an estimated high of 98 degrees, so...

3. M2: ...This is Jeff Leech, and it's time for the WBSQ weather update. It's rainy right now, with cloudy skies, so take an umbrella with you if you go out...

4. W2: ...Right now it's fine, but by this evening it'll be turning cloudy. Tomorrow it will be cold and snowy, so make sure that you...

4 Say It Right

Task A

❶ Explain how stress can change the meaning of an utterance by emphasizing the information the speaker considers important.

❷ Play the tape and let students listen to the examples.

support ········ Give other examples yourself before students do the exercise.

Task B

❶ Tell students they are going to hear five excerpts from weather reports.

❷ Ask students to individually check the columns.

❸ Have students compare their answers with a partner.

Task C

❶ Have students listen again and practice.

❷ Monitor as necessary.

(TRY THIS!) See tapescript above for the 5 sentences.

Tapescript

Example 1
W: It'll be fine tomorrow.

Example 2
W: It'll be fine tomorrow.

W: It'll be cold tonight.
W: It should be rainy tomorrow.
W: It'll be hot on the weekend.
W: Tonight'll be rainy.
W: This afternoon it'll be fine.

3 Listen In

A Which words do you think you might hear in a weather forecast? Circle them.

> ~~later~~   next year   ~~this afternoon~~
> last month   ~~tomorrow~~   right now

B Listen to the weather reports. Which ones describe the weather now? Which ones give a forecast? Circle *yes* or *no*.

	1	**2**	**3**	**4**
Now	~~yes~~/no	yes/~~no~~	~~yes~~/no	~~yes~~/no
Forecast	~~yes~~/no	~~yes~~/no	yes/~~no~~	~~yes~~/no

C Listen again. Check (✔) the words you hear in each report.

	1	2	3	4
hot		✔		
cold				✔
rainy	✔		✔	
fine	✔			✔
snowy				✔
sunny	✔	✔		
cloudy	✔		✔	✔

Let's go to the beach on Saturday.

I don't think that's a very good idea.

4 Say It Right

A Listen to the examples. Which is more important—the weather or the time?

B Listen and check (✔) the correct column.

	Weather	Time
Example 1	✔	
Example 2		✔

C Listen again and practice.

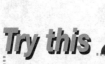 

Listen again. On a separate piece of paper, try writing the sentences.

	Weather	Time
1.	✔	
2.		✔
3.	✔	
4.	✔	
5.		✔

5 Focus In

A Look at the chart.

Let's and going to

What's the weather like?	It's hot and sunny.
What's the weather **going to** be like?	It's **going to** be cloudy.
What are you **going to** do on the weekend?	I'm not sure—maybe I'll play tennis.
Let's go on a picnic.	That sounds like a good idea.
Let's go to a ball game.	No, I don't think it's a good idea.

B Fill in the blanks to make conversations.

A: __Let__'s go to the beach tomorrow.
B: What's the weather _going_ to be like?
A: It's going _to be_ fine.
B: That _sounds like_ a good idea.

A: What _are_ you _going to_ do this weekend?
B: I'm not sure—maybe I'll _go_ shopping.
A: _That_ sounds like a good idea.
   Can I come with you?
B: Sure. _Let's_ go together.

C Write the number of the sentence next to the best response.

1. Let's go hiking this summer.
2. What's the weather like there?
3. Let's go to a ball game tonight.
4. What are you going to do tomorrow?
5. What's the weather going to be like?

__2__ It's cold and wet.
__3__ Sorry, I can't. I have to study this evening.
__5__ It's going to be sunny, I think.
__1__ That sounds like a good idea. I like mountains.
__4__ I'm not sure—maybe I'll stay home.

6 Talk Some More

A Write the words in the correct spaces.

(*tomorrow*) (*OK*) (*what's*) (*hot and sunny*)

Julia: Let's go on a picnic _tomorrow_.
Jeff: _What's_ the weather going to be like?
Julia: It's going to be _hot and sunny_.
Jeff: _OK_. That sounds like a good idea.

B Check your answers.

C Practice the conversation with a partner.
Then practice again using your own information.

5 Focus In

Task A

❶ Go through the chart with students.

❷ Elicit the meaning of *Let's*.

 ········ Present more examples as necessary, for students to grasp the rule.

Task B

❶ Have students fill in the blanks.

❷ Have them check with a partner.

❸ Have them practice the conversations.

Task C

❶ Have students complete the exercise.

❷ Have them check their answers with a partner.

❸ Go over answers with the class. Have students practice the sentences and responses in pairs.

6 Talk Some More

Task A

❶ Have students use the words to complete the conversation.

❷ Offer help as necessary.

Task B

❶ Play the tape.

❷ Have students check their answers.

Task C

❶ Have students practice the conversation.

❷ Have them practice again, using different outdoor activities and weather adjectives.

> **Tapescript**
>
> **W:** Let's go on a picnic tomorrow.
> **M:** What's the weather going to be like?
> **W:** It's going to be hot and sunny.
> **M:** OK. That sounds like a good idea.

7 Work In Pairs

See pages xii-xiii for suggestions on pair work.

Task A

❶ Divide students into pairs. Refer Student B to page 100.

❷ Have them look at the sentences.

❸ Have them say the sentences to each other, responding appropriately with *That sounds like a good idea,* or *I don't think it's a good idea.*

support ········▸ Write similar suggestions on the board, and have the class practice the appropriate response.

Sample

> **A:** It's going to be rainy tomorrow. Let's go on a picnic.
> **B:** No, I don't think it's a good idea. It's going to be cloudy tomorrow. Let's sunbathe.
> **A:** No, that's not a good idea. It's going to be rainy tomorrow. Let's stay in.
> **B:** Yes, that sounds like a good idea. It's going to be….

Task B

❶ Explain that Student A has a list of activities, Student B the weather forecast.

❷ Have them do the exercise, with Student B making the appropriate response to each suggestion.

❸ Monitor as necessary.

 Laredo: lɑreɪdou

Sample

> **A:** Let's go to a ball game on Thursday. The Sluggers are playing against the Swingers at the Laredo open-air stadium at seven o'clock.
> **B:** No, I don't think that's a good idea. It's going to be cloudy in the afternoon and then it's going to be rainy.
> **A:** OK. Then how about an outdoor concert on Friday? There's a Whispering Children concert at eight o'clock.
> **B:** That's a good idea. The weather's going to be fine then. How about Saturday?
> **A:** Let's go see a movie. Ships on the Horizon opens on Saturday evening at the Bel-Air Cinema.
> **B:** OK. It's not going to be rainy then, so let's go.
> **A:** And on Sunday, there's a rose exhibit at the Cultural Center Park. It's from ten o'clock in the morning to eight o'clock in the evening.
> **B:** Mm. It's going to be rainy and then cloudy in the morning. Let's go in the afternoon.

Task C

❶ Have students decide which activities they are going to do together.

❷ Go over their answers.

TRY THIS! You might want to have students brainstorm a list of outdoor and indoor activities before continuing with this exercise.

Work In Pairs   Student A

A Read the statements to your partner. Your partner will tell you if it's a good idea or not.

• *It's going to be rainy tomorrow. Let's go on a picnic.*
• *It's going to be rainy tomorrow. Let's stay in.*
• *It's going to be sunny tomorrow. Let's go to the park.*

B Suggest the following activities to your partner. Your partner will comment.

Thursday	Friday	Saturday	Sunday
Baseball: Sluggers play against the Swingers at the Laredo open-air stadium. 7:00 pm	**Outdoor Concert:** Whispering Children on tour. At the music hall. 8:00 pm	**Movies:** *Ships on the Horizon* opens at the Bel-Air Cinema. 7:15 & 9:15 pm	**Garden Shows:** Rose exhibit at the Cultural Center Park. One day only. 10:00 am– 8:00 pm

C Which activities are you going to do together?

Let's go on a picnic tomorrow.

Well...

What's the weather going to be like?

Try this

Think of two outdoor and two indoor activities. Suggest them to a partner. Write a conversation and practice it with your partner.

_____

_____

_____

_____

Work In Pairs (Student B)

Student A: Use page 99

A Read the statements to your partner. Your partner will tell you if it's a good idea or not.

- *It's going to be cloudy tomorrow. Let's sunbathe.*
- *It's going to be snowy tomorrow. Let's go to the beach.*
- *It's going to be snowy tomorrow. Let's make a snowman.*

B Listen to your partner's suggestions. Look at the weather forecast and give answers.

Thursday	Friday	Saturday	Sunday
AM	AM	AM	AM
PM	PM	PM	PM

C Which activities are you going to do together?

Let's go on a picnic tomorrow.

Well...

What's the weather going to be like?

Try this

Think of two outdoor and two indoor activities. Suggest them to a partner. Write a conversation and practice it with your partner.

_____

_____

_____

_____

100   Unit 12

Unit 12: What's the weather like?

7 Work In Pairs

See p. T99 for suggested instructions for this task.

Mid-Unit Assessment

Once your students have finished Work In Pairs, they will have covered approximately half of this unit. How well are they accomplishing the unit goals at this stage? You may wish to assess their ability on the points below before beginning the fluency task Express Yourself. Check (✔) the appropriate space in the chart for each goal.

Can your students...	Yes, all can.	Yes, most can.	Maybe half can.	Only some can.
1 ask about the weather? *e.g. What's the weather like?*	_____	_____	_____	_____
2 describe weather and weather predictions? *e.g. It's hot and sunny. It's going to be rainy.*	_____	_____	_____	_____
3 make suggestions? *e.g. Let's go on a picnic.*	_____	_____	_____	_____
4 use adjectives to describe the weather? *(see Get Ready for list)*	_____	_____	_____	_____
5 listen for and use stress for information cues? *(see Say It Right for examples)*	_____	_____	_____	_____
6 use *let's* and *going to* correctly?	_____	_____	_____	_____

If your students can already accomplish these fairly well, they're better prepared to expand their use of the target language in the tasks that follow. For those who are still having problems with particular items above, you may wish to direct them to the relevant areas of the unit on pages 96–100, to workbook pages 46–47, or to the online quiz on the *Expressions* website.

8 Express Yourself

Task A

 support ········ Brainstorm capital cities as a class, if necessary.

❶ Have students choose a capital city, but keep the information to themselves.

❷ Have them write weather forecasts for that city in the spaces provided.

❸ Monitor and assist as necessary.

Task B

❶ Have students form groups.

❷ Have them read out their weather forecasts to their group members.

❸ Have other students guess which city it might be. They could make their suggestions after each reading, or jot their ideas on a piece of paper. Share ideas at the end.

challenge ········ Set up a points system to make the guessing more of a competition: 2 points for a correct city, 1 point for a good guess, etc.

9 Think About It

❶ Have the students read the information and consider the answers to the questions. Discuss the questions as a class.

❷ Ask what other topics of conversation serve as small talk in their cultures.

10 Write About It

Task A

❶ Have students read the weather forecasts.

❷ Offer language support as necessary.

Task B

❶ Have students write their own forecasts.

❷ Monitor and offer language support as necessary.

 challenge ········ Have them write a long range forecast, taking in the next 7 days.

Express Yourself

(A) **Write weather forecasts for a famous capital city. Do not say where it is.**

Tomorrow	Next Month	In Six Months

 Group work

(B) **Take turns reading your forecasts. The group will try to guess which city it is.**

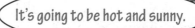

It's going to be hot and sunny.

 Think About It

In many cultures, the weather is a popular topic of conversation.

• How about in your culture? Do people talk about the weather?
• What other topics of small talk are common?

10 Write About It

(A) **Look at the weather forecasts.**

Pleasantville		High 27 Low 16	Blue skies: warm and sunny.
High Plains		High 15 Low 4	Cool to cold with cloudy skies. Rain later.
Winchester		High 23 Low 9	Some morning clouds. Afternoon sunny. Showers again at night.

(B) **On a separate piece of paper, make up a forecast for your city tomorrow.**

• *Strategy: Skimming*

Have you heard of Polar Bear Clubs?
Every January 1, their members celebrate the new year.
How? By going swimming in a freezing-cold river or lake!

This is the story of the Jacksonport Polar Bear Club (JPBC) in the United States.

It started in 1987 with a young boy named J.R. Jarosh. He jumped into Lake Michigan. The air temperature that day was -6°C, but J.R. went swimming anyway. He did the same thing for the next two years. In 1990, two more brave people joined him. Then the following year there were twelve. In 2000, six hundred people jumped into the freezing lake. And once again, J.R. Jarosh was one of them.

On the JPBC website, J.R. offers some important advice for future Polar Bears. He has learned all this from experience. He says they should wear shoes to protect their feet from the ice. They should bring warm boots to put on after swimming. And they should bring a blanket to sit on.

Answer the questions:

1. Who is this passage about? <u>Polar Bear Clubs</u>
2. What do they do every year? <u>They go swimming</u>
3. Where do they do it? <u>In rivers or lakes</u>
4. What day do they do it? <u>January 1</u>
5. What advice do they follow? <u>Wear shoes while swimming/bring warm boots/bring a blanket to sit on</u>

T alk About It ....

○ Why do you think people go swimming in freezing weather?
○ Do you think they are strange? Why or why not?
○ What kind of strange things do people do in your country?

11 Read On

Before the Reading

❶ Ask the class these warm-up questions. Alternatively, have students first discuss them in pairs or small groups.

What's the weather like today? What kind of weather do you like?

❷ Write these words on the board: *polar bear, club, freezing, jump, temperature, brave, experience, protect*. Elicit the meaning from the students, and help with words they don't know. Explain that the words are all from the Read On passage. In groups, have students discuss what they think the passage is about. Have each group give its predictions and note them on the board.

❸ Refer students to page 102. Have them look at the title of the reading, the headline, and the photos. Were their predictions correct? Write the five questions on the board, and explain that the students have to read the passage to find the answers to the questions.

During the Reading

❶ Monitor and offer language support where necessary.

❷ Have students compare their answers with a partner.

🌙 Jarosh: dʒɑrɒʃ

After the Reading

❶ Elicit answers from students, and write them on the board. Ask students to read out the sentence where they found each answer.

❷ Go over the meaning of each of the Talk About It questions. Have students work in pairs, asking and answering the questions. Then discuss the questions as a class.

Optional questions:
Would you join a Polar Bear Club? Why or why not?

Extension Activity

On the board, write a weather forecast for the next four days (or, elicit a weather prediction for each day from the students). In groups, have students decide what they will wear, where they will go, and what they will do on each day. Have each group report their ideas and note them on the board. Ask the class to decide which group has the most interesting plans.

Cultural Note

Since the original 'Polar Bear Club' started in Jacksonport, Wisconsin in 1987, many similar clubs have emerged in other parts of North America and Europe, including Belgium, Canada, Denmark, Sweden, England, Norway, and Poland. Ice festivals are generally popular in many parts of the world. Harbin in China, known as the 'Moscow of the Orient,' is famous for its annual Ice Carving Festival; Sapporo, in Japan, holds a similar ice sculpting festival every winter.

12 Vocabulary Review

Task A

❶ Have students complete the exercise. This could be done as a collaborative exercise if desired.

❷ Have students search back through the unit to check their answers.

Task B

❶ Have students express their own opinion.

❷ Turn this into a whole class session and encourage discussion.

 ⋯⋯⋯ Extend this activity to have students talk about their favourite season/month/festival, weather-related or otherwise.

12 Grammar Review

Task A

❶ Have students complete the exercise.

❷ Have students look back through the unit to check their answers.

Task B

❶ Have students look back to Work In Pairs, Student B.

❷ Have students write the weather forecast.

❸ Go through answers.

 ⋯⋯⋯ Have students write the weather forecast for either: various cities within your country or, various cities in the world. If students are able, have them 'present' their forecasts to the class.

Log On

Have students do the online activities for this unit on the *Expressions* website: **http://expressions.heinle.com**

Language Summary

For a more detailed review of the language practiced in this unit, refer students to the **Language Summary on page 141**. Encourage them to add new vocabulary in the **Word Builder** section.

1 Vocabulary Review

A Fill in the chart with words you learned in this unit.

Good Weather	Bad Weather

B What's your favorite kind of weather? Why?

2 Grammar Review

> What's the weather going to be like tomorrow?

> Maybe it'll be sunny!

A Fill in the blanks.

1. _Let's_ go to the beach.
2. _What's_ the weather going to be like?
3. Oh! _It's_ going to be cloudy and rainy.
4. I don't think _it's_ a good idea.

B Look back to Work In Pairs, Student B.
Write the weather forecast for Thursday and Friday.

On Thursday morning, it's going to be sunny.

On Thursday afternoon, it's going to be cloudy and then rainy.

On Friday morning, it's going to be cloudy.

On Friday afternoon, it's going to be sunny.

3 Log On

Practice more with the language and topics you studied on the *Expressions* website:

http://expressions.heinle.com

What can we get him?

1 Get Ready

A Look at the gifts in the list. Write the number next to the correct picture.

> **1.** a ticket to San Francisco
> **2.** some chocolates
> **3.** a tennis racket
> **4.** flowers
> **5.** a book
> **6.** some music

B What gifts could you buy someone who likes music? Or travel? Make two lists.

Music	Travel

2 Start Talking

A Look at the conversation and listen.

Alex: Max is leaving on Friday. What can we get him?
Gina: I don't know. What does he like?
Alex: Well, he likes music. Let's get him a CD.
Gina: Great idea. I'm sure he'll like that.

Pair work ➤ **B** Practice the conversation with a partner.
Than practice again using different names, likes and gifts.

Unit 13: What can we get him?

Workbook: pages 50–53

1 Get Ready

Task A

 ········· Ask students about gift-giving occasions in their countries: when, and what, they usually give.

❶ Go over the pronunciation and meaning of the suggestions in Get Ready.

❷ Have students individually match the suggestions with the pictures.

❸ Have them compare answers with a partner.

❹ Go over answers.

Task B

❶ Have students write three ideas for each category.

❷ Have students compare answers with a partner.

❸ Share answers as a class.

 ········ Give students other hobby/interest topics and have them think of gift ideas. Write some/all of their ideas on the whiteboard.

2 Start Talking

Task A

❶ Let students read the conversation.

❷ Play the tape while students listen to the conversation.

 ········ Rewind the tape and have students repeat the conversation after the tape.

Tapescript

M: Max is leaving on Friday. What can we get him?
W: I don't know. What does he like?
M: Well, he likes music. Let's get him a CD.
W: Great idea. I'm sure he'll like that.

Task B

❶ Have students practice the conversation.

❷ Have them practice the conversation in pairs, using different people, hobbies and gifts.

 ········ Refer students back to the ideas they thought of in Get Ready Task B, Challenge.

3 Listen In

Task A

1. Play the tape. Have students listen and write each person's likes and interests in the chart.

2. Go over answers.

Task B

1. Play the tape again. Have students listen and write the suggested gifts in the chart.

 support .... Pause the tape after each line of the conversation.

2. Have students check their answers together.

3. Go over answers.

challenge .... Ask students to say why the suggestions for gifts were rejected.

Task C

1. Have students work in pairs to decide who should receive what.

challenge .... Ask students if they can think of any other ideas for gifts.

Tapescript

1. **W1:** Julian is leaving on Friday. We'll have to get him a gift.
   M1: What does he like?
   W1: Well, he likes music.
   M1: OK, let's get him a CD.
   W1: No, he has hundreds of CDs.

2. **W2:** It's Annie's birthday next week. We should get her a gift.
   W3: What does she like?
   W2: She loves flowers.
   W3: So, let's buy her some roses.
   W2: No, I think everyone will get her flowers.

3. **M2:** John's going away on Sunday.
   M3: What can we get him?
   M2: He loves to eat out. How about taking him out to dinner?
   M3: No, he's on a diet.

4. **M4:** Sandy's leaving tomorrow. Let's get her a gift.
   W4: Well, she likes reading.
   M4: Let's buy her a book.
   W4: But we don't know what kind she likes.

4 Say It Right

Task A

1. Explain how reduced *is* and *does* can sound very similar in natural speech.

 support .... Give other examples yourself before students do the exercise.

2. Have students listen and check the questions they hear.

Task B

1. Play the tape.

2. Have students check their answers.

3. Have students compare their answers with a partner.

support .... Pause the tape after each sentence and correct line by line.

Task C

1. Have students practice saying and identifying the questions.

2. Monitor as necessary.

(TRY THIS!) Model saying the questions quickly before having students try.

Tapescript

1. **W:** What's he like?
   M: Kind of short.

2. **W:** What does he like?
   M: Music.

3. **W:** What does she like?
   M: Travel.

4. **W:** What's she like?
   M: Really nice.

5. **W:** What does she like?
   M: Reading.

   W: What's he like?
   W: What does he like?
   W: What does she like?
   W: What's she like?
   W: What does she like?

3 Listen In

(A) Listen and write each person's likes and interests in the chart.

	likes/interests	suggested gift
Julian	music	CD
Annie	flowers	roses
John	eating out	dinner
Sandy	reading	book

(B) Listen again and write the gifts people suggest in the chart above.

(C) Choose the best gift for each person. Write the person's name under the gift.

John

Sandy

Julian

Annie

4 Say It Right

(A) Some questions sound very similar in rapid speech.
Listen and check (✔) the question you hear.

1. __✔__ What's he like?   _____ What does he like?
2. _____ What's he like?   __✔__ What does he like?
3. _____ What's she like?   __✔__ What does she like?
4. __✔__ What's she like?   _____ What does she like?
5. _____ What's she like?   __✔__ What does she like?

Try this

Try saying the questions. Speak as quickly as you can. Your partner will answer. Was the answer correct?

(B) Listen again and check your answers.

(C) Listen again and practice.

5 Focus In

A Look at the chart.

Let's/how about...? and like	
What do you **like**?	I **like** pop music.
What does she **like** doing?	She **likes** playing football.
Let's get her a CD.	Great idea! She'll **like** that.
How about getting her a cookbook?	No, she already has a lot of cookbooks.

B Fill in the blanks to make four conversations.

A: It's Cathy's birthday. What can we get her?
B: ___Let's___ buy her a CD.

A: What do Bob and Gina like?
B: ___They like___ movies.

A: What should we get Geoff for his birthday?
B: ___How about___ getting him a new watch?

A: What does your brother like doing?
B: ___He likes___ playing golf.

C Suggest gifts for these people. Use *Let's* or *How about...?*

1. Ahmed likes reading.   ___Let's get him a book.___
2. Maria likes hiking.   _____
3. Jenny likes music.   _____
4. Steve likes flowers.   _____

6 Talk Some More

A Write the words in the correct spaces.

(likes) (getting) (has)
(like) (get)

Alex: It's Jo's birthday next week. I don't know what to ___get___ her.
Gina: What does she ___like___?
Alex: She ___likes___ cooking
Gina: How about ___getting___ her a cookbook?
Alex: No, she already ___has___ a lot of cookbooks.

B Check your answers.

Spotlight
We can also say *What about...?* instead of *How about...?*

Pair work

C Practice the conversation with a partner.
Then practice again using other people you both know.

5 Focus In

Task A

❶ Go through the chart with students.

❷ Explain that *Let's...* and *How about...?* can both be used to suggest something, but *Let's...* indicates a course of action to be taken by both parties in the conversation.

 .... Present more examples as necessary, for students to grasp the rule.

Task B

❶ Have students fill in the blanks.

❷ Have them check with a partner.

❸ Have them practice asking and answering the questions.

Task C

❶ Have students make suggestions for each person.

❷ Have them check their answers with a partner.

❸ Go over answers with the class. Answers may vary. Check for *-ing* verbs after *How about...?*

 .... Have pairs form sentences about other students in the class.

6 Talk Some More

Task A

❶ Have students fill in the blanks to make a logical conversation.

❷ Offer help as necessary.

Task B

❶ Play the tape.

❷ Have students check their answers.

Task C

❶ Have students practice the conversation.

❷ Have them practice again, using the ideas from Get Ready, Listen In, or their own information.

 .... Encourage students to close their books and continue practicing.

 .... Encourage students to vary their conversations by using different occasions as well as names and gifts.

(SPOTLIGHT) You might want to extend this and give *You/We could...* as a way of making a suggestion.

Tapescript

M: It's Jo's birthday next week. I don't know what to get her.
W: What does she like?
M: She likes cooking.
W: How about getting her a cookbook?
M: No, she already has a lot of cookbooks.

7 Work In Pairs

See pages xii-xiii for suggestions on pair work.

Task A

 ⟩········ In order to fully exploit the language presented in Talk Some More, have students think of three occasions to buy a present for their allotted person, and write them in the space given.

 ⟩········ Prompt students by writing occasions on the board. These might include: *birthday, leaving, Christmas, New Year's Eve/Day, new baby, new house.*

1 Divide students into pairs. Refer Student B to page 108.

2 Explain that Bill likes the things in the picture, but already has the things on the list.

3 Have Student A start the conversation by mentioning the occasion. (See sample dialog below.)

4 Have them listen to suggestions and agree upon a suitable gift.

> **Sample**
>
> **A:** It's Bill's birthday next week. What can we get him?
> **B:** Well, what does he like doing?
> **A:** He likes cooking, watching TV and playing tennis.
> **B:** How about getting him a cookbook?
> **A:** No, he already has a lot of cookbooks.
> **B:** Then let's get him a cooking video.
> **A:** That's a good idea.
> **B:** Or, we could get him some tennis balls.
> **A:** No, he already has...

Task B

1 Have students follow the same pattern for Connie.

2 This time have Student A make gift suggestions. If suggestions are refused, have them make further suggestions.

3 When a mutual agreement is reached, have them write the gift in the 'Suggestions' column.

> **Sample**
>
> **B:** It's Connie's leaving party on Monday. What can we get her?
> **A:** I don't know. What does she like?
> **B:** She likes working out, playing the piano, and painting.
> **A:** Let's get her a workout video.
> **B:** That's a good idea.
> **A:** Or, we could get her some CDs of piano music.
> **B:** No, she already has a lot of classical CDs.
> **A:** Then how about...?

Task C

1 Have each pair decide on the best present for Bill and Connie.

2 Go over ideas as a class, asking for reasons for each decision.

TRY THIS! This could be continued as a pairwork activity.

Work In Pairs
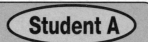

Student B: Use page 108

A Look at the information below. Describe what Bill likes to your partner. Your partner will suggest gifts for Bill. Decide which suggestions are good.

Bill likes...

He already has a lot of...
cookbooks
tennis balls
videos

B Listen to your partner and note down the things Connie likes. Suggest some gifts for Connie. Make a list of suggested gifts in the chart.

Connie likes...	Suggestions
exercising/working out	
playing piano	
painting	

C Decide with your partner which gifts you should get for Bill and Connie.

Try this
Which of the suggested gifts above would *you* like to receive? Why?

_____

_____

7 Work In Pairs   Student B

A Listen to your partner and note down the things Bill likes.
Suggest some gifts for Bill. Make a list of suggested gifts in the chart.

Bill likes...	Suggestions
watching TV/videos	
cooking	
playing tennis	

B Look at the information below. Describe what Connie likes to your partner.
Your partner will suggest gifts for Connie. Decide which suggestions are good.

Connie likes...

She already has a lot of...
workout clothes
art books
classical music CDs

C Decide with your partner which gifts you should get for Bill and Connie.

Try this

Which of the suggested gifts above would *you* like to receive? Why?

Unit 13: What can we get him?

7 Work In Pairs

See p. T107 for suggested instructions for this task.

Mid-Unit Assessment

Once your students have finished Work In Pairs, they will have covered approximately half of this unit. How well are they accomplishing the unit goals at this stage? You may wish to assess their ability on the points below before beginning the fluency task Express Yourself. Check (✔) the appropriate space in the chart for each goal.

Can your students...	Yes, all can.	Yes, most can.	Maybe half can.	Only some can.
❶ talk about what people like? *e.g. What does he like? He likes music. She likes cooking.*	_____	_____	_____	_____
❷ talk about gift giving? *e.g. Let's get him a CD. He'll like that. He already has a lot of CDs.*	_____	_____	_____	_____
❸ say the names of various gifts? *(see Get Ready for list)*	_____	_____	_____	_____
❹ recognize, pronounce and differentiate between the reduced form of *What does* and *What is?* *(see Say It Right for examples)*	_____	_____	_____	_____
❺ use *how about* and *let's* correctly?	_____	_____	_____	_____
❻ use *like* and *likes* correctly?	_____	_____	_____	_____

If your students can already accomplish these fairly well, they're better prepared to expand their use of the target language in the tasks that follow. For those who are still having problems with particular items above, you may wish to direct them to the relevant areas of the unit on pages 104–108, to workbook pages 50–51, or to the online quiz on the *Expressions* website.

Unit 13: What can we get him?

8 Express Yourself

Task A
1. Have students fill in the chart with real, or imaginary, hobbies.
2. Monitor as necessary and provide vocabulary, if required.

Task B
1. Tell students to form groups.
2. Have them work together to find suitable gifts for each person.
3. Monitor as necessary during the activity and provide vocabulary, if required.
4. Go over ideas with the class, asking each group about gifts they chose and reasons for choosing those gifts.

9 Think About It

1. Have the students read the information and consider the answers to the questions. Discuss the questions as a class.
2. Find out about gift-giving occasions in the students' culture(s), and conventions surrounding the giving and receiving of gifts.

10 Write About It

Task A
1. Have students read the thank you note.
2. Offer language support as necessary.

Task B
1. Have students think of a gift they were given. (This could be imaginary.)
2. Have them write a thank you note.
3. Monitor and provide language support as necessary.

 ········ Have students write a further note, thanking their classmates for the gift they received in Express Yourself.

8 Express Yourself

A Write three hobbies or activities that you like.

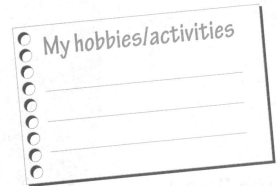

My hobbies/activities

What do you like doing?

Group work

B Ask each person in your group what they like to do.
Decide the best gift for each person.

9 Think About It

Oh, how sweet of you!

Oh, you shouldn't have.

Each culture has its own traditions about when you should give gifts, what you should give, and what to do and say when you get a gift.

• What are the traditions in your culture?

10 Write About It

A Look at the thank you note.

B Think of a gift you received in the past.
Now write a note thanking the person for the gift.

Thank You!

Dear David,
Thank you so much for the electronic currency calculator. It's just what I wanted! I'm sure it will be very useful on my trip to Singapore.
Chris

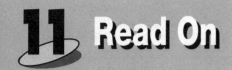

• *Strategy: Reading actively*

Read these statements. Then read the article to decide if the statements are *True* or *False*.

	True	False
• The Chinese never give knives.	✓	
• Chinese clocks are dangerous.		✓
• Two is good in Hong Kong but bad in Russia.	✓	
• Red roses mean romance in Germany.	✓	
• Two is bad in Russia and Germany.	✓	

Gift-giving Rules Around the World

Hong-Shin Wei, Hong Kong

You must never give a clock to a Chinese person, because the sound of the word for 'clock' is similar to the word for 'death' in Chinese. Also, don't wrap a gift in white, black, or blue paper, because these are the colors for funerals. Don't give a knife, because something sharp can cut a relationship.

Eugen Karpenko, Russia

If we give flowers as a gift, we have to give an odd number of them (one, three, five, etc.) because even numbers of flowers (two, four, six, etc.) are for funerals. If we give a gift of alcohol and the host opens it, we should empty it together. And we should always toast the bottle before we take a drink.

Rosie Kuhlmann, Germany

Flowers are a good gift to take to your dinner hostess, but don't take her red roses because it means you are in love with her. Don't take thirteen of anything because it's an unlucky number. Don't take an even number of anything, either. Don't wrap your gift in white, brown, or black paper.

Talk About It

○ Which of these gift-giving customs are the same in your culture?
○ Which times of the year do you give gifts?
○ Do you give special types of gifts at weddings? What?

11 Read On

Before the Reading

1 Ask the class these warm-up questions. Alternatively, have students first discuss them in pairs or small groups.

When do you receive gifts? What do you like to receive? What don't you like to receive?

2 List the students' suggestions on the board under two columns: *like* and *don't like*. Find out what is the most popular gift to receive in your class.

 ------- Ask students to give reasons why they like or don't like certain types of gift.

3 Refer students to page 110. Ask which three countries the passage refers to. Write the five statements on the board, and explain that students have to read the passage to decide whether each is true or false.

During the Reading

1 Monitor and offer language support where necessary.

2 Have students compare their answers with a partner.

🔊 Hong Shin Wei: hɔŋ ʃɪn weɪ, Eugen Karpenko: judʒɛn karpɛnkou, Rosie Kuhlman: rouzi kulmʌn

After the Reading

1 Elicit responses from students, and write the answers on the board. Ask students to read out the sentences that helped them decide.

2 Go over the meaning of each of the Talk About It questions. Have students work in pairs, asking and answering the questions. Then discuss the questions as a class.

Optional questions:
What's the most expensive gift you've given someone? What did the person say?

Extension Activity

Elicit types of gifts and list them on the board. Then, ask students to suggest different people they might give gifts to (e.g. *mother, father, grandmother, grandfather, girlfriend, boyfriend, husband, wife, colleague, classmate, teacher*), and list them on the board. In groups, have students decide which of the gifts they would give to each of the people listed. Call on students for their choices and note them on the board. Do the groups agree or disagree?

 ------- Ask students to give reasons for their choices.

Cultural Note

In the U.S., many couples planning to marry often register their names with a bridal registry in a particular department store. Here, an employee of the store helps the couple make a list of particular items that they would like to receive as wedding gifts, especially large items like dinnerware or cutlery. People who are invited to the wedding can visit the store and choose individual items they would like to buy for the couple from this list. This helps ensure that the couple receive the items they need or desire, and can make the shopping process much easier for the buyer.

12 Vocabulary Review

Task A

❶ Have students work individually, in pairs, or groups to think of gifts for each list.

❷ Have students look back through the unit to check their answers. Draw students' attention to correct spellings.

Task B

❶ Have students express their own opinion.

❷ Turn this into a whole class session and encourage discussion.

 ⟩········ Have students give reasons why. Then have students talk about the worst gift they ever received.

12 Grammar Review

Task A

❶ Have students complete all answers for each statement.

❷ Monitor for use of correct verb forms.

❸ Go through answers.

Task B

❶ Have students make suggestions for each person.

❷ Go through students' ideas as a class.

 ⟩········ Have students read out their suggestions. Counter with *S/he already has lots of...* and ask them to make a further suggestion.

Log On

Have students do the online activities for this unit on the *Expressions* website: **http://expressions.heinle.com**

Language Summary

For a more detailed review of the language practiced in this unit, refer students to the **Language Summary on page 142**. Encourage them to add new vocabulary in the **Word Builder** section.

12 Review

1 Vocabulary Review

A Fill in the chart with as many gifts as you can think of for people who like sports, music and travel.

Sports	Music	Travel

B What's the best gift you ever received?

How about getting him some shoes?

2 Grammar Review

A Fill in the blanks with the correct form of the verb.

It's Jo's birthday next week.

How about (*get*) ___getting___ her some flowers?
What about (*buy*) ___buying___ her a CD?
Let's (*give*) ___give___ her a gift certificate.

Sophia's leaving on Friday.

How about (*buy*) ___buying___ her a backpack?
Let's (*get*) ___get___ her a computer game.
What about (*give*) ___giving___ her a watch?

B Suggest gifts for these people.

1. Bill likes soccer. _____
2. Marie likes pop music. _____
3. Aya likes traveling. _____
4. Stephan likes studying. _____

3 Log On

Practice more with the language and topics you studied on the *Expressions* website:

http://expressions.heinle.com

We should go to the beach.

1 Get Ready

Buenos dias.

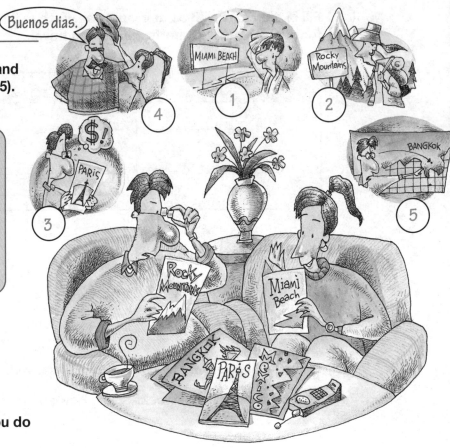

A Look at the sentences and number the pictures (1–5).

1. It's too hot.
2. I don't like hiking.
3. It's too expensive.
4. We don't speak Spanish.
5. It's too far.

B What activities could you do in these places?

Bangkok _____   Miami _____

Paris _____   Mexico City _____

2 Start Talking

A Look at the conversation and listen.

Dennis: Where should we go on vacation?
Renee: I think we should go to the beach.
Dennis: No, it's too hot. I think we should go hiking.
Renee: But I don't like hiking.

Pair work

B Practice the conversation with a partner.
Practice again using the other places in Get Ready.

112

Goals ➤ **Making suggestions** ➤ **Voicing objections**

Workbook: pages 54–57

1 Get Ready

Task A

 ········ Put these activities on the board: *going to the beach, going skiing, going hiking, going sightseeing, going abroad, staying home.* Ask students to put them in order of vacation preference. Use the results to stimulate discussion about vacations and generate vocabulary.

❶ Have students individually number the pictures using the objections in Get Ready.

❷ Have them compare answers with a partner.

❸ Go over answers.

Task B

❶ Have students write activities next to each city.

❷ Have students compare answers with a partner.

❸ Check answers as a class.

 ········ Have students brainstorm other cities/places and activities they could do there.

2 Start Talking

Task A

❶ Let students read the conversation.

❷ Play the tape while students listen to the conversation.

 ········ Rewind the tape and have students repeat the conversation after the tape.

Tapescript

M: Where should we go on vacation?
W: I think we should go to the beach.
M: No, it's too hot. I think we should go hiking.
W: But I don't like hiking.

Task B

❶ Have students practice the conversation.

❷ Have them practice the conversation in pairs, using different places and activities.

 ········ Have them continue with their books closed, using different ideas from Get Ready.

3 Listen In

Task A

❶ Direct students' attention to the 'Things To Do' column of the listening exercise.

❷ Have them note where they would choose to do these activities.

❸ Have them compare their ideas with a partner.

challenge ········ Turn this into a whole class discussion with students justifying their choices.

Task B

❶ Play the tape. Have students listen and fill in the four places mentioned in the chart.

❷ Go over answers.

Task C

❶ Play the tape. Have students listen and match the locations with the activities and objections.

support ········ Pause the tape after each line of the conversation.

❷ Go over answers.

(TRY THIS!) Play the tape again, as necessary. The word the man uses is *Well*.

Tapescript

W: Where should we go on vacation?
M: Well, I think we should go to Mexico City.
W: What can we do in Mexico City?
M: Plenty. They have great museums, good food, and wonderful nightclubs.
W: But we don't speak Spanish.
M: Well, then, let's go to Bangkok.
W: Bangkok? What can we do in Bangkok?
M: Oh, visit temples and markets.
W: Oh, no. It's too far.
M: Well, how about Paris? They have fantastic art galleries, and the shopping is wonderful.
W: Yeah, but it's too expensive.
M: Oh, well, then, how about staying close to home? We could go to the Rocky Mountains.
W: And?
M: Go hiking.
W: Hiking? I HATE hiking.
M: Well, let's stay home. At least it'll be cheap.

4 Say It Right

Task A

❶ Explain how *can* and *can't* often sound very similar in natural speech.

support ········ Give other examples yourself before students do the exercise.

❷ Have students listen and circle the words they hear.

Task B

❶ Play the tape.

❷ Have students check their answers.

support ········ Pause the tape after each sentence.

❸ Have students compare their answers with a partner.

Task C

❶ Have students practice saying other positive and negative abilities.

❷ Monitor as necessary.

(TRY THIS!) Encourage students to say their sentences to their partners as quickly as possible. Partners should try to identify which they heard, *can* or *can't*.

Tapescript

i.   **M:** I can't swim.
     M: I can go in July.
     M: We can't afford it.
     M: They can't speak Spanish.
     M: She can meet us at Christmas.

ii. **1. W:** We should go to the beach.
        M: But you know I can't swim.

     2. W: We should take our vacation in summer.
        M: OK. I can go in July.

     3. W: We should go to Bangkok.
        M: Oh, we can't afford it.

     4. W: They should go to Colombia.
        M: No, they can't speak Spanish.

     5. W: Your sister could join us in Miami.
        M: Good idea. She can meet us at Christmas.

iii. **M:** I can't swim.
     M: I can go in July.
     M: We can't afford it.
     M: They can't speak Spanish.
     M: She can meet us at Christmas.

3  Listen In

(A) Look at the *Things To Do* in the chart. Where would you go for these things? Check your ideas with your partner.

(B) Listen and write the names of the places Rick suggests.

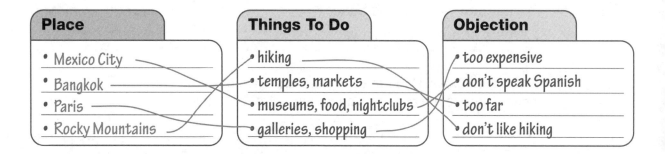

Place	Things To Do	Objection
• Mexico City	• hiking	• too expensive
• Bangkok	• temples, markets	• don't speak Spanish
• Paris	• museums, food, nightclubs	• too far
• Rocky Mountains	• galleries, shopping	• don't like hiking

(C) Listen again and match the places, things to do and objections.

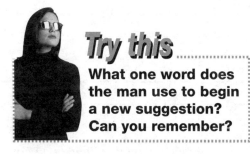

Try this

What one word does the man use to begin a new suggestion? Can you remember?

Where should we go tomorrow?

I think we should go shopping.

4 Say It Right

(A) The words *can* and *can't* often sound very similar. But their meanings are exactly opposite! Listen and circle the words you hear.

1. I **can** / **can't** swim.
2. I **can** / **can't** go in July.
3. We **can** / **can't** afford it.
4. They **can** / **can't** speak Spanish.
5. She **can** / **can't** meet us at Christmas.

(B) Listen again and check your answers.

(C) Listen again and practice.

Try this

Write down five things you can or can't do. Tell your partner.

5 Focus In

A Look at the chart.

Can and **should**	
Can you swim?	Yes, I **can**./No, I **can't**.
Can Maria speak English?	Yes, she **can**./No, she **can't**.
What **can** we do at the beach?	We **can** go swimming.
Where **should** we go on vacation?	We **should** go to the beach.

B Fill in the blanks. Use the words *should*, *can*, or *can't*.
Then practice the conversations with another student.

A: We ____should____ go to the beach.   A: Where ____should____ we go on vacation?
B: But I ____can't____ swim.   B: Maybe we ____can____ go hiking.

     A: That's a good idea.

C Can you ____? Fill in the blanks with *yes* or *no*. Then make complete sentences.

1. __No__ lift 1000 kg.   I can't lift 1000 kg._____
2. _____ tap dance   _____
3. _____ speak Turkish   _____
4. _____ play the guitar   _____
5. _____ cook   _____
6. _____ paint pictures   _____

6 Talk Some More

A Number the sentences to make a conversation (1–5).

Jim: __2__ I think we should go to the beach.
Jim: __4__ We can go swimming.
Julie: __3__ What can we do there?
Julie: __5__ But I don't like swimming.
Julie: __1__ Where should we go on vacation?

B Check your answers.

Spotlight
Instead of *I think we should*, we can also say *Why don't we...?*

C Practice the conversation with a partner.
Practice again suggesting different places to go.

5 Focus In

Task A

❶ Go through the chart with students.

❷ Point out the use of *can* for ability and *should* as a suggestion (perhaps contrast with/review the suggestion language of the previous unit).

 ········ Present more examples as necessary, for students to grasp the rule.

Task B

❶ Have students fill in the blanks.

❷ Have them check with a partner.

❸ Have them practice the dialogs in pairs.

Task C

❶ Have students fill in the blanks on the left. Offer language support as necessary.

❷ Have them write complete sentences on the right.

❸ Have them check their answers with a partner.

❹ Go over answers with the class.

 ········ Have students write three things they can do on a piece of paper. At least one statement must be false. Students should read their statements to the class. Their classmates should say which are true and which are false.

6 Talk Some More

Task A

❶ Have students number the sentences to make a logical conversation.

❷ Offer help as necessary.

Task B

❶ Play the tape.

❷ Have students check their answers.

Task C

❶ Have students practice the conversation.

❷ Have them practice again, using different places and objections.

 ········ Encourage students to close their books and continue practicing.

(SPOTLIGHT) This further extends language for suggestions from the previous unit. Draw students' attention to it and have them use it when practicing the dialog.

> ### Tapescript
>
> **W:** Where should we go on vacation?
> **M:** I think we should go to the beach.
> **W:** What can we do there?
> **M:** We can go swimming.
> **W:** But I don't like swimming.

7 Work In Pairs

See pages xii-xiii for suggestions on pair work.

Task A

❶ Divide students into pairs. Refer Student B to page 116.

❷ In order to prepare students for what they are likely to hear, have them write down three things they think they might do in Italy, and three things they might do in Singapore.

❸ Monitor and assist as necessary.

Task B

❶ Have students look at the places in the brochure.

❷ Have them suggest a vacation in Singapore to their partner, answering their partner's questions about things that can be done there.

> **Sample**
>
> **B:** Where should we go on vacation?
> **A:** Maybe Singapore would be nice.
> **B:** What can we do there?
> **A:** We can go shopping on Orchard Road. It's a shopper's paradise.
> **B:** Great. What else can we do?
> **A:** Well, we can go to the Night Safari.
> **B:** OK. That sounds interesting. What else?

Task C

❶ Change roles and have Student B tell their partner what they can do in Italy.

❷ Have Student A respond to suggestions by saying which activities they do and don't like.

❸ Have students work together to decide where they are going to go, and what they are going to do there.

❹ Share students' vacation decisions as a class.

 challenge ┈┈┈┈ Have students give reasons for their decision.

> **Sample**
>
> **A:** Where should we go on vacation?
> **B:** Maybe Italy would be nice.
> **A:** What can we do there?
> **B:** Well, we can see great works of art.
> **A:** No, that sounds boring.
> **B:** We can go shopping in the design houses.
> **A:** Yes, that sounds good.
> **B:** And we can…

(TRY THIS!) Ask students to write two sentences about the vacation plans they have just finalized.

Work In Pairs — Student A

A What things do you think you could do in Italy? Make a list.

Where should we go on our vacation?

Maybe Italy would be nice.

B Look at the brochure. When your partner asks you, suggest a vacation in Singapore. Tell your partner about the things you can do there.

Singapore

Visit the Night Safari for a close-up view of the animal kingdom.

Enjoy exotic flavors from a variety of cultures.

Botanical gardens delight visitors all year long.

Orchard Road— a shopper's paradise known around the world.

C Your partner has some information about Italy.
Ask what you can do there. Say which suggestions you like and which you don't.

Decide together which place is best for you.

Try this

Write two sentences about the country you are both going to visit and what you are going to do there.

We are going to visit...

_____

We should go to the beach.

Work In Pairs (Student B)

A What things do you think you could do in Singapore? Make a list.

Where should we go on our vacation?

Maybe Singapore would be nice.

B Your partner has some information about Singapore.
Ask what you can do there. Say which suggestions you like and which you don't.

Works of the great masters delight art lovers.

Italy's historical sites attract millions each year.

Italy

Italy's design houses tempt fashion lovers.

Discover a rich variety of cuisine.

C Look at the brochure above. When your partner asks you, suggest a vacation in Italy. Tell your partner about the things you can do there.

Decide together which place is best for you.

Try this

Write two sentences about the country you are both going to visit and what you are going to do there.

We are going to visit...

7 Work In Pairs

See p. T115 for suggested instructions for this task.

Mid-Unit Assessment

Once your students have finished Work In Pairs, they will have covered approximately half of this unit. How well are they accomplishing the unit goals at this stage? You may wish to assess their ability on the points below before beginning the fluency task Express Yourself. Check (✔) the appropriate space in the chart for each goal.

Can your students…	Yes, all can.	Yes, most can.	Maybe half can.	Only some can.
1 make suggestions? *e.g. I think we should go to the beach.*	_____	_____	_____	_____
2 voice objections? *e.g. It's too hot. I don't like hiking.*	_____	_____	_____	_____
3 say the names of various holiday destinations and activities? *(see Get Ready and Listen In for lists)*	_____	_____	_____	_____
4 recognize and pronounce the difference between *can* and *can't*? *(see Say It Right for examples)*	_____	_____	_____	_____
5 use *can* and *should* correctly?	_____	_____	_____	_____

If your students can already accomplish these fairly well, they're better prepared to expand their use of the target language in the tasks that follow. For those who are still having problems with particular items above, you may wish to direct them to the relevant areas of the unit on pages 112–116, to workbook pages 54–55, or to the online quiz on the *Expressions* website.

Unit 14: We should go to the beach.

8 Express Yourself

Task A

1 Tell students to form groups.

2 Have them work together to choose a vacation spot and brainstorm things to do there.

3 Monitor as necessary during the activity.

Task B

1 You might want to have students stand and mingle for this part of the activity.

2 Have them meet other group members and 'sell' their vacation spots by recommending everything that can be done there.

3 Turn this into a whole class activity. Poll students to find out which place was the most popular.

9 Think About It

1 Have the students read the information and consider the answers to the questions. Discuss the questions as a class.

2 Find out about vacations in the students' culture(s), and conventions surrounding taking time off work.

10 Write About It

Task A

1 Have students read the tour brochure.

2 Offer language support as necessary.

 Ask students if they would like to visit London, and have them give reasons why or why not. Have students talk about what they would do there.

Task B

1 Have students think of activities that can be done in their city/home area.

2 Have them write a tour brochure.

3 Monitor and provide language support as necessary.

 Have students 'present' their tour brochures to the class. If you divided students into groups or pairs for this activity, have the other students vote for which tour they would go on, and see whose is the most popular.

8 Express Yourself

(A) Choose a vacation spot anywhere in the world. Brainstorm a list of things to do there.

Destination: _____

Group work →

Activities

_____
_____
_____
_____

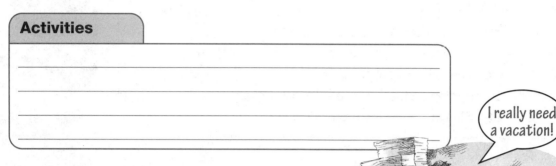

I really need a vacation!

(B) Talk to students from other groups. Who would like to come to your vacation spot?

9 *Think About It*

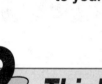

Different cultures have different ideas about how much time we should spend on vacation.

- How about in your country? What is the usual length of time?
- What are the most popular vacation spots?

10 Write About It

(A) Look at the tour brochure for London.

London

London is an exciting city. It has many superb areas for sightseeing.

Cruise down the River Thames to historic Greenwich.

Visit the Houses of Parliament and Westminster Abbey.

Go inside Big Ben, the world's most famous clock tower.

Travel around the city is easy and cheap—on a double decker bus.

London has something to offer visitors of all ages!

(B) On a piece of paper make a tour brochure for your own city or area.

We should go to the beach.

Read On Three All-American Roads

• Strategy: Inferring content

Read the article. Then read the statements and answer *True* or *False*.

	True	False
• There are many hotels on the Natchez Trace Parkway.		✔
• All of these roads have natural beauty.	✔	
• All of the roads have historical places.		✔
• You can go shopping on the Columbia River Highway.		✔
• The San Juan Skyway offers the most activities.	✔	

The United States government has named 20 roads 'All-American Roads.' These roads are especially natural or historical.

The Natchez Trace Parkway

About 200 years ago, today's Parkway was just a trail. People walked or rode horses. They slept on the ground. They carried their food with them. Sometimes robbers stole everything they had. They had to watch out for snakes, insects and wild animals. Today, a lovely road follows the old trail. There are no trucks, no shops or businesses—just forests and fields.

The Columbia River Highway

This little road goes through the mountains above the Columbia River, which is one of the largest rivers in the United States. The road passes many waterfalls. You can park and walk through the forest to the falls. There are lots of wildflowers in the spring. It's a wonderful place for a picnic. Don't forget your camera!

The San Juan Skyway

This road feels like the roof of the world. You drive very high, through the beautiful Rocky Mountains. You pass through little historic towns. The views of the mountaintops and the long valleys are amazing. You can see very old ruins of American Indian civilizations. You can stop to hike, camp, bicycle, fish, shop. Come in the autumn and see the golden leaves.

Talk About It

🔘 Which road do you think you would enjoy the most? Why?

🔘 Have you ever taken a trip on an interesting road? Talk about it.

🔘 What's your idea of a perfect vacation?

11 Read On

Before the Reading

❶ Ask the class these warm-up questions. Alternatively, have students first discuss them in pairs or small groups.

Can you drive? Do you like driving? Where do you like to drive?

❷ Tell the class to imagine they are driving in the countryside. Ask them what kinds of things they might see from the road. Write the words you elicit on the board. Include the following: *wild animals, snakes, forests, fields, rivers, waterfalls, wildflowers, views, valleys, leaves, towns,* and go over the meaning of each.

❸ Refer students to page 118. Write the five statements on the board, and explain that the students have to read the passage to decide whether each is true or false.

During the Reading

❶ Monitor and offer language support where necessary.

❷ Have students compare their answers with a partner.

🕪 San Juan: sɑn huɑn, Natchez Trace: nǣtʃɛz treɪs

After the Reading

❶ Elicit responses from students, and check the correct answers on the board. Ask students to read out the sentence that helped them decide each one.

❷ Go over the meaning of each of the Talk About It questions. Have students work in pairs, asking and answering the questions. Then discuss the questions as a class.

Optional questions:
What are some driving habits in your country? What rules do you have to follow?

Extension Activity

Tell the class that a visitor is coming to your town or city; he/she wants to see as much of the area as possible in the next five days. In groups, students should decide: 1) where they will take the visitor; 2) how long they will spend in each place; and 3) which route they will take to get there. Have groups present their plan to the class. (They could also draw a map of the route they will take.)

Cultural Note

In the U.S., hitchhiking was once practiced by many as a cheap way to get around the country. Nowadays, hitchhiking is illegal in many states. In these places, hitchhikers can risk getting fined if they're caught by a police patrol. In many other parts of the world, hitchhiking is still a fairly common practice. In places like Europe, however, it is starting to become less common, mainly due to concerns about safety.

Unit 14: We should go to the beach.

12 Vocabulary Review

Task A

① Have students complete the lists.

② Have them look back through the unit for more ideas, if necessary.

Task B

① Have students express their own opinion.

② Turn this into a whole class session and encourage discussion.

 Have students give reasons for their choices.

12 Grammar Review

Task A

① Have students complete the questions.

② Have them number the responses to each question.

③ Go through answers. Have students practice the questions in pairs.

 Have students make their own questions to ask their classmates. Set a rule that they have to make two questions for each target word.

Task B

① Have students write four activities.

② Monitor students and provide language assistance, as necessary. Draw attention to spelling, as well as grammer and punctuation.

Log On

Have students do the online activities for this unit on the *Expressions* website: **http://expressions.heinle.com**

Language Summary

For a more detailed review of the language practiced in this unit, refer students to the **Language Summary on page 142**. Encourage them to add new vocabulary in the **Word Builder** section.

12 Review

1 Vocabulary Review

A Make a list of vacation places and activities you learned in this unit. Can you add any more?

Vacation places

Vacation activities

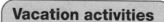

We should go to Japan on vacation.

B What are you going to do for your next vacation?

2 Grammar Review

A Complete the questions with *Can*, *What* or *Where*. Then write the number of the question next to the best response.

1. ___Can___ you dance?
2. ___What___ can we do in Paris?
3. ___Where___ should we go on vacation?
4. ___Can___ Leo speak Japanese?
5. ___What___ should we get Amy for her birthday?

___2___ Well, we can go shopping.
___3___ Let's go to Mexico.
___1___ No, I can't.
___5___ Let's get her some flowers.
___4___ Yes, he can.

B Write four activities which visitors can do in your country.

1. _____
2. _____
3. _____
4. _____

3 Log On

Practice more with the language and topics you studied on the *Expressions* website:

http://expressions.heinle.com

UNIT 15

Goals
- ○ Describing people and jobs
- ○ Using degrees of description

What's she like?

Get Ready

A The scrambled words in the picture are adjectives to describe people's personal qualities. Unscramble them and write them in the spaces.

B Write the number of each job in the correct place in the picture (1–4).

1. cashier
2. manager
3. mechanic
4. pump attendant

dohkirgwarn hardworking

esiusro serious

tenesinirtg interesting

nuynf funny

icne nice

ifedlrny friendly

Start Talking

A Look at the conversation and listen.

Dario: Did you meet the new cashier?
Mario: No, I didn't. What's she like?
Dario: Oh, she's really nice.
Mario: Really? I think I'll go and say 'hello.'

Pair work **B** Practice the conversation with a partner.
Then practice again, using different jobs and different adjectives.

Unit 15: What's she like?

Workbook: pages 58–61

1 Get Ready

Task A
 ········· Ask students to note down three adjectives to describe their best friend. Elicit suggestions and use to develop students' vocabulary.

❶ Refer students to the picture on page 120.

❷ Have students unscramble the adjectives in the boxes.

❸ Have students compare answers with a partner.

❹ Go over the meaning and pronunciation of the adjectives.

Task B
❶ Have students number the people in the picture.

❷ Have them check with a partner.

❸ Check answers as a class. Go over the meaning and pronunciation of the words.

 ········ Have students brainstorm other jobs and list them on the board.

2 Start Talking

Task A
❶ Have students read the conversation.

❷ Play the tape while students listen to the conversation.

 ········ Rewind the tape and have students repeat the conversation after the tape.

Tapescript

M1: Did you meet the new cashier?
M2: No, I didn't. What's she like?
M1: Oh, she's really nice.
M2: Really? I think I'll go say 'hello.'

Task B
❶ Have students practice the conversation.

 ········ Elicit and list personal adjectives and types of jobs on the board for reference.

❷ Have them practice the conversation in pairs, using different jobs and adjectives.

③ Listen In

Tapescript

1. **W1:** Did you meet the new designer?
   M1: No, I didn't. What's she like?
   W1: Oh, she's extremely interesting.
   M1: I guess I should go and meet her.

2. **W2:** Are you the new salesperson?
   M2: Yes, I am.
   W2: I heard you're really hardworking.
   M2: You did? (laughs)
   W2: Yes, I did. So, how's the new job?
   M2: It's fine.

3. **W3:** Who's that?
   M3: Oh, that's the new fitness instructor.
   W3: What's he like?
   M3: Very friendly. Come and meet him.
   W3: OK.

4. **W4:** Did you meet the new doctor yet?
   M4: No, I didn't. What's he like?
   W4: He's a she. And she's very serious.
   M4: Oh.

Task A

❶ Review the meaning of the six adjectives. Have each student decide which of the adjectives best describe him/herself.

❷ Have them write down any more adjectives they can think of.

❸ Elicit and list the adjectives on the board.

Task B

❶ Play the tape. Have students number the pictures to identify who's being talked about.

❷ Go over answers.

Task C

❶ Play the tape again. Have students match the people with the descriptions.

❷ Have students check their answers with a partner.

❸ Go over answers.

 ········ Ask students to describe what each person is like, and what each person isn't like, e.g. *The salesperson is hardworking; he's not lazy.*

TRY THIS! Play the tape again, as necessary. The word is *extremely*.

④ Say It Right

Tapescript

W: Your boss is really funny?
W: My job is kind of boring.
W: The new receptionist is extremely nice.
W: Her sister's really serious?
W: Your job is boring?

Task A

❶ Explain how intonation can show the difference between a statement and a question, i.e. falling indicates a statement; rising indicates a question.

 ········ Read through the examples yourself before playing the tape.

❷ Ask students to individually punctuate each sentence with a question mark (?) or a period (.).

❸ Have students compare their answers with a partner.

Task B

❶ Play the tape. Have students check their answers.

❷ Have students repeat after the tape, if necessary.

Task C

❶ Have students listen again and practice.

TRY THIS! In pairs, have students practice saying the sentences with different intonation.

A Which of the adjectives below describe *you*? Can you add more?

nice friendly hardworking

serious interesting funny

B Listen. Who are the people in the conversations talking about? Number the pictures (1–4).

C Listen again. Draw lines to match the people with the descriptions above.

Try this

There was one more word with the same meaning as *very* and *really*. What was it? Can you remember?

 Say It Right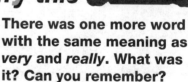

A Listen. Are these questions or statements? Add a question mark (?) or a period (.) at the end of each sentence.

1. Your boss is really funny ?
2. My job is kind of boring .
3. The new receptionist is extremely nice .
4. Her sister's really serious ?
5. Your job is boring ?

B Listen again and check your answers.

C Listen again and practice.

Try this

Say all five sentences to your partner. Your partner will say *Question* or *Statement*.

5 Focus In

A Look at the chart.

Adverbs of degree + adjectives
What's she like?

She's **nice**.
She's **very kind**.
She's **not very interesting**.
She's **sort of serious**.

B Write the number of the question next to the correct answer.

1. What's your father like?   **3**   She's funny.
2. What are her parents like?   **4**   It's boring.
3. What's Pete's new girlfriend like? **1**   He's nice.
4. What's your job like?   **2**   They're friendly.

C Add an adverb to the answers in part B and write them in the spaces.

1. (really)   _She's really funny._
2. (extremely)   _It's extremely boring._
3. (kind of)   _He's kind of nice._
4. (very)   _They're very friendly._

6 Talk Some More

A Write the correct expressions in the correct spaces.

(kind of serious)   (very funny)

(really nice)   (really friendly)

Mario: So, how's the new job?
Norma: It's _really nice_. I just met Larry. He seems _kind of serious_.
Mario: Oh no! He's _very funny_. He makes us laugh all the time!
Norma: Really? How about Jim, the mechanic?
Mario: He's _really friendly_.
Norma: Great! I think I'll go say 'hello.'

Spotlight

With adjectives which can be negative, like *serious* or *boring*, use *kind of* to make them sound softer.

B Check your answers.

Pair work

C Practice the conversation with a partner. Then practice again using different adjectives.

5 Focus In

Task A

❶ Go through the chart with students.

❷ Explain that when describing people, we often use phrases to soften or intensify the adjective. You might want to ask if they do this in their own language(s).

❸ Give students more examples, if necessary, to help them understand when and how to use the adverbs of degree with adjectives.

Task B

❶ Have students number the correct answers.

❷ Have them check with a partner.

❸ Go over the answers as a class. Have them practice asking and answering the questions.

Task C

❶ Have students rewrite the answers, adding the intensifier/softener.

❷ Go over answers.

❸ Have students practice asking and answering the questions in 'B' above. This time, students should answer using the adverbs listed.

6 Talk Some More

Task A

❶ Have students fill in the blanks with the expressions given.

❷ Offer help as necessary.

Task B

❶ Play the tape.

❷ Have students check their answers.

Tapescript

M: So, how's the new job?
W: It's really nice. I just met Larry. He seems kind of serious.
M: Oh no! He's very funny. He makes us laugh all the time!
W: Really? How about Jim, the mechanic?
M: He's really friendly.
W: Great! I think I'll go say "hello."

Task C

❶ Have students practice the conversation.

 .... Brainstorm other adjectives students know to describe people. Include: *dull, lazy, talkative, easy-going.* Write them on the board for reference.

❷ Have them practice again, using different adjectives and different jobs.

 .... Have students close their books, change partners and continue practicing using their own imagination. Make sure students are using intensifiers, as well as varying the adjectives they use and the jobs.

(**SPOTLIGHT**) Reinforce the need for care with adjectives that may be potentially offensive/rude.

Unit 15: What's she like?

7 Work In Pairs

See pages xii-xiii for suggestions on pair work.

Task A

❶ Divide students into pairs. Refer Student B to page 124.

 Elicit job vocabulary from students and list them on the board for reference.

❷ Have students look at the pictures.

❸ Have them write down a job for each of the people pictured.

Task B

❶ Explain that they are going to talk about new colleagues.

 Draw their attention to the language in the speech bubbles.

❷ Model the dialog first, with a student. Demonstrate how to start the conversation using 'So, how's the new job?'

❸ Have pairs ask and answer questions about the people in the photos.

> **Sample**
>
> **A:** So, how's the new job?
> **B:** It's OK. How about you?
> **A:** It's fine.
> **B:** Did you meet Robert?
> **A:** No, what's he like?
> **B:** He's really nice. He smiles and says 'hello' every morning. And he likes telling stories, too.
> **A:** Mm, he sounds very friendly. I just met Tom.
> **B:** Oh, yeah? What's he like?
> **A:** Well, he doesn't smile much. And he always stays in the office until nine o'clock.
> **B:** Wow, he sounds really hardworking. Did you meet…?

Task C

❶ Have them decide on adjectives to describe each person. Encourage students to use intensifiers.

❷ Have them check their answers together.

❸ Go through answers with the class. See if students have similar or different opinions about the people.

 As you are going over the adjectives, have students give reasons as to why they chose those adjectives.

(**TRY THIS!**) Use this as an opportunity to review some of the language students' learned in Unit 3. Have them describe the appearance of their classmate, as well as their personality.

Work In Pairs

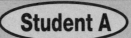

Student B: Use page 124

A Think of a job for Tom, Rebecca and Shawn.

Write them here:

Tom is a(n) _____

Rebecca is a(n) _____

Shawn is a(n) _____

Tom	Rebecca	Shawn

- Doesn't smile very much.
- Always stays in the office until 9:00 pm.

- Likes helping other people.
- Tells great jokes.

- Always says hello.
- Usually leaves work early.

B You and your partner both started work in the same office recently. Use the information above to talk about the people you met there.

C What words would you use to describe the people above? Does your partner agree?

Did you meet Kim, the manager?

No, what's she like?

Try this

Think of a person in your class. Write your description. Then describe him/her to your partner. Your partner will guess who you are describing.

_____

_____

_____

_____

What's she like? **123**

Work In Pairs Student B

A Think of a job for Robert, Gina and Sandy.

Write them here:

Robert is a(n) _____
Gina is a(n) _____
Sandy is a(n) _____

Robert

- Likes telling stories.
- Smiles and says hello every morning.

Gina

- Never says hello.
- Is always in front of the computer.

Sandy

- Listens to other people.
- Always arrives at the office first.

B You and your partner both started work in the same office recently. Use the information above to talk about the people you met there.

C What words would you use to describe the people above? Does your partner agree?

Did you meet Kim, the manager?

No, what's she like?

Try this

Think of a person in your class. Write your description. Then describe him/her to your partner. Your partner will guess who you are describing.

_____
_____
_____
_____

7 Work In Pairs

See p. T123 for suggested instructions for this task.

Mid-Unit Assessment

Once your students have finished Work In Pairs, they will have covered approximately half of this unit. How well are they accomplishing the unit goals at this stage? You may wish to assess their ability on the points below before beginning the fluency task Express Yourself. Check (✔) the appropriate space in the chart for each goal.

Can your students...	Yes, all can.	Yes, most can.	Maybe half can.	Only some can.
❶ describe people and jobs? *e.g. She's really nice. It's pretty interesting.*	_____	_____	_____	_____
❷ use intensifiers to indicate degrees of description? *e.g. very, sort of, extremely*	_____	_____	_____	_____
❸ say the names of occupations and use descriptive adjectives? *(see Get Ready and Listen In for lists)*	_____	_____	_____	_____
❹ listen for intonation to distinguish between statements and questions? *(see Say It Right for examples)*	_____	_____	_____	_____
❺ use adverbs of degree with adjectives correctly? *e.g. kind of boring, really funny*	_____	_____	_____	_____

If your students can already accomplish these fairly well, they're better prepared to expand their use of the target language in the tasks that follow. For those who are still having problems with particular items above, you may wish to direct them to the relevant areas of the unit on pages 120–124, to workbook pages 58–59, or to the online quiz on the *Expressions* website.

Unit 15: What's she like?

8 Express Yourself

Task A

support ⟶ Encourage students to think of all the adjectives learned so far, and list them on the board.

1. Do this exercise individually or with students in pairs.
2. Have students think of adjectives to describe the people and situations in the ovals.
3. Monitor and assist as necessary. Make sure students use intensifiers as well as adjectives.

Task B

1. Divide students into groups.
2. Have them talk about the people and situations in Task A.

challenge ⟶ Encourage students to give reasons why they would use those adjectives. Have them continue describing people or situations not listed, i.e.: *my co-worker, my neighbor,* etc.

9 Think About It

1. Have students read the information and consider the meaning of the expression.
2. Have students answer and discuss the questions as a class. Ask whether they have similar expressions in their own language(s).
3. Ask about rules for describing people's characters in their culture(s).

challenge ⟶ Ask students if they know any other expressions used to describe people, i.e.: *two-faced, a dark horse,* etc. Try to use idioms that are easy to explain and grasp the meaning of.

10 Write About It

Task A

1. Have students read the email.
2. Offer language support as necessary.

Task B

1. Have students write a similar message.
2. Monitor and assist as necessary.
3. Have students read their email messages to each other.

8 Express Yourself

 A How would you describe...

your boss or teacher?   your job or class?   your best friend?

learning English?   a brother or sister?   your daily life?

Use these words, or any others you know.

• *very*	• *kind of*	• *funny*	• *nice*	• *interesting*	• *boring*
• *really*	• *not very*	• *hardworking*	• *friendly*	• *serious*	• *smart*

 Group work

 B Share your information with the other people in your group.

9 Think About It

Don't judge a book by its cover.
This expression means that we can't always
tell what someone is like by looking at them.

• Do you believe this is true?
• Do you have a similar expression in your language?

10 Write About It

 A Look at this message.

B On a piece of paper,
write to a friend or
family member telling
them about your
English class, and
the people
you study with.

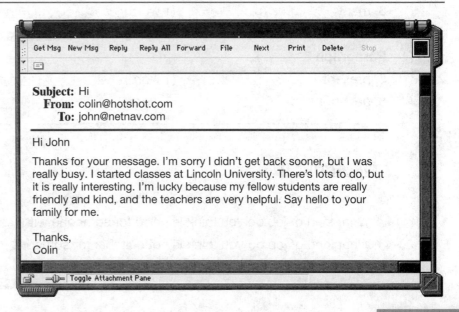

Subject: Hi
From: colin@hotshot.com
To: john@netnav.com

Hi John

Thanks for your message. I'm sorry I didn't get back sooner, but I was really busy. I started classes at Lincoln University. There's lots to do, but it is really interesting. I'm lucky because my fellow students are really friendly and kind, and the teachers are very helpful. Say hello to your family for me.

Thanks,
Colin

Read On   Finding The Ideal Partner

• Strategy: Inferring vocabulary

How important is personality in a business partnership?

Amy Nelson, Police Officer

My partner just got promoted, so I'm getting a new person soon. In my business, my life sometimes depends on my partner. I need someone who is always paying attention to what's happening around us. A good police officer must really understand human nature.

Sarah Freeland, Caterer

I provide the food for parties and banquets. My business has grown a lot, and I'm looking for a partner. I need someone who can do several things at the same time. My partner must show up for work on time and work long hours. I need someone who can work fast, and will never be impolite to our customers.

Jonathan Mead, Resort Owner

I own a little resort in the mountains. I have five cabins on a lake. I advertise, rent the cabins, clean them, rent boats, and operate a little store. I'm looking for a new partner now because my current partner is getting married. I need someone who really likes people, who doesn't lose his temper, and who loves nature.

Find words in the text that mean the same as:

Paragraph 1

1. got a better job	(2 words)	*get promoted*
2. the way people think and act	(2 words)	*human nature*

Paragraph 2

3. many	(1 word)	*several*
4. rude or bad mannered	(1 word)	*impolite*

Paragraph 3

5. present	(1 word)	*current*
6. get angry	(3 words)	*lose (one's) temper*

Talk About It

○ What kind of person are you? Describe your personality.

○ What kind of job do you think is good for someone with your personality? Why?

○ What kind of job do you think is not suitable for someone with your personality? Why?

11 Read On

Before the Reading

1. Elicit some different jobs and write them on the board. Then, ask the class these warm-up questions. Alternatively, have students first discuss them in pairs or small groups.

   What type of person would be good for each of these jobs? Would <u>you</u> be good for these jobs? Why? Why not?

2. Write the adjectives you elicit next to each job. Add the following phrases to the board: *can do several things at the same time, shows up for work on time; likes people; works fast; pays attention.* Elicit the meaning of each, and have students decide which job(s) the phrases match best.

3. Refer students to page 126. Write the six phrases on the board, and explain to students that they are to find words in the reading that have the same meaning.

During the Reading

1. Monitor and offer language support where necessary.

2. Have students compare their answers with a partner.

After the Reading

1. Elicit responses from students, and write the correct answers on the board.

2. Go over the meaning of each of the Talk About It questions. Have students work in pairs, asking and answering the questions. Then discuss the questions as a class.

   Optional questions:
   Some companies use personality tests at interviews. Do you think this kind of testing is useful? What kinds of questions do you think they ask?

Extension Activity

Write these words on the board: *good-looking, wealthy, patient, good sense of humor, responsible, caring, hardworking, reliable, generous.* Ask students to think about their ideal partner (for work, dating/marriage, etc.), and rank the attributes from the most important to the least important. Have students compare their lists in groups. Survey the groups and note the most important and least important attributes within the class. Ask individuals to give reasons for some of their choices.

Cultural Note

There are many tests designed to assess people's personality. Some are so widely accepted that many companies include them as part of their normal screening process for potential employees, although many doubt their validity. Some people look to other methods like signs of the zodiac, in which your star sign, based on the position of the planets on the date of your birth, determines your personality. Chinese astrology, which determines your attributes based on your birth year, is also used. In Japan, many people believe that personalities are decided by a person's blood type.

Unit 15: What's she like?

12 Vocabulary Review

Task A
1. Have students try and fill in the chart from memory.
2. Have students search back through the unit to complete the chart.

Task B
1. Have students circle the relevant adjectives.
2. Turn this into a whole class session and encourage discussion.

 challenge Have students stand up individually and describe themselves using their chosen adjectives. The other students in the class should say if they agree or disagree. If they disagree, they have to say why.

12 Grammar Review

Task A
1. Have students complete the exercise.
2. Allow students to look back through the unit to check their answers.
3. Have students practice asking and answering the questions in pairs.

Task B
1. Have students work through the exercise and form the sentences.
2. Have students look back through the unit to check their answers.

 challenge Have students practice the sentences in pairs using the question *What's the new ___ like?* Have students make their own conversation and practice it in pairs.

Log On

Have students do the online activities for this unit on the *Expressions* website: **http://expressions.heinle.com**

Language Summary

For a more detailed review of the language practiced in this unit, refer students to the **Language Summary on page 143**. Encourage them to add new vocabulary in the **Word Builder** section.

1 Vocabulary Review

A Fill in the chart with adjectives you learned in this unit.

Positive Adjectives	Negative Adjectives	Positive or Negative Adjectives

B Which of these words describe *you*?

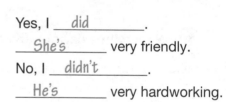

What's the new teacher like?

2 Grammar Review

A Fill in the blanks.

1. ___Did___ you meet the new boss?   Yes, I ___did___.
2. ___What's___ she like?   ___She's___ very friendly.
3. ___Did___ you meet the new designer?   No, I ___didn't___.
4. ___What's___ he like?   ___He's___ very hardworking.
5. ___Did___ you meet the new mechanic?   No, I ___didn't___.
6. ___What's___ he like?   ___He's___ extremely funny.

B Make up sentences using the words shown.

1. (kind of/doctor/serious)   The new doctor is kind of serious.
2. (cashier/really/interesting)   The new cashier is really interesting.
3. (kind of/manager/boring)   The new manager is kind of boring.
4. (pump attendant/funny/very)   The new pump attendant is very funny.
5. (smart/extremely/teacher)   Our new teacher is extremely smart.

3 Log On

Practice more with the language and topics you studied on the *Expressions* website:

http://expressions.heinle.com

UNIT 16

Goals

○ *Talking about what you did*   ○ *Asking about past events*

I lost my cell phone.

1 Get Ready

A What did Greg do today? Write the number next to the correct picture (1–5).

1. Took out some money
2. Picked up shirts
3. Worked out
4. Had lunch with Cindy
5. Bought flowers for Mom

Pair work **B** Work with a partner and make up one more activity for each place Greg went today.

○ _____
○ _____
○ _____
○ _____
○ _____
○ _____

2 Start Talking

A Look at the conversation and listen.

Greg: Oh, no! I lost my cell phone.
Pete: Oh, that's terrible, Greg! Where did you go today?
Greg: Well, first, I went to the dry cleaners. Then, I went to the bank. Next, I had lunch with my girlfriend...

Pair work **B** Practice the conversation with a partner. Practice again, but extend the conversation to talk about everything Greg did today.

128

Unit 16: I lost my cell phone.

Goals ➤ Talking about what you did   ➤ Asking about past events

Workbook: pages 62–65

1 Get Ready

Task A

 Ask students to note down three things things they did today since they got up. Elicit responses and note any key vocabulary on the board.

1. Have students look at the pictures and read the list in Get Ready.

2. Have students number the pictures.

3. Have students compare answers with a partner.

4. Check answers as a class. Draw students' attention to the past tense forms of the verbs in the list.

Task B

1. Have students work together to think of more activities. Possible answers are: *Flower shop; buy a plant, Rosie's Grill; have a cup of coffee, Bank; pick up traveller's checks, Fitness center; take a sauna, Cleaners; take in shirts.*

2. Monitor and assist as necessary.

3. Elicit suggestions and go over answers as a class.

2 Start Talking

Task A

1. Have students read the conversation.

2. Play the tape while students listen to the conversation.

 Rewind the tape and have students repeat the conversation after the tape.

Task B

1. Have students practice the conversation.

2. Have them practice the conversation in pairs, using the other places Greg went.

challenge ⊳ Extend this activity by having students use the other activities they thought of in Get Ready 'B.'

> **Tapescript**
>
> **M1:** Oh, no! I lost my cell phone.
> **M2:** Oh, that's terrible, Greg! Where did you go today?
> **M1:** Well, first I went to the dry cleaners. Then I went to the bank. Next I had lunch with my girlfriend...

Unit 16: I lost my cell phone.

3 Listen In

Task A

1. Have students work in pairs to write a location for each action.

2. Write a list of places on the board, e.g. *bank, gift shop, dry cleaners, flower shop, restaurant, department store, gym,* and have students decide which activities could be done in which places.

3. Elicit ideas from students and go over them as a class.

Task B

1. Play the tape. Have students circle the activities they hear.

2. Have them compare answers with a partner, then go over answers as a class.

 Ask students to tell each other, or you, what Greg did and didn't do. For example, *Greg had hamburgers. He didn't have pizza.*

Task C

1. Play the tape again. Have students number the places in order.

2. Have students check their answers with a partner.

3. Go over answers.

Tapescript

M1: Oh, um, hi. My name is Greg Dennison. I had lunch at your place today, and ...we had hamburgers, and... yeah, that's right. Anyway, I wondered—did I leave my cell phone there? Oh, OK, I see. Thanks. Yes, my name is Greg Dennison. I bought some flowers there this afternoon. I was wondering—did I leave my cell phone there. No? OK. Thank you. Al, this is Greg. Hi... Yeah, I had a great workout this morning. Listen, did I leave my cell phone there? Yeah, ask Bill. No, oh, OK. Hello, Mrs. White? This is Greg Dennison—yeah, the guy with all the dirty shirts. I picked them up today. Did I leave my cell phone there? I didn't. Oh, OK, well thanks for your time. Yes, my name is Dennison... D-E-N-N-I-S-O-N. I picked up a credit card this morning. Did you find a cell phone lying around? You didn't. Well, sorry to bother you. Greg Dennison... Oh, Cindy, hi! What's that noise? Are you at a payphone? What? Where are you? On the bus? Do you mean you... Oh, really? ...Oh, great!

4 Say It Right

Task A

1. Explain to students that they are to listen for the difference in vowel sounds.

 Read through the examples yourself before playing the tape.

2. Ask students to individually circle the word with the different vowel sound in each group.

3. Have students compare their answers with a partner.

Tapescript

W:	l<u>o</u>st	b<u>ou</u>ght	s<u>aw</u>	sh<u>u</u>t
W:	p<u>i</u>cked up	w<u>e</u>nt	s<u>ai</u>d	l<u>e</u>ft
W:	l<u>a</u>y	<u>a</u>te	c<u>a</u>lled	m<u>a</u>de
W:	p<u>u</u>t	f<u>ou</u>nd	t<u>oo</u>k	l<u>oo</u>ked

Task B

1. Play the tape. Have students check their answers.

2. Have students repeat after the tape, if necessary.

Task C

1. Have students listen again and practice.

 In pairs or groups, have students draw up sets of four words, each of which contains a word with a different vowel sound. Have them exchange lists and find the word in each set which has a different sound.

TRY THIS! The odd one out is *spoke.* Answers: 1. brought; 2. read; 3. paid; 4. cooked

3 Listen In

A Look at the activities below. Where do people do these things?

> • *picked up a credit card* • *bought chocolates* • *picked up shirts*
> • *bought flowers* • *had pizza* • *bought workout clothes* • *had a hamburger*
> • *picked up pants* • *picked up an ATM card* • *worked out at the gym*

B Listen and circle the things Greg did.

C Listen again and number the places in the order you hear them (1–5).

4 Say It Right

A Circle the word with the different vowel sound in each group.

1.	lost	bought	saw	(shut)
2.	(picked up)	went	said	left
3.	lay	ate	(called)	made
4.	put	(found)	took	looked

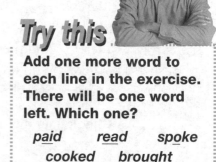

Try this

Add one more word to each line in the exercise. There will be one word left. Which one?

p<u>ai</u>d   read   sp<u>o</u>ke
c<u>oo</u>ked   br<u>ou</u>ght

B Listen and check your answers.

C Listen again and practice.

I lost my cell phone. **129**

5 Focus In

A Look at the chart.

Simple past	
How **was** your day? What **did** you do today?	It **was** busy. First, I **went** to the bank. Then, I **picked** up my cleaning. Next, I **had** lunch with my boyfriend. Finally, I **studied** for my test.

B Write the correct past verb forms in the spaces.

go	went	have	had	pick	picked
is	was	work	worked	make	made
are	were	study	studied	put	put
do	did	buy	bought	read	read

C Think of four things you did yesterday. Write sentences in the blanks.

First, I got up and _____.
Then, _____.
Next, _____.
Finally, _____.

6 Talk Some More

A Fill in the missing information.

Spotlight
What for? has the same meaning as *why?*

Pete: So, Greg, how was your day?
Greg: It was busy. I went to the bank.
Pete: What for?
Greg: <u>I picked up a credit card</u>. Then I went to the fitness center.
Pete: What did you do there?
Greg: <u>I worked out</u>.
Pete: Uh huh.
Greg: And then I went to Rosie's Grill for lunch.
Pete: Who did you have lunch with?
Greg: <u>My girlfriend, Cindy</u>.

B Check your answers.

C Practice the conversation with a partner.
Practice again using information about your own day.

5 Focus In

Task A

1 Go through the chart with students. Ensure students are aware of regular and irregular past tense verbs.

2 Review the use of sequencers (covered in Unit 8).

Task B

1 Have students write the past tense verb forms in the spaces.

2 Have them check answers with a partner. Go over answers and check spellings.

Task C

1 Have students write about their day.

2 Monitor and assist as necessary.

 challenge ········· Have students work in pairs to talk about what they did using the model in 'A.'

6 Talk Some More

Task A

 support ········· Play the Listen In recording again to remind students of the activities that Greg does.

1 Have students fill in the blanks with activities Greg mentions.

2 Offer help as necessary.

Task B

1 Play the tape.

2 Have students check their answers.

Task C

1 Have students practice the conversation.

support ········· Describe your own day. Then ask a few students to describe what they did at various points in the recent past, e.g. *before the class, during the coffee break,* etc. Note any useful vocabulary on the board.

2 Have them practice the conversation again, using information about their own day.

challenge ········· Have students close their books, change partners and continue practicing. Have students think of different information so as to use as many past tense verbs from Focus In 'B' as they can.

(SPOTLIGHT) Point out that *What for?* is a little more direct than *Why?*

Tapescript

M2: So, Gregg how was your day?
M1: It was busy. I went to the bank.
M2: What for?
M1: I picked up a credit card. Then I went to the fitness center.
M2: What did you do there?
M1: I worked out.
M2: Uh-huh.
M1: And then I went to Rosie's Grill for lunch.
M2: Who did you have lunch with?
M1: My girlfriend, Cindy.

7 Work In Pairs

See pages xii-xiii for suggestions on pair work.

Task A

❶ Divide students into pairs. Refer Student B to page 132.

❷ Have them write the phrases on the correct lines.

❸ Have them check their answers with a partner.

Task B

❶ Write these question prompts on the board: *Who did ____ see yesterday? Where did ____ go yesterday?*

❷ Have them ask about the people in the chart.

❸ Have them fill in the chart with the information they receive.

> **Sample**
>
> **A:** Who did Pete see yesterday?
> **B:** He saw his boss, his secretary and his co-workers.
> **A:** OK. And what did Sandy do yesterday?
> **B:** She went to a birthday party, and had lunch at her mom's house.
> **A:** Who did Bill...?

Task C

❶ Have Student B ask about the people in the chart.

❷ Have them fill in the chart with the information they receive.

> **Sample**
>
> **A:** Where did Pete go yesterday?
> **B:** He went to the office, and then he went to the movies.
> **A:** And who did Sandy see yesterday?
> **B:** She saw her friends and her family.
> **A:** What about Bill? Where did he go yesterday...?

TRY THIS! Have them look back to the sequencers in Focus In to help them write the sentences.

 challenge ⟶ ········ Have students read what their partner did to the rest of the class.

Work In Pairs (Student A)

A Write the words and expressions in the correct order below.

(tomorrow) (the day before yesterday) (the day after tomorrow) (yesterday)

<u>the day before yesterday</u> , <u>yesterday</u> , **today,** <u>tomorrow</u> , <u>the day after tomorrow</u>

B Ask your partner questions. Note what the people did and who they saw yesterday.

NAME	WENT	SAW
Pete	office, the movies	boss, secretary, co-workers
Sandy	birthday party, lunch at mom's	friends, family
Bill	gym, school	instructor, teachers, students
Gina	supermarket, medical center	cashier, doctor, nurse

C Answer your partner's questions about the people in the chart.

Where did you go today?

Well, first I went to the office...

Try this

Now ask your partner about his/her day. Get as much information as you can and write it here. Note the things your partner did in the correct order.

_____

_____

_____

_____

I lost my cell phone.   **131**

7 Work In Pairs (Student B)

A Write the words and expressions in the correct order below.

(tomorrow)   (the day before yesterday)   (the day after tomorrow)   (yesterday)

the day before
____yesterday____ , ____yesterday____ , **today,** ____tomorrow____ , the day after
____tomorrow____

B Answer your partner's questions about the people in the chart.

NAME	WENT	SAW
Pete	office, the movies	boss, secretary, co-workers
Sandy	birthday party, lunch at mom's	friends, family
Bill	gym, school	instructor, teachers, students
Gina	supermarket, medical center	cashier, doctor, nurse

C Ask your partner questions. Note what the people did and who they saw yesterday.

Where did you go today?

Well, first I went to the office...

Try this

Now ask your partner about his/her day. Get as much information as you can and write it here. Note the things your partner did in the correct order.

_____

_____

_____

_____

Unit 16: I lost my cell phone.

7 Work In Pairs

See p. T131 for suggested instructions for this task.

Mid-Unit Assessment

Once your students have finished Work In Pairs, they will have covered approximately half of this unit. How well are they accomplishing the unit goals at this stage? You may wish to assess their ability on the points below before beginning the fluency task Express Yourself. Check (✔) the appropriate space in the chart for each goal.

Can your students...	Yes, all can.	Yes, most can.	Maybe half can.	Only some can.
1 talk about what they did? *e.g. I went to the bank. I had lunch.*	_____	_____	_____	_____
2 ask about past events? *e.g. How was your day? What did you do?*	_____	_____	_____	_____
3 use past tense verbs? *(see Get Ready, Listen In and Focus In for lists)*	_____	_____	_____	_____
4 recognize and say similar vowel sounds? *(see Say It Right for examples)*	_____	_____	_____	_____
5 use past and future time expressions correctly?	_____	_____	_____	_____

If your students can already accomplish these fairly well, they're better prepared to expand their use of the target language in the tasks that follow. For those who are still having problems with particular items above, you may wish to direct them to the relevant areas of the unit on pages 128–132, to workbook pages 62–63, or to the online quiz on the *Expressions* website.

8 Express Yourself

Task A

 ········ Help students think of past tense verbs learned so far. Go over spellings of irregular verbs.

❶ Emphasize that the events and people can be real or imaginary.

❷ Have students fill in the lists.

❸ Monitor and assist as necessary.

Task B

❶ Divide students into groups.

❷ Have them talk about their weekends.

challenge ········ Have students in each group decide who had the most interesting weekend. Then, have one student from each group stand up and report that student's activities to the rest of the class.

9 Think About It

❶ Have the students read the information and consider the answers to the questions.

❷ Discuss the questions as a class.

challenge ········ Expand the discussion by asking students how they think people will communicate in the future.

10 Write About It

Task A

❶ Have students read the diary entry.

❷ Offer language support as necessary.

Task B

❶ Have students write a similar entry.

❷ Monitor and assist as necessary.

 ········ Have students read their diaries to a partner. Encourage students to correct each other's verb tenses if they think their partner has made a mistake.

Express Yourself

A Make a list of the places you went and the people you talked to last weekend.

Places I went

People I saw

Group work **B** Take turns asking and answering about the places you went and the people you saw. Who in the group had the most interesting weekend?

And where did you go yesterday?

Think About It

People say the world is getting smaller. Our social networks are changing. In these days of e-mail and cell phones, although we talk to more people, we see them less.

- What do you think about this trend? Do you think it will continue?
- Do you like using cell phones and e-mail? Why or why not?

Write About It

A Look at the diary entry.

B Now write a diary entry about what you did yesterday.

Dear Diary,

Dear Diary,
Today was a beautiful, sunny day. At the end of class in the morning, I had lunch in a cafe with some of my classmates. In the afternoon I studied, and then I went to the fitness center and worked out. Around six o'clock my friend Mike phoned and invited me to go see a movie. It was a science fiction movie and it was really exciting. After the movie we went to an Italian restaurant for pizza. What a great day!

• *Strategy: Identifying reference words*

Did you ever lose something on an airplane trip?
Did you wonder what happened to it?

Every year travelers lose things on airplanes. In 1970, a man and a woman had a great idea for a business. They bought unclaimed lost items from the airlines. Then they sold them in their store in Scottsboro, Alabama, U.S.A. They named the store 'Unclaimed Baggage.'

There's nothing like this store, and the prices are great. Shoppers can buy used clothing, cameras, jewelry, glasses, electronics, sporting goods, and books. Of course, they can buy lots of used suitcases too!

Sometimes the store owners buy strange things. They have no idea what they are, so they put pictures of them on their website. If you can identify one of these things, they will send you a free 'Unclaimed Baggage' T-shirt.

When you buy something from them, it's yours. So a woman was very surprised when her little girl pulled the head off of a Barbie doll that she bought there. Inside the body they found $500.

Some things are sold online. But the best place to buy is at the store itself, which is very large. If you're ever in Alabama, you should go there. You might find something you lost!

**Look at these sentences from the reading passage.
What does the underlined word mean in each one?**

1. They bought unclaimed lost items from the airlines.   The man and woman
2. Of course, they can buy lots of used suitcases, too.   Shoppers
3. They have no idea what they are.   The strange things
4. Inside the body they found $500.   The woman and her daughter
5. If you're ever in Alabama, you should go there.   The Unclaimed Baggage Store

---

Talk About It ....

◗ Have you ever lost something on a trip? What and where?

◗ Have you ever found something interesting? What and where?

◗ Do you think that a store like this would be popular in your country? Why or why not?

Unit 16: I lost my cell phone.

11 Read On

Before the Reading

❶ Ask the class these warm-up questions. Alternatively, have students first discuss them in pairs or small groups.

Do you often lose things? What do you lose? Where and when did you last lose something?

❷ On the board draw two columns headed *things you wear* and *things you use*. Elicit words from students to put in each column. Include *jewelry, cameras, glasses, electronics, suitcases, clothing*.

❸ Refer students to page 134. Have students look at the title, photos, and opening questions. Ask if any students have lost anything on a plane trip. Then write the five sentences on the board, and explain that they have to read the passage to find out what the underlined words mean. Point out the example.

During the Reading

❶ Monitor and offer language support where necessary.

❷ Have students compare their answers with a partner.

🕐 Scotsboro: sk<u>o</u>tsbərə

After the Reading

❶ Elicit responses from students, and write the correct answers on the board.

❷ Go over the meaning of each of the Talk About It questions. Have students work in pairs, asking and answering the questions. Then discuss the questions as a class.

Optional questions:
Do you often take airplane trips? What do you like about air travel? What things don't you like?

Extension Activity

Divide the students into groups. Explain that someone in the group is going on a plane trip to a sunny resort for a 5-day vacation. The group must decide together what the person should take in his/her carry-on luggage (he/she has already packed all their clothes into a suitcase). Tell them there is a 4kg weight limit for carry-on luggage. List the items to choose from on the board with weights (or elicit these from the students). For example: *video camera (1.5kg), cell phone (.5kg), camera with film (1kg), sunglasses (0.1kg), guide book (1.2kg), novel (0.6kg), magazine (0.3kg), sunscreen lotion (0.2kg), sun hat (0.1kg), diary (0.7kg), snacks (0.2kg), CD player with CDs (0.5kg), laptop (2.5kg), umbrella (0.4kg)*. Include a weight for the bag itself, e.g. 0.4kg. Have groups report their choices to the class.

 ········ Ask each group to give reasons for their choices.

Cultural Note

Losing baggage is a common fear among air travelers. Although most lost baggage is returned within 24 hours, it can take much longer, or else never reappear. The air travel industry offers some tips on how to avoid the hassle of lost luggage: pack valuable items in your carry-on luggage; share your items with a traveling companion, if possible; label your luggage on the inside and outside; and, arrive at the airport early (losing luggage is more common among people who arrive late).

Unit 16: I lost my cell phone.

12 Vocabulary Review

Task A
❶ See if students can do this exercise from memory, first. Have them work in pairs or groups if need be.

❷ Have students look back through the unit to check they have listed all the verbs mentioned.

Task B
❶ Have students add any more verbs they know to the correct columns.

❷ Go over answers with the whole class.

 ········· Check spellings of irregular verbs by either: 1) having students use the book to check each other's spellings, or 2) holding a mini spelling bee in class.

12 Grammar Review

Task A
❶ Have students complete the exercise.

❷ Have pairs check they have the right answers by practicing the conversation.

❸ Go over answers as a class.

Task B
❶ Have students write about their day.

❷ Have pairs ask and tell each other about what they did yesterday using the conversation in 'A' above as a model.

Log On

Have students do the online activities for this unit on the *Expressions* website: **http://expressions.heinle.com**

Language Summary

For a more detailed review of the language practiced in this unit, refer students to the **Language Summary on page 143**. Encourage them to add new vocabulary in the **Word Builder** section.

12 Review

1 Vocabulary Review

A Fill in the chart with the verbs you learned in this unit.

Regular Verbs		Irregular Verbs	

B Can you add any more verbs to the two columns?

2 Grammar Review

A Fill in the blanks in the conversation.

A: How __was__ your day?

B: Busy. I __went__ to the fitness center.
and __worked__ out hard.

A: What __did__ you __do__ next?

B: I __had__ lunch with my friend.
We __went__ to Colin's Café.

A: What __did__ you __eat__?

B: A hamburger and french fries.

B Write four sentences about what you did yesterday.

1. _____

2. _____

3. _____

4. _____

3 Log On

Practice more with the language and topics you studied on the *Expressions* website:

http://expressions.heinle.com

Am I in the right class?	Yes, you are.
	No, you aren't. You're in Class B.
Are you Pat?	Yes, I am.
	No, I'm not. I'm Peggy.
Is he/she Pat?	Yes, he/she is.
	No, he/she isn't.
Are they sisters?	Yes, they are.
	No, they aren't. They're friends.

What's	your his her	name?		My His Her	name is...

○ **WORD BUILDER**
Write down any new words from this unit you want to remember.

Is	this that	your family? your husband?	Yes, it is. No, it isn't.
Are	these those	your children? your parents?	Yes, they are. No, they aren't.

Do you have any brothers or sisters?	Yes, I do.
	No, I don't.
	I have one brother and two sisters.

○ **WORD BUILDER**
Write down any new words from this unit you want to remember.

Do you know Amy?

Do you know Amy?	Yes, I do.
	Yes, I know her.
	No, I don't.
	No, I don't know her.

Does he/she have short hair?	Yes, he/she does.
	No, he/she doesn't.
	No, he/she has long hair.

| Is he/she tall? | Yes, he/she is. |
| | No, he/she isn't. |

| What does he/she look like? | He/She's | tall. |
| | He/She has | blond hair. |

○ **WORD BUILDER**
Write down any new words from this unit you want to remember.

Where are you from?

Where are you from?	I'm from Mexico.
Where do you come from?	I come from Mexico.
Where is he/she from?	He's/she's from Canada.
Where does he/she come from?	He/she comes from Canada.

| What do you do? | I'm a teacher. |
| Where do you live? | I live in Singapore. |

○ **WORD BUILDER**
Write down any new words from this unit you want to remember.

| Come in. Make yourself at home. | Thank you. Thanks a lot. |

| Would you like some juice? | Yes, please. No, thank you. |
| Would you like orange or apple juice? | Apple, please. |

| May I have some water? | Sure. Here you are. |

○ WORD BUILDER

Write down any new words from this unit you want to remember.

| How much | is this sweater? is it? | It's $16. |
| | are the shoes? are they? | They're $79. |

| How many T-shirts do you need? | One. |
| How many pairs of shoes do you need? | I need two pairs. |

| I'll take this shirt. | That'll be $30, please. |

| Do you take credit cards? | Yes, we do. No, we don't. |

○ WORD BUILDER

Write down any new words from this unit you want to remember.

Is there a pool?

Excuse me.	Yes, sir? Yes, ma'am?

Is there a business center in this hotel?	Yes, there is. No, there isn't.

Where is it?	It's on the second floor. It's next to the coffee shop. It's between the pool and the health club.

How do I get there?	Take the stairs to the second floor. It's next to the health club.

◯ **WORD BUILDER**
Write down any new words from this unit you want to remember.

First, you turn it on.

Do you know how to use a computer?	Yes, it's easy. No, it looks difficult.

Do you know how to use a VCR? I can't turn on the VCR.	First, you need to plug it in. Then, you have to press the *on* button. Finally, press the *play* button.

◯ **WORD BUILDER**
Write down any new words from this unit you want to remember.

UNIT 9 — Language Summary — *I get up early.*

What's the matter?	I'm tired.

Why are you tired?	I get up at 5:30 every morning.
How come?	I have an early morning class.

What do you do in the morning?	I go to school.
What time do they study in the afternoon?	They study at 3:00.
What does she do in the afternoon?	She reads the newspaper.
What does he do at night?	He watches TV.

○ WORD BUILDER
Write down any new words from this unit you want to remember.

UNIT 10 — Language Summary — *I'd like a hamburger.*

Can I help you?	Yes, I'd like a hamburger, please.
	No, thanks.

What size would you like?	Medium, please.
	I'll have a medium, please.

Would you like ketchup and mustard on that?	Yes, please.
	I'll have some ketchup, but I don't want any mustard.
	No, thank you.

Is that all?	Yes, thanks.
	No, I'll have an iced tea.

○ WORD BUILDER
Write down any new words from this unit you want to remember.

Do you want to see a movie?

| What are you doing tonight? | I'm going to a concert. |
| What's Pete up to this evening? | He has to work late. |

Do you want to see a movie?	What's playing?
	Which one?
Do you want to go to a concert?	Who's playing?

Do you want to see a movie tonight?	That sounds good.
How about seeing a movie tonight?	I'd love to.
	Sorry, I'm going to a party tonight.
	Oh, no. I have to work tonight.

○ **WORD BUILDER**
**Write down any new words from
this unit you want to remember.**

What's the weather like?

| What's the weather like? | It's hot and sunny. |
| What's the weather going to be like? | It's going to be cloudy. |

Let's go on a picnic.	OK. That sounds like a good idea.
	I don't think it's a good idea. It's going to rain tomorrow.
What are you going to do on the weekend?	I'm not sure. Maybe I'll play tennis.

○ **WORD BUILDER**
**Write down any new words from
this unit you want to remember.**

UNIT **13** Language Summary — *What can we get him?*

What do you like?	I like painting.
What does he/she like doing?	He/She likes playing tennis.

What can we get him/her?	Let's get him/her a CD.	Great idea. I'm sure he'll/she'll like that.
	How about getting him/her a CD?	No, he/she already has a lot of CDs.

○ **WORD BUILDER**
Write down any new words from this unit you want to remember.

UNIT **14** Language Summary — *We should go to the beach.*

Can you swim?	Yes, I can. No, I can't.
Can Mario speak English?	Yes, he can. No, he can't.

Where should we go on vacation?	I think we should go to the beach.

What can we do at the beach?	We can go windsurfing.

We should go to the mountains.	But I don't like hiking.

○ **WORD BUILDER**
Write down any new words from this unit you want to remember.

| Did you meet the new cashier? | Yes, I did. |
| | No, I didn't. |

| What's he/she like? | He's/She's | extremely
very
really | nice
interesting
boring |
| How's your new job? | It's | kind of
sort of
not very | |

○ **WORD BUILDER**
**Write down any new words from
this unit you want to remember.**

| I lost my wallet. | That's terrible! |

| How was your day? | It was busy. |
| What did you do? | First, I ate breakfast.
Then, I went to school.
Next, I did my homework in the library.
Finally, I met some friends and we had dinner. |

○ **WORD BUILDER**
**Write down any new words from
this unit you want to remember.**

Congratulations! *You've finished Book 1.*

A What did you enjoy about *Expressions*?

⚫ Check (✔) the boxes.

	Not at all	A little	A lot
I enjoyed the speaking activities.			
I enjoyed the listening activities.			
I enjoyed the reading activities.			
I enjoyed the writing activities.			
I enjoyed the grammar activities.			
I enjoyed the vocabulary activities.			
I am now a better English learner.			

B Preferences

⚫ Which were the most useful for improving your English? Put them in order (1–6).

_____ Working on my own   _____ Role plays

_____ Pair work   _____ Review activities

_____ Group work   _____ Internet activities

C Assess

⚫ Now look back at the chart on page 7. Are any of your choices different now? How?

⚫ How will you continue to improve your English? Write down four ideas.

Good luck with your continued English studies!

Workbook Answer Key

Unit 1   Are you Dr. Lowe?

WORKING WITH WORDS

A 1. Dr. Scott, 2. Ms. Harris, 3. Mr. Shih, 4. Yang Shih, 5. Mrs. Shih, 6. Prof. Morales

B 1. Bill, 2. friend, 3. Prof., 4. brother, 5. friend

C Answers may vary.

LOOKING AT LANGUAGE

B 1. A: Is, B: isn't; 2. A: Are, B: am; 3. A: Are, B: 'm/'m; 4. A: Are, B: aren't

C 1. I'm not, 2. they are, 3. Areyou/I'm not/I'm, 4. you are

READING AND THINKING

B 1. F, 2. T, 3. T, 4. T, 5. F, 6. T

C 1. Tran, 2. Tam, 3. William, 4. Lamountain, 5. LaMontagne

SHOWING WHAT YOU KNOW

A 1. Yes?, 2. How do you spell that?, 3. Nice to meet you., 4. Hello., 5. No, I'm not., 6. Y-O-U-N-G.

B **brother** — sister, **family name** — first name, **nickname** — real name, **men** — women, **father** — mother

C Excuse me., Are you (name)?, Are you from (country)?, Answers may vary.

Unit 2   Is that your family?

WORKING WITH WORDS

A 1. Lee, 2. Megan and Bernie, 3. Megan and Bernie, 4. Connie, 5. Laura and Carlos, 6. Connie

B **your mother** — your father's wife, **your sister** — your mother's daughter, **only child** — someone with no brothers or sisters, **triplets** — three brothers or sisters of the same age, **your mother's brother** — your uncle

C Answers may vary.

LOOKING AT LANGUAGE

B 1. that, 2. it, 3. those, 4. they, 5. these, 6. they

C **That's my husband** – 2, **That's your husband** – 1, **These are your glasses** – 5, **Those are my glasses** – 6, **Those are your children** – 3, **Those are my children** – 4

READING AND THINKING

B 1. c, 2. f, 3. a, 4. d, 5. b, 6. e

C 1. Small family, 2. Small family, 3. Big family, 4. Small family, 5. Small family, 6. Big family

SHOWING WHAT YOU KNOW

A 1, 5, 3, 7, 6, 4, 2.

B sets of twins, Yes, we do., No, they aren't., How about you?, only child

Unit 3   Do you know Amy?

WORKING WITH WORDS

A **dark hair:** Manny, Leo, **straight hair:** Ken, Leo, **short hair:** Manny, **mustache:** Manny, **earring:** Ken, **glasses:** Leo

B 1. glasses, 2. middle-aged, 3. young, 4. tall, 5. curly

C Answers may vary.

LOOKING AT LANGUAGE

B 1. A: Do, B: don't; 2. A: Does, B: doesn't; 3. A: Do, B: don't; 4. A: Does, B: doesn't

C Answers may vary.

READING AND THINKING

B 1. The boy is surprised by the picture of his father.
2. The boy looks different than his father did.

C 1. T, 2. F, 3. T, 4. F, 5. F

SHOWING WHAT YOU KNOW

A **Conversation 1:** A: My new boss is Mr Davidson., B: Mr. Davidson? Is he short?, A: No he isn't. He's tall and he has an earring., B: Oh, is that him over there?, A: Yes, it is.
Conversation 2: A: What does your brother look like?, B: He has dark hair and he wears glasses., A: Does he have a mustache?, B: Yes, he does.

B Answers may vary. Suggestions: Ken: He is tall. He has long, straight, blond hair; Manny: He has short dark hair. He has a mustache; Leo: He has long, dark hair. He wears glasses.

Unit 4   Where are you from?

WORKING WITH WORDS

A Japan, India, Australia, United States, Canada, Mexico, Brazil, Italy

B **Time words:** date of birth, 1786, 19th century, **Place words:** capital, home address, town, **Vacation words:** tourist, visit, ski

C Answers may vary.

LOOKING AT LANGUAGE

B 1. A: do, B: in; 2. A: is, B: from; 3. A: does, B: in; 4. A: are, B: from

C 1. A: Is, B: isn't; 2. A: Do, B: don't; 3. A: Are, B: aren't; 4. A: Are, B: are; Extra word: does

READING AND THINKING

B 1. F, T, F, 2. F, T, T

C 1. Alaska, 2. Hawaii, 3. Alaska, 4. Alaska, 5. Hawaii, 6. Hawaii, 7. Alaska, 8. Hawaii

SHOWING WHAT YOU KNOW

A 1, 7, 5, 9, 3, 6, 2, 4, 8

B 1. How much money do you make?, 2. What do you do?, 3. Where are you from?, 4. What are you doing?, 5. Are you married?

C Answers may vary.

Workbook Answer Key

Unit 5   Make yourself at home.

WORKING WITH WORDS

A **Pic 1:** living room, coffee, orange juice, sandwich. **Pic 2:** kitchen, bread, plate, cookies. **Pic 3:** bedroom, glasses, gift, flowers

B **foods:** cookies, apple, orange, sandwich, bread. **rooms:** bedroom, living room, bathroom, kitchen, classroom

C Answers may vary.

LOOKING AT LANGUAGE

B some, Would, please, may, Of course, Thanks

C **1. Q:** Would you like a sandwich? **A:** Yes, please. **2. Q:** May I use the bathroom? **A:** Of course, it's the first door on the left. **3. Q:** Would you like tea or coffee? **A:** Tea, please. **4. Q:** Would you like some bread? **A:** No, thanks. May I have some cookies, please?

READING AND THINKING

B **1.** b, **2.** d, **3.** c, **4.** e, **5.** a

C **1.** Levent's father, **2.** Levent's sister, **3.** Diane, **4.** Levent, **5.** Levent's mother, **6.** Roy

SHOWING WHAT YOU KNOW

A **Conversation 1:** A: Come In. Make yourself at home. B: Your apartment is really nice. A: Thanks, I like it a lot, too.
Conversation 2: A: Would you like an orange? B: No, thanks. But may I have an apple? A: Of course. Here's your apple.
Conversation 3: A: Would you like cola or juice? B: Cola, please. A: Here you are.

B **1.** Your new house is really nice. **2.** No, thanks. **3.** May I use the bathroom (please)? **4.** May I have a cookie, please? **5.** Yes, please.

Unit 6   How much is this sweater?

WORKING WITH WORDS

A **1.** shirt, **2.** coat, **3.** necktie, **4.** belt, **5.** pants, **6.** shoes, **7.** sweater, **8.** jacket, **9.** T-shirt, **10.** jeans, **11.** shorts, **12.** socks

B **1.** white, **2.** T-shirt, **3.** skirts and dresses, **4.** jeans, **5.** checked

C Answers may vary.

LOOKING AT LANGUAGE

B **2.** Correct **3.** Incorrect - How many sweaters do you need? **4.** Correct **5.** Incorrect - That'll be $60, please.

C **1. Q:** much, **A:** It's; **2. Q:** many; **3. Q:** much, **A:** They're; **4. Q:** much, **A:** They're; **5. Q:** many

READING AND THINKING

B **1.** You can save money on expensive clothes at an outlet mall. **2.** Outlet malls are different from department stores.

C **1.** T, **2.** F, **3.** F, **4.** F, **5.** T

SHOWING WHAT YOU KNOW

A 1, 7, 9, 5, 3, 8, 4, 2, 6

B **1.** They're $22.50., **2.** It's $50., **3.** No, thanks., **4.** No, we don't., **5.** Three, please., **6.** I need a new necktie.

C Answers may vary.

Unit 7   Is there a pool?

WORKING WITH WORDS

A **First Floor (clockwise, from left):** restaurant, laundry, pool, newsstand **Second Floor (clockwise, from left):** business center, health club, coffee shop, game room

B **front desk** — ask for a room, **newsstand** — buy a magazine, **coffee shop** — have breakfast, **business centre** — send a fax, **laundry** — get clean clothes

C Answers may vary.

LOOKING AT LANGUAGE

B **1.** It's next to the front desk. **2.** Is there a coffee shop in this hotel? **3.** It's on the third floor. **4.** It's between the restaurant and the newsstand. **5.** No, there isn't. **6.** Take the elevator to the third floor.

C **1.** next to, **2.** on, **3.** in, **4.** between, **5.** on, **6.** on/next to

READING AND THINKING

B **1.** d, **2.** b, **3.** a, **4.** e, **5.** c

C is expensive; the hotel, is quiet; the cabin, is modern; the hotel, has a lake; the cabin, has a game room; the hotel, has sailing; the cabin, has two rooms; the cabin, has cable TV; the hotel

SHOWING WHAT YOU KNOW

A **1.** Yes, sir? **2.** Uh, is there a bookstore in this hotel? **3.** Just go down the stairs and turn left. **4.** It's on the second floor, next to the newsstand. **5.** You're welcome, sir. **6.** I'm sorry, there isn't.

B **1.** The health club. **2.** The game room. **3.** The newsstand. **4.** The restaurant. **5.** The business center.

C **1.** It's on the first floor, next to the restaurant. **2.** It's on the second floor, to the right of the elevator/next to the game room. **3.** It's on the first floor, to the right of the elevator/next to the newsstand.

Unit 8   First, you turn it on.

WORKING WITH WORDS

A **1.** telephone, **2.** computer, **3.** photocopier, **4.** cassette player, **5.** coffee machine

B **2.** Correct. **3.** Incorrect - Put in a disk. **4.** Correct. **5.** Incorrect - Plug in/ Unplug the cord. **6.** Correct.

C Answers may vary.

LOOKING AT LANGUAGE

B How do I use the computer? First, turn on the computer. Then, put in a disk. Next, you have to open a file. Now, you have to save your work. Finally, you can close the file.

C **1.** on, **2.** how, **3.** Turn, **4.** in, **5.** Dial, **6.** Press

READING AND THINKING

B **1.** T, **2.** T, **3.** F, **4.** F

C **1.** Fixing a paper jam., **2.** Turning on the copier., **3.** Fixing a paper jam., **4.** Putting in paper., **5.** Turning on the copier/Putting in paper/Fixing a paper jam., **6.** Turning on the copier.

SHOWING WHAT YOU KNOW

A 1, 5, 9, 7, 3, 6, 4, 2, 8, 10

B Answers may vary.

C Answers may vary. Suggestions: next to the coffee machine, to the left of the computer, between the computer and the coffee cup

Workbook Answer Key

Unit 9   I get up early.

WORKING WITH WORDS

A (top row) Picture 1: 8, Picture 2: 3, Picture 3: 1, Picture 4: 5
(bottom row) Picture 1: 6, Picture 2: 2, Picture 3: 7, Picture 4: 4

B 1. make dinner 2. start the bus 3. leave school 4. What's that?
5. start

C Answers may vary.

LOOKING AT LANGUAGE

B 1. arrive/I arrive at school at 8:00. 2. start/Class starts at 8:20. 3. have/Yes, I do. 4. get/They get to class at 8:45. 5. do/She goes jogging.

C 1.Q: What does she do in the morning? A: She takes a shower. 2.Q: What time do your parents get up? A: They get up at 6:30. 3.Q: What do they do on Friday nights? A: They visit friends. 4.Q: What does he do on the weekends? A: He goes jogging or does homework. 5.Q: What time do you leave home in the morning? A: I leave home around 7:00.

READING AND THINKING

B 1. F, 2. T, 3. T, 4. T, 5. F

C 1. c, 2. b, 3. c, 4. a, 5. b, 6. c, 7. a, 8. c

SHOWING WHAT YOU KNOW

A 1. I am. I got up at 5:00. 2. By bus. 3. How come? 4. I'm really busy. 5. At 10:00.

B 1, 5, 3, 6, 2, 4

C Answers may vary.

Unit 10   I'd like a hamburger.

WORKING WITH WORDS

A 1. salad, 2. pizza, 3. hot dog, 4. sandwich, 5. fries, 6. hamburger, 7. iced tea, 8. apple

B Gina: hot dog, fries, (small) iced tea, Fernando: hamburger, salad, (medium) iced tea, Karen: a sandwich, an apple, (large) iced tea

C Answers may vary.

LOOKING AT LANGUAGE

B 1. a, 2. thanks, 3. 'd like, 4. an, 5. some, 6. 'll

C A: May I help you? B: Yes, I'll have a chicken sandwich. A: Would you like a drink with that? B: Yes, I'd like an iced tea. A: What size would you like? B: Large, please.

READING AND THINKING

B 1. The first McDonald's was quite successful, but there were problems.
2. The brothers made changes which saved time and money.

C 1. a, 2. e, 3. c, 4. b, 5. d

SHOWING WHAT YOU KNOW

A Conversation 1: A: I'd like a pizza, please. B: A large or a small? A: Large, please. B: One large pizza. Do you want extra cheese? A: No, thank you.
Conversation 2: A: May I help you? B: Yes, please. I'd like a hot dog. A: Would you like mustard or ketchup on that? B: I'll have mustard. A: Here you go.

B Answers may vary.

Unit 11   Do you want to see a movie?

WORKING WITH WORDS

A 1. Scary Summer: thriller 2. Life on Mars: science fiction
3. Laughing all the Way: comedy 4. One True Love: drama

B 1. cry, 2. true, 3. funny, 4. laugh, 5. kiss

C Answers may vary.

LOOKING AT LANGUAGE

B 1. Q: going, A: 're going; 2. Q: going, A: have to; 3. Q: seeing, A: has to visit; 4. Q: play, A: have to go

C 1. A: I can't, I have to work late. 2. A: I'm sorry (I can't). I'm going to the movies. 3. A: No, he has to study for an exam. 4. A: They're visiting relatives in New York. 5. A: She's going to the beach.

READING AND THINKING

B Winston: Thriller: Out of the Unknown Jerry: Science Fiction: Search for a New World Emi: Comedy: Judy and Jim

C 1. F, 2. T, 3. F, 4. F, 5. F

SHOWING WHAT YOU KNOW

A 1. Do you want to go to a concert tonight? 2. How about a thriller?
3. Do you want to go to a science fiction movie? 4. What are you doing tonight? 5. Mrs Richards can go, but her husband can't.

B Answers may vary.

Unit 12   What's the weather like?

WORKING WITH WORDS

A 1. cold/snowy/0/-15 2. cloudy/rainy 3. hot/sunny/35/25

B Time words: next month, tomorrow, this weekend Temperature words: hot, warm, cool Types of weather: snowy, cloudy, rainy

C Answers may vary.

LOOKING AT LANGUAGE

B 1. A: Let's go to a ball game. B: No, I don't think it's a good idea. 2. A: What's the weather (going to be) like today? B: It's (going to be) warm and rainy. 3. A: Is the weather going to be rainy tomorrow? B: No, it's going to be sunny. 4. A: What's the weather going to be like tomorrow? B: It's going to be cold. 5. A: Let's go to the library. B: That sounds like a good idea.

C 1. Let's go to a concert. 2. What's the weather going to be like tomorrow?
3. Maybe it'll be snowy. 4. What's the weather like there?

READING AND THINKING

B 1. c, 2. a, 3. d, 4. b

C 1. T, 2. F, 3. F, 4. T

SHOWING WHAT YOU KNOW

A 1. What's the weather like now? 2. It's cloudy and cool. 3. Let's go to a movie on Friday. 4. That sounds like a good idea. 5. What's the weather going to be like? 6. It's going to be snowy and cold.

B Answers may vary.

Workbook Answer Key

Unit 13   What can we get him?

WORKING WITH WORDS

A Laura — a dozen red roses, **Alan** — a French dictionary, **Levent** — concert tickets, **Carlo** — a pot/wok, **Barbara** — running shoes, **Li Ping** — a new watch

B 1. cooking, 2. painting, 3. cycling, 4. flowers, 5. roses

C Answers may vary.

LOOKING AT LANGUAGE

B 1. Q: getting, A: has; 2. Q: does, A: traveling; 3. Q: Let's, A: He'll; 4. Q: like, A: swimming; 5. Q: get, A: them

C A: doing B: likes A: going B: has A: Does B: wants A: go B: stay

READING AND THINKING

B 1. c, 2. a, 3. e, 4. d, 5. b

C 3, 6, 1, 4, 2, 5

SHOWING WHAT YOU KNOW

A 1, 5, 7, 3, 6, 4, 8, 2

B 1. What's he like? 2. What does she like? 3. What are they like?

C Answers may vary.

Unit 14   We should go to the beach.

WORKING WITH WORDS

A (top row) 7, 1, 3, 8
(bottom row) 2, 5, 4, 6

B 1. terrible 2. hate 3. boring 4. United States 5. studying

C Answers may vary.

LOOKING AT LANGUAGE

B 1. A: can, B: can; 2. A: should, B: don't; 3. A: Can, B: can't; 4. A: Can, B: can; 5. A: should, B: don't (or can't)

C 1. Q: Can you play chess? 2. Q: What can they do at the zoo? 3. Q: What can we do at the pool? 4. A: You can go sightseeing. 5. A: No, you/I can't.

READING AND THINKING

B 1. T, 2. T, 3. F, 4. F, 5. F, 6. T

C 1. Most people can afford a youth hostel vacation.
2. Hostels help you understand people from other countries.

SHOWING WHAT YOU KNOW

A 1. We should go to the beach. 2. What can we do at the beach? 3. They have superb art galleries. 4. Can we afford an expensive vacation? 5. How about going to Mexico? 6. I don't like playing soccer.

B Answers may vary.

C Answers may vary.

Unit 15   What's she like?

WORKING WITH WORDS

A 1. F, 2. T, 3. F, 4. T, 5. T

B 1. nice — kind, 2. boring —not interesting, 3. funny — not serious, 4. current — present

C Answers may vary.

LOOKING AT LANGUAGE

B **Adjectives:** serious, kind, lucky, helpful, funny, nice
Adverbs of Degree: really, kind of, sort of, very, extremely, not very

C 1. They're not very interesting. 2. What's she like? 3. He's sort of boring. 4. What are they like? 5. They're kind of interesting.

READING AND THINKING

B 1. long hours 2. friendly 3. serious 4. manager 5. receptionist

C 1, 4, 3, 7, 6, 2, 8, 5

SHOWING WHAT YOU KNOW

A **Conversation 1:** 1, 3, 5, 2, 6, 4 **Conversation 2:** 1, 5, 3, 2, 4, 6

B 1. how's the new job? 2. I'll go and say hello. 3. you meet her yet? 4. us laugh.

C Answers may vary.

Unit 16   I lost my cell phone.

WORKING WITH WORDS

A 1. picked up/dress, 2. bought/cell phone, 3. had lunch, 4. lost/credit card, 5. did/homework, 6. watched/television

B 1. classmate, 2. doctor, 3. jewelry, 4. gym, 5. bank

LOOKING AT LANGUAGE

B **Regular Past Tense:** worked, picked up, called, watched
Irregular Past Tense: had, bought, went, did

C 1. Q: did, A: went 2. Q: was, A: was 3. Q: do, A: visited 4. Q: did, A: bought 5. Q: were, A: were

READING AND THINKING

B 1. T, 2. T, 3. F, 4. T, 5. T

C 4, 1, 3, 5, 2

SHOWING WHAT YOU KNOW

A 1, 10, 2, 4, 5, 11, 7, 6, 8, 3, 9

B Answers may vary.

C Answers may vary.